GOD'S
LOVE AFFAIR
WITH THE
GUILTY

"ALL ARE WEIGHED DOWN WITH BURDENS THAT ONLY CHRIST CAN REMOVE. ... IF WE WERE LEFT TO BEAR THIS BURDEN, IT WOULD CRUSH US. BUT THE SINLESS ONE HAS TAKEN OUR PLACE. ... **HE HAS BORNE THE BURDEN OF OUR GUILT.**"

—ELLEN G. WHITE, *THE DESIRE OF AGES*, P. 328.

BILL LEHMAN

HEALTH MINISTRY FOUNDATION

Main Distributor of Bill Lehman Books and Sermons:
Health Ministry Foundation, Inc.
Loma Linda, California USA

Copies of this book may be obtained from several Adventist Book Center
locations, other book sellers, but primarily from this website:
www.PastorBillLehman.org

Information Contact Email:
JWLsermons@gmail.com

All Scripture quotation from KJV unless otherwise noted.
Italics provided by the transcriber.
This Amazon edition has an updated book cover.

This book is a transcript of a 14-sermon series preached by the late Pastor Bill
Lehman at the Auburn Academy in Auburn, Washington. Every effort has been
made to transcribe the audio recordings in a way that preserves the meaning of
the original content. Thanks to Okay Hill for providing the sermon transcripts
that were used to produce this book.

Published in the USA
ISBN: 978-1-61455-022-8

CONTENTS

Chapter 1: Why Do I Feel So Guilty? 5

Chapter 2: Blessed Are the Guilty 19

Chapter 3: No Punishment for the Guilty 37

Chapter 4: The Judgment and the Guilty 55

Chapter 5: The Greatest Sinner 69

Chapter 6: Freedom for the Guilty 83

Chapter 7: The Guilty and the Law 99

Chapter 8: God's Love Affair with the Guilty 111

Chapter 9: God's Gift to the Guilty 125

Chapter 10: How the Guilty Get Into Heaven 137

Chapter 11: When You Offend Your Lover, What Do You Say? 149

Chapter 12: Communion: Worthy or Unworthy? 159

Chapter 13: Good News for the Guilty 163

Chapter 14: A Safe Place for the Guilty 177

Chapter 1: Why Do I Feel So Guilty?

I'm not pulling your leg when I say this is God's love affair with the guilty. I really mean that. It's not just a title that we use for evangelism or something like that. Our title is a question that many have: "Why Do I Feel So Guilty?"

I believe with all my heart that some of the most serious problems both in and out of the church are the ones with guilt. If you could sit where I have sat, and talked to as many people as I have in counseling, you would agree with me. Those who do not think this is a problem are afraid to admit it. I have discovered that this is a major problem. We hide from this; we just don't like to talk about it. I'm not going to talk about your sins, not one of them. I'm not going to put a guilt trip on you; I'm hoping to take the loads off. So just don't get worried about it, will you? But I do think that, more than legalism, there are other causes to guilt that perhaps you haven't thought about—that there is often a misunderstanding, a misinterpretation, or sometimes a lack of understanding of doctrine.

I think that there are other causes beyond that, too—beyond parents who are dictatorial and teachers in school. There are many other causes of guilt. Perhaps you will see some as you read through this book. Some of our topics are on theology and doctrine. Why do we feel so guilty? I'll try to be specific about the guilt as we go along, but let's be general to start with.

Why do we feel guilty? How can we have guilt trips, as they call them nowadays? How can a person feel guilty about the same act for weeks, months, or years? Isn't that true? There are many who don't know what I'm talking about. I have found out that there are some people who don't like talking about guilt, or else they won't admit it. I'm talking about stuff they understand. I don't know which one it is; I can't read minds. And so the guilt goes on and on and on.

By the way, in my estimation, it's worse in the churches that have higher standards than in other churches. If you come to me for counseling, I'd ask you to what church you belong. There is something about this in religion that causes us to have serious guilt trips. Why do we feel so guilty?

I would like to begin with this verse: "And the Lord God commanded the man, saying, Of every tree of garden, you may freely eat. But of the tree of the knowledge of good and evil, thou shall not eat of it: for the day that thou eatest thereof, thou shalt surely die." Genesis 2:16-17. That doesn't seem very restrictive.

What was the knowledge of good and evil? I was amazed when I first learned the definition for this, because it had always been fuzzy in my mind. I had no idea what it was about, but here is a good definition for guilt: "The knowledge which

God did not want our first parents to have was the knowledge of guilt." *Selected Messages,* Book 1, p. 214. That is a good one, isn't it? "The knowledge which God did not want our first parents to have was the knowledge of guilt." Don't forget this definition as you progress through this book. God never wanted a human being to ever feel guilty or have any knowledge of guilt whatsoever. Never!

The Bible says that God never changes. He is the same yesterday, today and forever. So He still doesn't want us to have the knowledge of guilt, right? Do you know the God who doesn't want us to feel guilty, or do you know a different God? I mean that, really. Do you know the One that never wants you to feel guilty? Or is your God a different one? You know, we don't all worship the same God. We really don't. Sometimes we think that we do, but we have vastly different concepts of God. We have different concepts that are wide apart. We're not similar at all in that one teaching on the subject of guilt. He never wanted one human being, ever, no matter how sinful, to have the knowledge of guilt. Never! Then why do we feel so guilty, if God didn't want it?

If you study the story there in Genesis, it's obvious the devil had a different idea. He said, "If you eat of that tree, your eyes will be opened. You will become as gods … knowing what? Good and evil. God is depriving you. He is robbing you of something that will be a great blessing to you." So the devil painted a rosy picture about eating from that tree. God did not have a rosy picture. One said, "It's bad." The other said, "It's good." One said, "Don't do it." The other said, "It's wonderful; try it out." And it's amazing what happened to Adam and Eve as soon as they partook of that tree. In a very short time, the two lovers started accusing each other. So Satan has different ideas about guilt than God has, and yet, whenever we feel guilty, we usually think that it is God Who has caused us to feel guilty, don't we?

We have all kinds of human logic established that it must be God. I'm trying to change your mind about God and about guilt. I'm trying to convince you of something good, and not of something bad. It's very difficult to change minds, let me tell you. We are extremely hard to convince. I'll have to theologically twist your arms until they almost jump out of their sockets before you'll say, "Ouch! I believe, I believe!"

Let me tell you a little bit more about Satan. Zechariah, chapter 3, is a marvelous chapter on the activity of Satan regarding guilt, and the activity of Christ regarding guilt. Please, don't forget some of these precious books in the Bible that shed light on guilt. Chapter 3, beginning in the first verse (I will mostly use the King James Version, but some modern versions help us understand some things better. I'll explain some of the words from modern versions.): "He showed me Joshua the high priest standing before the Angel of the Lord." Here Joshua, the leader of God's people, presents all his people before God. And it says that Satan was "standing at his right hand to resist him." There is the devil at Joshua's right hand, to resist him to the Angel of the Lord.

You must look up words in the dictionary, and also realize that some modern translations have a better word for "resist." When I looked up "resist" in the dictionary, this is what it said: "To oppose, to accuse, and to hate." So Satan is standing there to oppose Joshua representing all his people, to accuse him, and to hate him. All of that is involved in the word "resist." That is what Satan is doing as he stands there before the Angel of the Lord.

What does the Lord do under these circumstances? Note verses 2 and 4 of that chapter: "And the Lord said unto Satan, the Lord rebuke thee." Now, who is there accusing, opposing and hating? "O Satan, even the Lord that hath chosen Jerusalem rebuke thee: Is not this a brand plucked out of the fire?"

What is that? What is "a brand plucked out of the fire"? Even modern translations say "a brand plucked out of the fire." If you have some wood burning in a fireplace or stove, and you pull out one of those burning sticks, you have a brand in your hand. But the picture here is like someone burning up a lot of things. You see something very precious in that fire. It's already on fire, but you risk putting your hand in to pull it out, to save it because it's so good and so precious to you. That is the symbolism of a brand plucked out of the fire.

So the Lord says to Satan about us, "Aren't these souls so precious to Me? They're like brands pulled out of the fire. To Me they were burning up, and I've come to save them and risk My own life to do it. That is how precious they are to Me." So the verse is talking about how valuable we are in the mind of Jesus. We often forget that, don't we? If we forget that we are brands plucked from the fire, we can lack self-worth, but it says we are extremely valuable. If God gave the most valuable possession in all of heaven for us, then God's estimation of every soul is extremely high, right? Extremely high—and please don't forget that.

If we remember how precious God thinks we are, it's very difficult to feel guilty, and it's very difficult to stay that way. If we *forget* that is the way God feels about us, it's easy to feel guilty. I'm afraid that this is a basic misunderstanding—brands plucked from the burning fire.

In verse 3: "Now Joshua was clothed with filthy garments" representing the sins of his people. He doesn't come to God in righteousness. He doesn't come spotless. He doesn't come as a perfect man. He comes in all the sinfulness of the people.

It continues in verse 4: "And He answered and spake unto those who stood before Him, saying, Take away the filthy garments [all the sins] from him. And unto him He said, [This is the first time He talks to Joshua.] Behold, I have caused thine iniquity to pass from thee, and I will clothe you with a change of raiment." In other words, "I've taken away all your sins, and I've clothed you with change of raiment." Then the Lord says to the devil, "The Lord rebuke thee, Satan. Get off his back. Shut up. Be quiet. Let him alone. This is someone so precious to Me that I pulled him right out of the fire. I cannot let him die. He is too valuable to Me."

I wish there was some way to take one of those big syringes the doctors use and shoot this into your brain so that you never forget it, because in five minutes you will have forgotten everything I said about this, and you will be back under guilt again. Our biggest problem, just like the Jews, is unbelief. Our problem is not with the Bible; we just don't believe it. The Bible says it so clearly, so wonderfully well. We just don't believe it.

Now, please remember the two roles of God and Satan: God is exonerating, God is forgiving, God is taking away sin; but the devil is accusing, opposing, hating, and resisting. Be careful to whom you are listening, will you? Be careful. Sometimes, and I think it is most of the time, we think it's God doing the work of Satan whenever we feel accused and guilty. If someone comes along and forgives us so quickly, we think that it is the devil. It's too easy. Isn't that right? "I haven't been doing right yet. I haven't taken care of the whole thing. It must be the devil telling me this, and so I don't like that, either." God has a terribly hard time convincing us of His mercy and grace and love. He really does. I hope as you read on that He does a better job with us than I've sometimes seen in the past.

These two roles are more different than we sometimes think. The Lord says that they (His people) are precious. The devil hates us and despises us. Remember the following verse—and I know some of you have already considered this: "For God sent not His Son into the world to condemn the world, but that the world through Him might be saved." John 3:17. Isn't that precious? Again, "For God sent not his Son into the world to condemn the world, but that the world through Him might be saved." Will all the sinners say "Amen!"?

"God sent not His Son into the world to condemn the world." He never sent Jesus to condemn us, but that all of us through Him might be saved. Please tack that onto John 3:16, will you? Take it with you wherever you go. That was Jesus speaking, right? This is Christ. How little we understand about Him, as well as about His Father.

Satan's attacks are graphically described in Revelation 12:10, and I want to put our discussion back into this context. Don't forget about his accusations. "And I heard a loud voice saying in heaven, 'Now is come salvation, and strength, and the kingdom of our God, and the power of his Christ: for the accuser of our brethren is cast down, which accused them before our God day and night.'" The accuser of our brothers is cast down. He accuses them before our God day and night. I want to tell you that he accuses them not only before God, but before the people themselves. He accuses them day and night. The devil's attacks are long-term, never-ending, and persistent. I knew a girl who could hear the devil talk to her audibly, day and night, every hour, nonstop for two solid weeks. She audibly heard him. The psychiatrist said she didn't really hear the devil talking to her; she just *thought* she heard the devil talking to her. But she said to me, "Elder Lehman, doesn't the doctor know the devil can talk to people?" The devil *can* talk to us.

"He [Satan] knows that those who seek God earnestly for pardon and grace will obtain it." *Testimonies for the Church*, Volume 5, p. 470. The devil knows that. He knows that those who seek God earnestly for pardon and grace, and learn the truth about forgiveness, will obtain it. The devil knows that, too. Therefore, he presents their sins before them to discourage them. Who does that? The devil. He presents our sins before us to discourage us, because if he doesn't discourage us, we are going to find pardon and grace. He doesn't want us to find that. So far as Satan is concerned, it's automatic. We seek for pardon and grace, and we are going to have it. So he tries to discourage us so we will not seek for those things.

He is constantly—and that means every second—seeking occasion against those who are trying to obey God. Even their best and most acceptable services, he seeks to make appear corrupt. Have you ever noticed that when you try to do better... *bang*, you fail. Isn't that right? Almost immediately, you fail. Then you give up and say that there is no hope for you. "Even their best and most acceptable services, he seeks to make appear corrupt. By countless devices, the most subtle and the most cruel, he endeavors to secure their condemnation." Ibid., p. 471.

A fellow came to me in academy during a week of prayer. I think he was about fifteen, but he was about six-feet-two—thin, nice fellow—and looked extremely serious. He waited from something like 8:45 p.m. on Friday night until after midnight to talk to me. I sat in the front row of the chapel, counseling nonstop for four hours the last night I was there. This fellow waited until last because I think he thought he was lost. Some of you know what I mean by that. He sat beside me there on the front pew in a chapel with old wooden theater seats. He told me a very sad story about how he had been kicked out of three academies in quite rapid succession over a period of a year and a half. Finally, he told me that the previous spring, he was kicked out of a fourth academy.

His mother, who was single at that time, despaired of anything for her son. She said he probably would have to go to public school, but by some hook or crook of the Lord, he was accepted into yet another academy, a boarding school—the one where I was doing the counseling. He said that he had resolved that last fall to really serve God for the first time in his life. He said that the Lord had really blessed him for a month or two, but in July of that year he was driving his best friend's British sports car convertible south of Napa, California. He said he and his friend were coming back home from a short trip. The ragtop was down; it was a nice day. He wasn't speeding, but was just talking. Then, while driving along, he suddenly came up too fast on the back end of a semi truck. He slammed on the brakes, but the car slid under the back of the semi and his best friend was decapitated.

I don't know what that is like, do you? I really don't know. But he sat there beside me, trying to regain his composure in order to continue. Somehow the Lord enabled him to recover emotionally to some extent from that accident. Then he said that he had come to the new school in September, still resolving to do better—that God was still with him by some means or other. He had a roommate who also had had a lot of problems in the past, and who also had been kicked out of a few schools. I don't know if the faculty of the new school he was in knew that and stuck them together, or what happened, but they were together, both resolving to do better.

For every test and for every class, they really boned up on things, back and forth drilling each other. Finally, it came around to the first major exam in biology. For days they drilled each other back and forth, asking each other questions and digging out the answers. They were going to do better, at last. They were going to get good grades if it killed them. So they really worked hard. They took the exam in biology, and a day later the teacher called them into his office and asked, "How come you both got an A on the test, and your scores were only one point apart? You cheated. You cheated!" And he flunked them both on the test.

The fellow paused, and I asked, "What do you want me to do? Talk to the teacher?" And he said, "Nah. I've had so many failing grades, one more won't hurt me a bit." He said he had had so many failing grades for years, but that was the first time he ever had a possibility of getting a good grade.

I asked, "Then what do you want?" He said, "I have a question for you. How do you ever stand up once you have fallen down? Nobody will let you up. They just keep knocking you back down. How can you ever stand up once you've been down?" After all that, he was on the verge of giving up hope entirely. He continued, "Your parents won't let you up. The faculty won't let you up. The preacher won't let you up. The church won't let you up. How do you ever get back up? How can you ever walk again when you have been down?" That is a big question, isn't it?

May I suggest to you that part of the answer is what I quoted earlier: "The devil is constantly seeking occasion against those who are trying to obey God. Even their best and most acceptable services, he seeks to make appear corrupt. By countless devices, the most subtle and the most cruel, he endeavors to secure their condemnation." You and I can become a tool of the devil. I wonder how many times I've been that. I really do.

There is a passage from the book *The Ministry of Healing* where we are told that people that are just about ready to collapse go to church often. They hear the pastors, who give them another little push right over the brink to the chasm below. We ministers don't even know it. We think we are doing God's service and God's work, blessing people. Don't blame those who do it wrongly. We don't even know we're doing wrong. We don't know a better way. I mean that; we don't. Don't condemn our ignorance any more than you do yours. We ought to do better. We ought to know better, but we don't. Parents operate ignorantly for years, too. That is all they know. If you don't believe it, wait until you're a parent. You'll find out how ignorant you are. It's not as easy as it looks. We continue to do so many things wrong. So the devil is constantly on the attack and constantly there to harass us, to find all kinds of fault.

Do you know the literal translation of the word *Satan* from the Greek? *Satan* is not an English word. A literal translation means *accuser*. That is his literal title. If you want to become more expressive than that, it's one who looks down at you. That's graphic. Don't you love people who come and look down their noses at you? Those who just make you feel like a worm of some kind? That is what the devil is—one who looks down upon us. His very attitude is accusatory, accusing us day and night. That is his activity.

I want to remind you of a couple of things that you already know, but that you probably forget sometimes. First, this is enemy territory. There are beautiful places in this world we call home, perhaps with lots of green trees and everything else that is so beautiful. Think of a day with no clouds and only sunshine. How can you beat that? But this is enemy territory, isn't it? The Bible calls Satan the "god of this world." 2 Corinthians 4:4. He is the prince of this earth. Ellen White called him the "prince of darkness." *Child Guidance*, p. 200. Satan rules the people on this earth, unless we give our hearts to Christ. He operates down here on the earth. All the fallen angels are down here. They're not up there in space somewhere; they're down here. This is their place of operation.

If you believe in the great controversy, you know that there is a war going on over us and this earth, right? It's not peace, at all. Just because some countries are not fighting doesn't mean there is peace. There are all sorts of fighting going on down here. That is why there is so much trouble in nations, churches, and homes. That is why there is so much divorce. The devils, all of them, are on the job all the time. They don't sleep, either. They are supernatural powers that can come down and deceive in very tricky, subtle ways.

We often blame each other for what *they* do. Do you know that? Not always, but often. We act like they don't exist, and think that our miserable wives or our husbands are causing our problems. It's not our wives or husbands. And although we can't always say "the devil made me do that," far more often than anyone realizes, he does. Far more often. There are things that we do and say that we wish a thousand times that we had never said or done. Isn't that right? Immediately after I do something, I ask, "Why did I do a stupid thing like that?" There are reasons why. The devil is warring, and the Bible says that. "And the dragon was wroth [angry] with the woman [God's church], and went to make war with the remnant of her seed, which keep the commandments of God, and have the testimony of Jesus Christ." Revelation 12:17.

He is especially angry at one group—the remnant. If we don't think there is a war on, we really have trouble with eyesight. We ought to ask God to open our eyes so that we may discern and see. There are tremendous misunderstandings at every level in this church. Just tremendous problems! If we would be able to see both sides and then listen to the stories, we would say, "Who could ever straighten this mess out?" It's because we don't believe each other anymore, do we? We just don't believe each other about many, many things, and we do believe so many things that we shouldn't believe.

If a close friend tells you something, you believe it because that person is a good friend, but he or she may not have heard the truth in the first place. That friend also may have heard it from a good friend, who heard it from a friend. We pluck something out of a conversation, and it tells us something different than if we had heard the whole conversation, doesn't it? The context that makes so much difference is left out. So-and-so said this and this and this. We are so sure that we are accurate and that the person did it. But when put into context, it sounds different. We tend to believe each other if we are good friends, and it's very difficult to be objective in this.

This is enemy territory. Please, don't forget that there are spiritual booby traps everyplace. Everything is trapped. It's not that someday we are going to have deceptions. We've been having them in the church for a hundred years or more. Did you know that? Deceptions are all around us. They may not be the theological traps that we often see, but something else.

Some of the things in basic Christianity we hardly understand at all. Really, it's true. We can't even discuss the fundamentals in Christianity anymore. And we're so hardheaded about our beliefs that we cannot let others teach us when we need to be teachable. There are all kinds of land mines, every place we go. The enemies are here all the time—in our homes; with our children, husbands and wives; with conferences; with pastors, committees, and boards. Just all kinds of booby traps. If you have never fought in a war with booby traps, go read about how dangerous they are. Avoid booby traps. I think that spiritual booby traps can be just as deadly as real ones.

Most of us believe that our guilt is the result of the Holy Spirit accusing us. Because of our lack of understanding of something that Jesus said, speaking of the Holy Spirit, we think our guilt is from the Holy Spirit. Jesus said, "When He is come, He will reprove the world of sin...." John 16:8. This means that the Holy Spirit comes to *convince* of sin, or to *convict* of sin. We probably think that we understand the English language quite well, but there are some words that we do not properly understand.

Reprove of sin means something other than you may think it means. First, the Bible teaches that the Holy Spirit will "reprove the world of sin." John 16:8. The Bible does not say that the Holy Spirit will reprove *sinners*. We *think* it says "reprove sinners," don't we? But it doesn't say that. It says "reprove of sin." So He doesn't put down the sinner. He brands the sin. That is all; it's not so bad. The Holy Spirit is against sin, but not against sinners. The devil is against sinners, not against sin. Make sure you don't listen to the wrong party. Make sure of that. So this text does not say what some people try to make it say. When you look up that word *reprove*, you will find it says something much different than we try to make it say.

What does *convince* mean? And what does *convict* mean? In the dictionary, *convince* means "to persuade; to satisfy by evidence or argument; to cause to feel certain; to overcome doubts." So it's to persuade. In other words, the Holy Spirit is persuading us about sin, but not about guilt or about sinners. In other words, "Is it a sin or is it not a sin?" The Holy Spirit says, "Yes, it is a sin."

The word *reprove* means "to express disapproval or to speak in disapproval, or refuse to approve, or to have or express an unfavorable opinion." I don't like that television program. Does that make you feel bad? I don't like cruelty to animals. Do you have a hang-up about that? I don't like not being on time. These are disapprovals—unfavorable opinions.

When you begin to look at it, it's not bad at all. There are a lot of things that you don't like that do not make people feel guilty. Not a bit. *Reprove* is not a bad word. When I reprove, I'm just saying that I don't think that something is the right thing to do. I disapprove. That's all. No hang-ups. No guilt trips. *Convince* conveys the same idea, but *convict* is a little stronger. That means to bring home to the conscience an understanding, a comprehension, that something is wrong. Therefore, the Holy Spirit convinces of sin, but not of guilt.

The devil has a different activity, which is to cause guilt. God does not lead us into guilt trips—something on our backs that rides on us all day long. Not at all. If He did that, Jesus would have misrepresented the Holy Spirit. Jesus, through the Holy Spirit, comes to sinners—not to condemn, but to save, as it reads in John 3:17. So the Holy Spirit will not be condemning us. He may disapprove or convince us of sin, but that is not condemnation. We must rightly divide the words.

The Holy Spirit and the devil do not say what we often think that they say. They do not. Please, don't make them say what they do not say. Bringing realization of sin is far different than accusing of sin day and night, or what is called giving a guilt trip, when we can't get rid of it. Realization of sin is much different than that.

I'm begging you to go back and examine these things, because I know you won't believe me. You should divide the work of the Holy Spirit from that of Satan. They are not similar. They are totally dissimilar. There is no likeness at all to each other. They are total opposites. God is not like Satan. Satan is not like God, nor is the Holy Spirit like Satan. They are so different. And what bothers me is that so many of us think that the voice of guilt is the voice of the Holy Spirit.

One reason we believe the devil's words is that because he is so logical, we think he must be right. Jesus said about him, "When he speaketh a lie, he speaketh of his own: for he is a liar, and the father of it." John 8:44. He is a liar and the father of liars. He is the source of all lies. We can't believe a word he says, but he has a way of making everything appear so logical, so true, that we buy into and accept what he has to say. He sounds so true.

Say, for instance, that this morning at 9:00 o'clock, I lost my temper. Tonight, when I'm ready to go to bed, the devil starts harassing me about my temper. I say, "Oh, that must be the voice of God. I did lose my temper this morning. That is true. So it must be God." I think that it cannot be the devil, or it wouldn't be so accurate.

Now, please go back and read the Scriptures, will you, and read them carefully. The devil sends counterfeits, which are mixtures of truth and lies. They're not total fakes, right? A counterfeit is very much like the real—so much like the genuine that only the experts can tell the difference. The devil doesn't deal in total phonies. He doesn't do that. You know, even a child can tell the difference between a total phony and a counterfeit. The devil doesn't do that. He is a lot smarter than that. Don't make him this horned animal, you know, with the tail and pitchfork. He's not that stupid. So sometimes he just doesn't tell the whole story. He just tells part of it.

The Bible tells us what God knows about us, and how and why we sin. I'll tell you more about it later, but here is what the Lord says about us: "He knoweth our frame [our bodies]. He remembereth that we are dust." Psalms 103:14. We are weak, helpless human beings. God understands what it's like to battle against a supernatural power. We wrestle not against flesh and blood, but against principalities and powers. Those are supernatural powers. He knows that if it were not for Jesus, we would be helpless in their grasp.

It's like you have a watchdog, and a man comes by at night, and the dog doesn't even bark. He puts his tail between his legs and goes whimpering back under the porch someplace. You need to get rid of the dog. But if a great big lion comes by and weighs three times as much as the dog, and the dog takes one look at him and heads to the back porch, you ought to commend the dog.

So it is with us. God knows that our enemy is supernatural. He is enormous compared to us, and he has an unfair advantage. I must not blame you when the devil takes advantage of you and overcomes you, because you don't have a chance, except for Jesus. And our kids don't have a chance, either, by the way, except for Jesus.

When an evil, supernatural power comes along, people get beaten up unless they know Jesus and walk with Him day by day. Isn't that right? The Christian hymn says, "I need Thee every hour." I can't make it alone. There is no way. And yet we expect people to do better or to do perfectly, totally forgetting that there is an enemy camped around, watching every minute. You say to your children, "How can you do such stupid things? I told you again and again." What you tell your wife or children, the enemy hears, too. And *bang*, he is going to get you disturbed, as well as the child or your spouse, right? Everybody gets all upset because someone didn't do what he or she was supposed to do.

I'm convinced that we give up on alcoholics and those on drugs too soon, when we ought to recognize that the devil is giving them nothing but fits, day and night. We give up on them so easily. These people might be ever so sincere and really trying, but they fail. And we say, "Oh, there's no hope for that person." We say that, then too often we just walk off and leave them, never realizing that they are battling an enemy. Were it not for Jesus, they would be whipped all the time. Do we really bring Christ into their lives as an ever-present Person, protecting them, camping around about them, blessing them? Do we do that?

Weak sinners dishonor Christ by their unlikeness to their Redeemer, and therefore Satan endeavors to frighten those souls with the thought that their cases are hopeless, and that the stains of their faults will never be washed away. He hopes to so destroy their faith that they will continue to yield to his temptations, to turn from their allegiance to God, and to someday receive the mark of the beast. He points out everything wrong with them. Everything! The whole list, as long as your arm, and then we wonder why people feel guilty.

We say about ourselves, "Well, you know, I've done some pretty bad things, and for a long time." Don't forget that the devil twists everything, but remember that God knows our humanity, that we are but dust. He knows the enemy better than any of us, and how unfair it is to be matched up against him. He knows that.

One more quotation: "The people of God have been in many respects very faulty. Satan has an accurate knowledge of the sins which he has tempted them to commit, and he presents these in the most exaggerated light." *Testimonies for the Church*, Volume 5, p. 474. Satan has an accurate knowledge of the sins he has tempted us to commit. Has he never presented to you your sins, extremely exaggerated? He always does so to me. It wasn't my sins so much as it was just his representation of them.

We cannot whitewash our sins and paint them up nicely. We can't do that, so don't argue with the devil about your sins. Satan can make our sins look a thousand times worse than they really were and just blot out any ray of hope we possibly had. And we believe him. How unfortunate that is for us. We must conclude that the devil is a dirty fighter—really rotten, right to the core. Unfortunately, we act like he doesn't exist. Now, don't get a guilt trip because you have been ignorant about his devices. Forget it. The Lord enlightens us. Thank God for the light (truth) that He gives. The Lord will bless us. He always wants to bless us. The Bible teaches, "We are saved by hope." Romans 8:24. Can you say that? Say often that we are saved by hope, and not by guilt. It is the goodness of God that leads to repentance—not His criticism, and not His accusations. The goodness of God leads us to forsake sin, which is what repentance is all about.

Never forget what Romans 8:24 teaches—that we are saved by hope, and not by guilt. Don't try to stop your children from sinning by telling them how bad they are. That is the wrong method. Cease telling alcoholics, or those who use tobacco, how bad they are. We are saved by hope, not by guilt. The Bible says that. We are never going to help ourselves by being on guilt trips—not at all. This won't help us a bit. We do not believe in penance; we believe in *repent*ance. There is a vast difference between those two. Some people just eat worms; they put themselves through all kinds of misery—all day long. That won't help them. That is just buying the devil's pitch. That's all it is.

The Bible predicted that Jesus would come to undo the heavy burdens. He said, "My yoke is easy and My burden is light." There is a song I learned as a child. "His yoke is easy; His burden is light. I've found it so; I've found it so. His service is my sweetest delight; His blessings ever flow." I can remember only the chorus. That is a beautiful song. "His yoke is easy and His burden is light. I found it so." What a marvelous song.

Jesus criticized the Pharisees, "for they bind heavy burdens and grievous to be borne, and lay them on men's shoulders; but they themselves will not move them with one of their fingers." Matthew 23:4. That is the devil's work. He, and sometimes even we, bind heavy burdens upon others, leaving them with a huge load of guilt that is grievous to be borne. They just crush a person, and we won't lift even one little finger to lighten their load of guilt. Jesus said to the Pharisees, "But woe unto you" (verse 13), didn't He? Woe on you, whoever lays guilt trips on others. Christ came to lift the burdens, to make them light, and to take away the guilt.

You can do some tremendous things for other people. Do you know that? You don't have to flatter people. Just explain to those who are burdened with guilt what the activity of the devil is in the great controversy, and that we have hope in Jesus—that enormous hope in Christ. He came to lighten our load. If they will just go to Him, the load gets lighter. Immediately! He came not to condemn but to save, and we are saved by hope. We are under His grace, and where sin does abound, grace does much more abound. Today we need a tidal wave of grace, don't we? One that sweeps from the Pacific Ocean all across the United States to Europe and everywhere else. Just an enormous tidal wave, higher than the tallest mountain, just sweeping over us.

Grace does much more abound. Grace is much more powerful than sin. I say it again: grace is bigger than any sin. We offer grace to others piecemeal—just little portions of grace to great sinners—and wonder why they don't join our church. We have given almost nothing when it comes to grace. Yet they say, "Man, my sins are big. Your grace is for midgets. I need someone to come and help me out. Where is the big God? Where is the mighty God that is abundant and able to save by hope?"

I would like to recommend that we all join in the battle, because the war is on, whether you like it or don't like it. It's going to continue until Jesus comes and triumph comes at last. We all fight against demonic powers, rulers of darkness in high places. There are many things we do that we would never do by choice. We really wouldn't. There are many things we blame each other for that we really didn't want to do. There are many things about which we feel guilty that God did not have a thing to do with. In fact, it's unbelief that allows us to feel guilty. This nagging, harassing, lengthy guilt is not from God. When the Holy Spirit speaks to our hearts, the guilt lasts but a moment, for He leads us immediately to Christ, who takes away the sins of the world. We never have to stay guilty very long when the Holy Spirit speaks to us. Not a bit. The devil, though—he will grind us down over a long, long term until we want to take our own lives.

Friends, let's help each other, shall we? Let's pray for each other. Let's intercede on each other's behalf. Let's intercede on behalf of our children. Let's stop blaming each other. Let's lift up the fallen. Let's take off the loads, and put them on Jesus. He can handle them. Let us do the work of Christ. Let us believe with all our hearts in the magnificent One. He came to save us by hope, and not by condemnation. May God bless you as we join hands, fighting this war until Christ comes and takes us home where there is total peace, total hope, and absolutely no condemnation.

CHAPTER 2: BLESSED ARE THE GUILTY

If you have the devotional book *Sons and Daughters of God*, take a look at page 120: "Blessed is the soul who can say, 'I am guilty before God: but Jesus is my Advocate.'" That is blessed. That is good. That is wonderful. Blessed are the souls who can say they are guilty before God, but that Jesus is their Advocate. Each ones says, "I have transgressed His law. I cannot save myself, but I can make the precious blood that was shed on Calvary all my plea."

I'd like to give a little detour from this. I came to the conclusion a few years ago that God never deals in blame. I'm still talking about guilt. God never deals in blame for our bad deeds, nor in credit for our good deeds. If He dealt in credit, there would be no such thing as grace. If we stacked up some brownie points to earn our way to heaven, there would be no grace whatsoever. If we can earn it, there is no grace. God never deals in blame or in credit. Never; not even once. And that is because all have sinned, and all have come short of the glory of God. "There is none righteous, no, not one." Romans 3:10. If He dealt in blame, we would all be lost eternally, right? There would no hope for even one human being. We would all be lost if God dealt in blame.

And He doesn't deal in comparative religion, either. You know—better than, holier than, or more righteous than. I wish you could discard automatically all ideas of blame and credit. Throw them out the window and never look back. There is no such thing as blame and credit in God's mind. There is not. Try to prove me wrong, but take a year to do it, will you? Don't just jump to a conclusion. That helps me a little bit. Blessed are the souls that can say, "I am guilty before God."

This is a very difficult thing for us to accept. From almost the time that we are born, our parents and almost everyone else have treated us according to what we deserve. If we are guilty, we get spanked or something else. If we speed down the highway, a flashing light comes up behind us, and someone writes out this little piece of paper, and we may have to appear before a judge. There is always a penalty of some kind for wrongdoing. Don't you just love penalties? The worst thing about guilt is that punishment always follows. We are guilty, and *bang*, we are going to get it. We do everything we possibly can to avoid punishment, which means we try to avoid guilt. Guilt is just one step away from punishment, right? Children very early in life learn to avoid punishment. They say, "I'm not guilty." Very early they become experts at avoiding guilt by lying. We all have lied to avoid guilt and punishment, haven't we?

Unfortunately, this carries over into Christianity, and Christianity is totally unlike that. In life we are accustomed to being punished if we do wrong. That's what we think that we deserve—punishment. We think that God treats us the same way, but He doesn't. If he did, we would all be hopelessly lost. When it comes to God, we must divorce ourselves entirely from the way we usually think about blame and credit, and from thinking that because we are guilty, we won't make it to heaven.

Let me illustrate. Imagine me when I was about seven or eight years of age. Across the street from my home lived one of my friends, whose name was Dean. He was the same age as I, and we often played together. One morning he was out behind his house, where there was an old shed. We used to goof around in the shed a lot. One morning Dean was all alone. Boys that age like to throw rocks, and he was throwing rocks at the old building and at trees. All of a sudden, a rock went right through the only window in the back of the shed, and right away, Dean was filled with terrible fear. He wondered what his dad would do to him when he saw that. What would he tell him? And then he began to think, "Well, Dad doesn't come out to the shed very often. Maybe once a month. He won't see it for a really long time." That made him feel better. You know how it is—the heart stops pounding and the lump goes out of your throat, and you get a little peace. So Dean went about the day very happily. No more guilt. All gone. He had rationalized it all away.

When his father came home that evening, for some very strange reason, he went out to the shed. He rarely went there. He opened the door and there was glass all over the ground inside the shed. He went back into the house very quickly and asked, "Where is Dean?" Dean, of course, came out to see his father. He was thinking, "What's wrong now?" He didn't know that Dad had been out in the shed. "Who broke the window in the shed?" You know how dads can talk sometimes, don't you? We imagine our heavenly Father talks the same way, but He doesn't. Right away, Dean was surprised. He never anticipated Dad would ask him so quickly, or find out so soon what had happened.

What do you do when are you surprised? Well, you say the first thing that comes into your mind. "Billy did it." Of course, I was the "Billy" he was accusing. They still call me Billy, even at my age, when I go home to visit. "Billy did it." So his dad went right out the front door before he sat down to eat supper. He came over to our house and knocked on the door. My dad went to the door and said, "Hi, Mel. What's going on?" Dean's dad asked, "Where is Billy?" My dad asked why he wanted to know. And he said, "Billy broke the window on our shed." Dad replied, "Oh, I see. When did that happen?" "This morning." Then Dad said, "That's strange. Billy has been at his grandmother's for a week."

Poor Dean. His dad went back across the street faster than he came over to our house, and before supper, you could hear the yowls coming out of that house. I wasn't there, but I heard about the whipping, I don't think he got spanked for breaking the glass, do you? He got spanked for lying to his dad. Something similar has probably happened to most of us.

If you think you can escape from the wrong things you've done, then when you are feeling really well someday, ask God to tell you all about yourself. We just let our minds flee away from the reality of some things that we have done in our lives. We don't like to think about some of the bad things for five seconds, do we? We can't hang onto them. We don't want to listen; it bothers us. We have all kinds of ways of evading the truth. Many people speak evasively almost constantly, or they tell you one-twentieth of the story. You arrive at certain conclusions by that one-twentieth, that little fraction of the truth. A month later, you hear a little bit more about the truth—maybe another one-twentieth—and you change your mind about what was said at first. You hear another one-twentieth and you change your mind again. That continues until you hear the whole story, and you ask, "*Why didn't you tell me that in the first place?*"

The reason we are so adept at this is the fact that that practice is about six thousand years old. The Lord asked Adam, "Who did it?" Adam replied, "*She* did." Do you think that it was Eve that caused Adam to sin? Adam, after only one sin, accused his wife, the one God made for Him, as the culprit. And they both blamed God, didn't they?

The most fantastic example in the Bible of evasively trying to get out of responsibility for sinning is found in Exodus chapter 32. You ought to like this one, because poor Aaron was so much like we are. Some of you know the story already, but let's read it. It's about the people's worshiping of the golden calf when Moses came down from Mt. Sinai. "Moses said unto Aaron, What did this people unto thee, that thou hast brought so great a sin upon them? And Aaron said, Let not the anger of my lord wax hot." Exodus 32:21-22. "Don't get furious with me. Don't lose your temper. You know the people." How easy it is to blame everybody else; they are bad people. "For they said unto me, make us gods, which shall go before us; for as for this Moses, the man that brought us up out of the land of Egypt, we wot not what has become of him." (Verse 23.) Moses had been up in the mountain for forty days and forty nights.

Aaron continued with his evasive talk: "I said unto them, whosoever hath any gold, let them break it off. So they gave it to me: then I cast it into the fire, and there came out this calf." (Verse 24.) Aaron didn't mold it? He only cast the gold into the fire? Nothing else, and there it was? "It was the fire, it was the people—but I had nothing to do with it." Aaron accused those really wicked people.

"Dishonesty is practiced all through our ranks, and this is the cause of lukewarmness on the part of many who profess to believe the truth." *Testimonies for the*

Church, Volume 4, p. 309. That is not a very nice commentary on the condition of the church. I would like to explain that I think one of the reasons for this dishonesty is a terrible fear of guilt and punishment. It really is. If we didn't have to fear experiencing guilt and, as a result, punishment, we could be quite open, couldn't we?

Over the past fifteen years, the God I have conceived of in my mind has been growing in His great ability and love. I used to serve a pygmy god. I have a little book that on the cover shows a baby playing with little alphabet blocks on the carpet. The title is *Your God is Too Small*. My God was too small for many years. He is not to blame; I was to blame. My concept was of a miniature god of some kind who could only forgive little sins, but could not forgive big ones—not even moderate-sized sins. He surely couldn't forgive me. If somehow I could shrink my sins small enough, then God could forgive me. That is a terrible concept of God, isn't it?

"This is a faithful saying, and worthy of all acceptation, that Christ Jesus came into the world to save sinners; of whom I am chief." 1 Timothy 1:15. The Bible says that God can forgive the chief of sinners. We're always trying to make ourselves look like little sinners. I think that this fear of guilt and punishment leads us to not only excuse or justify our sins, but also it can lead to addictions such as alcoholism. I'm certain it leads to drug addiction, for I have heard many of those involved with drugs who have testified to it as the truth.

I'm also certain it leads to many emotional problems such as suicide, to hopelessness and despair, to failure to attend church or Bible classes. "Why should I go if they are going to make me feel guilty?" Do you wonder why they stay away? They stay away because we have a unique ability in our classes and in church to make people feel guilty. We do. So when guilty people go to church, it's like they are saying, "Hurt me; hurt me. I enjoy that." And sometimes we think God is using us when we hurt people. They don't come to church because they know that eventually someone will hurt them. So they don't come. Maybe your children don't come because they know how many things they are doing wrong. They don't know how to attain the victory. They don't know Jesus. They think, "Why go and be a hypocrite? Why go and be constantly reminded of my problem so I can go on another guilt trip? No way. I've been trying to get rid of that miserable problem. You want to drag me to church, but it only makes me feel guilty again. Let me have a little peace once in a while." Sometimes they find more peace staying away than they do going to church. And it's difficult nowadays to escape from guilt, because so many of us do such a fine job of making people feel guilty. It has caused many to detest even the mere mention of one word: sin. Preachers don't talk about this anymore, because people just hate to hear that word. It's a reminder of their many failures in their lives. We have now changed the word *sin*, by the way. It is no longer *sin*. It's our *failures*. It's our *weaknesses*. It's our *mistakes*. But we never sin. *Sin*'s a bad word. I'm not trying to be ridiculous about this. Really, we have come to a place where we cannot talk about sin because it gives people hang-ups, and we call talking about it negativism and other terms.

Have you seen the book by Karl Menninger, the famous psychiatrist from Topeka, Kansas? The title of the book is *Whatever Became of Sin?* I found it to be an extremely interesting book. Dr. Menninger explains how all the new cures that people have invented for the last forty years for our hang-ups and our problems have failed to bless people. Psychiatrists are saying it now, not just preachers. We have said that we've excused sin with every kind of explanation and word and title we could use for it, but we never dealt with it, and, as a result, people have not been blessed. Dr. Menninger asked, "Whatever became of sin, and God's method of taking care of sin?" Read the whole book if you can. Check it out at a public library. You'll find it very intriguing, for he is trying to turn psychiatry back to religion— back to Christianity and hope in Christ, rather than treatment of symptoms in human beings, which is sometimes an evasion. I found the book a great blessing to me in my ministry.

Today some people cannot stand to talk about negative things. They feel we must always be positive. And I'm wondering if we can no longer face reality. When we can no long face reality, we may become spiritual schizophrenics. Do you know that? There is a danger that, when we cannot face reality, we will practice escapism for so long that we actually can have other personalities. However, God can enable us to face hard reality and not become despairing or discouraged or depressed. When I really know Jesus, I don't have to fear reality—not one bit. And as I hear people talking about some of these things nowadays, I ask myself if they really know Jesus. Why is reality so fearful? Why? The true gospel doesn't make us afraid of it. We can come nose-to-nose with it, and not have to run away and hide at all. But if you don't know Christ, you cannot run fast enough to get away from reality. I think that the correction we need, and the help we need, involves going back and finding Jesus. He can bring a marvelous peace into our lives.

There is a song titled *Sweet Peace, the Gift of God's Love*. The lyrics are:

> There comes to my heart one sweet strain,
> A glad and a joyous refrain,
> I sing it again and again,
> Sweet peace, the gift of God's love.

Through Christ on the cross peace was made,
My debt by His death was all paid,
No other foundation is laid.
For peace, the gift of God's love.

When Jesus as Lord I had crowned,
My heart with this peace did abound,
In Him the rich blessing I found,
Sweet peace, the gift of God's love.

In Jesus for peace I abide,
And as I keep close to His side,
There's nothing but peace doth betide.
Sweet peace, the gift of God's love.

Chorus:
Peace, peace, sweet peace,
Wonderful gift from above,
Oh, wonderful, wonderful peace,
Sweet peace, the gift of God's love.
                    (Lyrics and music by Peter Philip Bilhorn.)

I cannot manufacture peace. I cannot accomplish it by positive thinking. I can only receive it as a gift from heaven. Fantastic peace, like a river. A tranquility that calms the soul. No anxiety, no worries. He takes care of everything—all of it. Take your burdens to the Lord and leave them there.

So how do you deal with guilt? What does the Bible say we must do with guilt and, of course, with the fears of punishment? What do we do with failure and stigma, and with constant habits of sin? How do we get rid of these things? How can we escape from guilt trips? How can we get off the merry-go-round once we are on it? What can we do about that? What can we do when we have sinned, which produces guilt?

First of all, we must admit that the methods many of us have been trying do not work. We have to discard some of the things that we've tried for years and years—those thing that really haven't been effective. Secondly, we must do what the Bible says. I want to recommend to you a text that you may at first think is fearful: "He that covereth his sins shall not prosper: but whoso confesseth and forsaketh them shall have mercy." Proverbs 28:13.

Remember back in the previous chapter that I gave a most marvelous quote: "Blessed is the soul who can say, 'I am guilty before God.'" *Sons and Daughters of*

God, p. 120. The above verse in Proverbs is like that. It talks about people who cover their sins and how, in doing so, they will not prosper. I can cover my sins by excuses, by explanations, by justifications, by evasions, and in all sorts of ways. Whoever covers sins is not going to prosper, and is not going to be blessed, but the one who confesses and forsakes them, he shall have mercy. God recommends that we go to Him, confessing our sins.

I am going to share with you something that it took the Lord many years to teach me. In the book of John there is a statement that John the Baptist made. When he saw Jesus coming down to the river Jordan where he was baptizing, he said, "Behold the Lamb of God, which taketh away the sin of the world." John 1:29. That text had been testing my understanding for years. I have had problems understanding what it is all about. I probably still don't fully understand it, but now it says something special to me. Why did John the Baptist call Jesus the "Lamb of God"? "Well," you say, "He was going to die." It's more than that.

If you had lived in the days of Jesus, when the sanctuary was there in Jerusalem, or back in the days of Moses, you would have seen people go to the sanctuary with lambs. "Behold the lamb of Bill Lehman." What does that mean? That means I have sinned. I am on the way to the sanctuary to offer a sacrifice for my sins. That is what it means. The lamb of Bill Lehman means that Bill Lehman has sinned. He is going to confess his sin, and offer this animal in his place. But John the Baptist called Jesus not "the lamb of sinners," not "the lamb of human beings who sinned," but "the Lamb of God." Had God sinned? Never! Then why did God sacrifice? The people sacrificed only when they had sinned. They didn't have to sacrifice if they hadn't sinned. And John the Baptist called Jesus the Lamb of God, as though God had sinned. You have to think about that for a little while, but it's very precious.

Until you find that out, perhaps you will never really understand confession. Until you understand, perhaps you never will really escape from guilt. Jesus is called the Lamb of God for a very good reason. The Bible says, "All we like sheep have gone astray; we have turned every one to his own way; and the Lord hath laid on Him [Jesus] the iniquity of us all." Isaiah 53:6. The Father did that. In the Garden of Gethsemane, the Father laid upon Jesus our sins, and Jesus prayed, "O my Father, if it be possible, let this cup pass from Me: nevertheless not as I will, but as Thou wilt." Matthew 26:39. The Father *did* give Jesus our sins. The Father laid on Jesus, the Lamb of God, all of our sins. It was the Father's will that Jesus died for your sins and mine.

How did He do that, and why? When Adam and Eve sinned, God had a problem, just like parents have with their children. Would He let the children suffer and die for their sins, or would He, as their parent or their heavenly Father, do something about their sins? You see, in some societies parents can be held accountable for their children's crimes. If you don't believe it, let your minor child drive your car down the highway and have an accident and destroy some property and see who pays. And see what the judge says in the court. The courts hold the parents accountable for their minor children's crimes. Parents are accountable for their children.

God had a problem. Would He accept the responsibility for His children's sins? Or would He let *them* suffer the consequences for their sins? What would He do? Legally, He could be held accountable because He was the Father. They were His children, were they not? He could justly volunteer to take the responsibility for their punishment, or He could let them suffer. We can be thankful that God *volunteered* to take our punishment. The entire Godhead was involved. The Lord said that if man had to take responsibility for his own sins, God would lose His children *eternally,* right? God didn't want to lose His children; He would take the responsibility for their crimes. And that is why God offered Christ for a sacrifice. God says, "I take responsibility for man's sins. I will offer a sacrifice because they are Mine." You will see this symbolized in the Bible. In the old patriarchal system, the oldest living father offered the sacrifice for all the children and grandchildren and great, great grandchildren. The offspring did not offer sacrifices under the patriarchal system; it was the family patriarch that offered the sacrifice.

You can see the same thing in the Old Testament sanctuary system when the high priest offered the sacrifice for all of the congregation's sins. Remember that the sins of the people were not taken care of until the Day of Atonement. The high priest offered the sacrifice for the whole congregation on that day. The people did not offer the sacrifice; the high priest did! One man took the responsibility for all.

"And he shewed me [the prophet Zechariah] Joshua the high priest standing before the angel of the Lord, and Satan standing at his right hand to resist him. And the Lord said unto Satan, The Lord rebuke thee, O Satan; even the Lord that hath chosen Jerusalem rebuke thee: is not this a brand plucked out of the fire?" Zechariah 3:1, 2. There was Joshua, the high priest, who took responsibility for all the sins of the people of God. In the same way, God said, "I am responsible," and He offered a Sacrifice to take care of all the people. The Sacrifice offered by the Father was that His precious Son took upon Himself all the punishment for your sins and mine for all eternity. And so we come confessing our sins in the name of Jesus, acknowledging that God has paid the penalty in the person of Jesus for our sins. And we literally lay our sins on Jesus as we confess our sins in His name; we acknowledge that God has taken the responsibility, and we don't have to have them anymore. *Isn't that fantastic?* You may not quite believe it, but if you study it enough, you will find out that it's true. It is completely true. The reason for confession is that God says, "I take the responsibility. If you believe that, confess your sins in My Son's name and lay them on Him, and believe that He has already taken care of your sins." God doesn't say that He will take care of our sins *someday*. He has already done it on Calvary. Do you believe that? This is why we come confessing. If we confess our sins and forsake them, we will find mercy. What a precious word. Don't forget it.

This Bible method of confession frightens us. Don't you just love to confess your sins to somebody when you have wronged them? Do you have no problem at all confessing your guilt? We have a terrible time confessing our guilt! But the Bible says that if we confess our sins rather than covering them up, we will prosper and find mercy.

How can this be an escape from punishment? You may be asking, "But if I have sinned, will I not get punished when I acknowledge my sins?" You need to understand something about confession which I think is poorly understood by many Christians. We understand so many beautiful doctrines, but I do not think we understand confession at all.

Suppose that you get a ticket from a traffic violation on the way home from work or church. You go to court on a set date. There is a nice judge smiling down at you. The clerk reads the charges against you. You were speeding on a highway, going sixty miles an hour in a thirty-mile-an-hour speed zone. The first thing the judge asks is, "How do you plead?" Have you ever been in a courtroom and listened to that procedure? It's educational to watch other people and see how much they are like us. I have watched people in courtrooms several times, and sometimes the person will not answer the question of the judge. Instead, he or she begins to explain to the judge what happened.

The judge asks again, "How do you plead? Guilty or not guilty?" And again the person begins to explain. So the judge asks again, "How do you plead? Guilty or not guilty?" And the person just will not plead guilty or not guilty. He or she will not do it. And the judge tries and tries, and finally he says, "If you do not plead one way or the other, I will hold you in contempt of court." Well, if that was you avoiding the judge's question, that puts you in deeper water than before.

You think you have to squirm out of it somehow. Some people just have a terrible time deciding whether to plead guilty or not guilty. Now, the reason you must plead guilty or not guilty is that if you plead not guilty, then they must have a court trial to discover your guilt or innocence. The court is obligated to prove your guilt if you plead not guilty. So if you have an attorney and you plead not guilty to some serious crime, but the court finds you to be guilty, then your lawyer is going to beg for clemency. Clemency is something that you have to beg for. You never deserve it, by the way. That is grace. You beg for clemency. You begin to describe, through your attorney, all of the extenuating circumstances, including your background, your home life, the poor environment you lived in, the poor school you went to. You can describe how bad your parents were, how dire economic conditions were, and all sorts of things—all in an effort to show that you didn't have a fair chance in life—all the reasons why the judge ought to be merciful to you, and not throw the book at you. That is called asking for clemency or mercy. The same plea for mercy can be made if you plead guilty in the first place and forego a trial.

The same thing is true in the heavenly court. If you come pleading not guilty, there is no reason to confess. Only the guilty confess, right? There is nothing to confess if you're innocent. And no explanation is needed if you are innocent. You don't have to explain one thing at all. But if you confess, you are saying that you are guilty. That's not an explanation. It's not an excuse; it's not an evasion. It's simply saying, "I am guilty." Remember, "Blessed is the soul who can say, 'I am guilty before God, but Jesus is my Advocate. I make His precious blood all my plea.'" You are pleading for mercy or clemency.

So when I sin, I must say I am guilty. If you do not say you are guilty, then you have not confessed yet. Some don't want to confess, but want to offer many explanations and excuses. Why? Is God mean? Is He critical? Is God demanding? Is He exacting? Is He a tyrant? Does God like to punish? Does He dislike His children? God is not like that at all! He knows a lot more things than we give Him credit for. If I really believe in a God of mercy and love, who gave His only begotten Son to die for me that I might not have to die eternally, then I can come boldly to the throne of grace and find mercy and help in time of need. I can come *boldly*. Why? Because He is a God of grace. He is a God of mercy. He forgives quickly. If we confess our sins, He is faithful and just to do what? To forgive us our sins and to cleanse us, too. He is faithful and just. We can trust Him to do it. He said, "I promise I will do it. Do you trust Me?" Then come boldly, not digging your toes into the ground and getting choked up, with goose bumps on your back. You don't have to go to God that way. The Lord has taken care of sin through the sacrifice of His beloved Son.

If we trust Him and His love, we ought to come boldly to the throne of grace because *it is the throne of grace*. It is not a throne of wages or merit. I'm concerned that we don't believe very much in God's grace. Grace is not permissiveness to sin. Not at all. Grace is vastly different from that. When I confess my sins and plead with the Lord for mercy, I show that I believe in a God of mercy. If I do not believe in a God of mercy, I must believe in a God of wages, and then I will have to earn my way to heaven. But God does not forgive us because we are deserving. He forgives us because He is so good, and *there is no other reason.* We must somehow get these basic things in Christianity embedded in our minds, or we will never get rid of guilt.

We judge people from human perspectives and human viewpoints. Are they deserving or undeserving of mercy? We have all sorts of ways of looking at it. God doesn't see humans as we see ourselves and each other. He reads the heart. He knows all the things there. God knows that humans are weak in the flesh (Romans 8:3). That means we are helpless when it comes to overcoming sin.

God knows how miserably weak we humans are. Believe me, we are weak. When I was in college during a week of prayer, one morning about 10 o'clock, one of the faculty, a tall man who weighed about 250 pounds, was leading the song service. That guy had a pretty bad reputation, at least according to the gossip. Whether it was deserved or not, I do not know. He stopped the song service and began to confess his sins, not in detail but in generalities, and he went on and on. He is the only faculty member at any college that I have ever heard confess his sins in public. And when he was finished, he begged us to forgive him. And he said, "I suppose you wonder why I said these things." And this big man said, "I'm just that weak." You know, to me he grew about ten feet that day. There are not many people big enough to say that in front of anybody else.

We are all weak, but God knows our helplessness. Do we know our helplessness? He does. It's when we come confessing our sins that He says, "I know how weak you are. I know all about that. You don't have to explain to Me. I know it better than you do."

Most people sin because of their weakness and their helplessness, not because they like to sin. Have you discovered that? For years as a minister, I thought people sinned because they liked to sin. I mean, sin is enjoyable, but I know that most people want to stop. But often they can't. Sin is a weakness of the human race. It is a real revelation to find many, many people in a variety of sins who continue sinning because they are so weak—just plain helpless. When we discover that, by the way, people suddenly look different. That is an insight into people's hearts and minds that very few have nowadays. We are so judgmental, you know? You can't read minds and I can't, either. We assume we can, but we cannot. We don't even know ourselves. We just think we do.

When my wife Rose and I were counseling a certain case, a marriage difficulty, the wife went and talked to her a few times. One night I came home in the wee hours of the morning from talking to that family, and Rose asked, "Well, what happened?" I usually don't tell her because repetition embeds it in the mind, and some things are not easy to forget. There are a lot of things that we should forget. Don't repeat them. That helps. Memorization comes by repetition, so just don't repeat them, and you can forget faster. Some things we should remember, but some things we should forget. So I began to tell her about this, and it seemed there was a very basic thing in life that they had problem with. Rose said to me, "Well, what do you think about that?" When I told her, she said, "*You don't believe that!*" We had been married for over twenty years. We dated a long time. We grew up in the same neighborhood. My father went to school with her mother. Rose didn't want to believe what I thought about the couple's situation.

She finally looked at me and said, "You *do* believe that!" She never would have thought it. There were many things I did not know about her, either. When you think you know someone, you had better take another look. We judge too much by externals and words; and some of our actions are only externals, and not necessarily the intent of the heart. We often don't tell what is in our hearts. We tell things that are just a little shade off. That is called "buying a pig in a poke," as they say down south. It means paying for something specific, but it is in a sack, so you don't really know what you're getting.

We are evasive about very sensitive things in life, and we don't understand even our spouses—not nearly as much as we think we do. We just assume we do, and that is a bad assumption. We don't understand fellow Christians, either. We don't know why they do things. We might know what they have done, but not why. Please, don't judge motive. Only God is able to do that, right? Isn't that marvelous—that only He knows? That is tremendous. He is an enormous God of marvelous grace and sensitivity. So I don't know why people do the things they do, and most people don't realize how weak they are. I sin because I am weak. I am so helpless. The devil knows that, and the Lord knows that. God can gladly show me mercy because He knows my weakness. We don't expect a weak child to do strong things; neither does God. So He comes to help me. When I'm weak and realize it, then I'm strong because I depend on Him and not on me. He is trying to get me to depend on the strong One, not on myself. He knows that I was born in a sinful place with sinful parents, without any choice on my part. If environment or hereditary have anything to do with life, He knows I'm going to be a sinner. I was born in a sinful world to sinful parents. How can I be anything else? I can't.

"Can the Ethiopian change his skin, or the leopard his spots? then may ye also do good, that are accustomed to do evil?" Jeremiah 13: 23. Who is not accustomed to doing evil? Some think that they have not been evil. They don't realize that with humans, it is impossible to do good of themselves. Please don't leave out that impossibility in your Bible studies to people. Please don't think that when you have educated them, they can do it. The Bible doesn't say we are saved by education, even though the Lord did tell us to teach all nations. We are saved by Jesus. Without Him, we can do nothing, but we can do all things through Him. Without Him, we're helpless. Christ came down to give us abilities we do not have in ourselves. When we find ourselves failing and falling, it simply means we are walking alone, without Jesus. We are trusting in ourselves. Early in my conversion, I thought I could do everything the Lord asked me to do. My head is hard, and after many years of failing, I still tried to find some method whereby I could do it. We're always looking for new methods so we can perform. There aren't any, by the way. We can do all things only through Christ. Without Him, we're helpless. We must learn that very difficult lesson.

We go on feeling guilty over our failures, and the Lord is always there waiting to help us. We just don't trust Him to do it. We say *we* must do it, and we can't. "Wherefore in all things it behoved Him to be made like unto His brethren, that He might be a merciful and faithful high priest in things pertaining to God, to make reconciliation for the sins of the people. For in that He Himself hath suffered being tempted, He is able to succour them that are tempted." Hebrews 2:17-18. The Lord came down and took our humanity so that He might be able to succor us. That means that He might understand us. That He might know what it is like to struggle against the enemy and supernatural power. Evil angels know a lot of things about human weakness. Christ understands our proneness to sin. It is just part of us. We are born that way; we cannot help it. God knows all these things.

The Ministry of Healing is a fantastic book. When you have time, read some of the chapters. There are a few paragraphs I wish to share about God's understanding of why we have so much trouble with sin:

"We should strive to understand the weakness of others. We know little of the heart trials of those who have been bound in chains of darkness and who lack resolution and moral power. Most pitiable is the condition of him who is suffering under remorse; he is as one stunned, staggering, sinking into the dust. He can see nothing clearly. The mind is beclouded. He knows not what steps to take. Many a poor soul is misunderstood, unappreciated, full of distress and agony—a lost and straying sheep. He cannot find God, yet he has an intense longing for pardon and peace.

"We become too easily discouraged over the souls who do not at once respond to our efforts. Never should we cease to labor for a soul while there is one gleam of hope. Precious souls cost our self-sacrificing Redeemer too dear a price to be lightly given up to the tempter's power.

"We need to put ourselves in the place of tempted ones. Consider the power of heredity, the influence of evil associations and surroundings, the power of wrong habits. Can we wonder that under such influences many become degraded? Can we wonder why they should be slow to respond to efforts for their uplifting?" *The Ministry of Healing*, p. 168.

From the same book, here is another quote that I like very well:

"We need more of Christlike sympathy; not merely sympathy for those who appear to us to be faultless, but sympathy for poor, suffering, struggling souls who are often overtaken in fault, sinning and repenting, tempting and discouraged. We are to go to our fellow men, touched, like our merciful High Priest, with the feeling of their infirmities." Ibid., p. 164.

It was the outcasts, the publicans, and the sinners that Christ called, and by His loving kindness compelled them to come unto Him. Those outcasts, publicans, and sinners were the one class that He sought after. He would never countenance those who stood apart in their self-esteem and looked down upon others.

Years ago I used to have a system of tagging people. I never told anybody about it. I was sure that I knew exactly who was going to go to heaven and who was not. Thank God that it has been over thirty years since the days when I judged many people whom I knew almost nothing about. One time I was with a group of pastors who were coming back to Union College in Minnesota. We had been on a recruitment trip to get students to attend school there. There were three pastors in the front seat—two student pastors and one faculty member who was also a pastor—talking about holy, sacred things, mainly theology. We pastors can find great pride in doing that. The deeper the theology, the more exalted we think we are. On a Sunday afternoon, after a long trip, we just indulged it for mile after mile. In the backseat, a man who was a singer and a girl who played the piano were sound asleep, or at least I thought the girl was. As we drove on, I noticed that the girl was leaning over the back of the front seat, listening. When the conversation came around to a key place, she began to talk for the first time in hours, and she expressed a love for Jesus that I had never had. I had put a tag on her that she wasn't going to make it.

She talked and talked about her love for Christ in very sincere terms. I slipped down lower and lower in the seat, and I wished I could find a hole and crawl out of the car. She talked so sincerely and calmly and humbly. It made me realize that with all my theology, I didn't know Jesus. It embarrassed me. I'm not saying Christianity is indefinite. We don't know the heart, do we? We don't know why people do what they do; we can't read minds. The Lord looks on the heart. The Bible says that, right? He is looking for heart religion, not just external words and behavior. What is seen and heard on the outside will follow what is in the heart. God knows all about me; therefore, He can show me mercy. He knows why I deserve clemency. It's because there is no other way. If He doesn't show me mercy, I am hopelessly lost. He knows that.

There are many quotations about why God shows great mercy. "Grace is an attribute of God exercised toward undeserving human beings. We did not seek for it, but it was sent in search of us. God rejoices to bestow His grace upon us, not because we are worthy, but because we are so utterly unworthy. Our only claim to His mercy is our great need." *The Ministry of Healing*, p. 161. Does that seem like a contradiction? Our only claim to His mercy is our great need. Our great need! I am helpless; He is the strong One. He comes to bless me and to rescue me and to save me.

"In some who presented the most hardened exterior, He discerned hopeful subjects. He knew that they would respond to the light, and that they would become His true followers." *Gospel Workers*, p. 48.

"Beneath an appearance of hatred and contempt, even beneath crime and degradation, may be hidden a soul that the grace of Christ will rescue to shine as a jewel in the Redeemer's crown." *Mount of Blessing*, p. 130. Rescued from crime and degradation, a soul will gleam in His crown.

"Our Redeemer has opened the way so that the most sinful, the most needy, the most oppressed and despised, may find access to the Father." *Desire of Ages*, p. 113.

"Often we regard as hopeless subjects the very ones whom Christ is drawing to Himself. Were we to deal with these souls according to our imperfect judgment, it would perhaps extinguish their last hope." *Christ Object Lessons*, pp. 71-72.

"However wretched may be the specimens of humanity that men spurn and turn aside from, they are not too low, too wretched, for the notice and love of God. Christ longs to have care-worn, weary, oppressed human beings come to Him. He longs to give them the light and joy and peace that are to be found nowhere else. The veriest sinners are the objects of His deep, earnest pity and love." Ibid., p. 226.

"Many will come from the grossest error and sin, and will take the place of others who have had opportunities and privileges but have not prized them. They will be accounted the chosen of God, elect, precious; and when Christ shall come into His kingdom, they will stand next His throne." Ibid., p. 236.

And finally, "We are to present the word of life to those whom we may judge to be as hopeless subjects as if they were in their graves." *Testimonies for the Church*, Volume 6, p. 308. The Lord can still rescue them.

It has been a few years since Rose and I were missionaries in Africa. I wish you could all go to the Congo (now called Zaire) and work with the Congolese people; they are different. We have always had only few converts in the Congo because they are a hardened, heathen people. Just look at their eyes and their faces, and you'll see what I mean. I shall never forget one camp meeting we went to. It was my first sermon, and we had a call that lasted over three hours. The reason that call lasted so long is that I kept asking for people to come down and accept Christ, and one or two at a time would make their way to the front. I invited them to take studies and join the church. I asked that after my *first sermon*. That was the first sermon that many people there had ever heard from anybody. I asked them to accept Christ. I can remember that experience to this day.

The church in which I was preaching was planning to close down because they had so few converts over many years. It was a partially finished building with bamboo walls. It had no roof on it yet, so they put palm fronds on long bamboo poles to shade us from the jungle sun. That is where I preached. There was a sub-chief there who sat in the back. There was an aisle going about three-fourths of the way back to where the sub-chief sat; he was a dignitary there. He laughed and joked and teased all through my sermon. The people just roared with laughter at what he would say. They had to laugh when the sub-chief made jokes; if they didn't laugh, they might end up in jail.

So they all laughed, and I thought to myself, "That fellow is going to tear up my meetings." He just continued joking and teasing. He would go up to someone and tap him on the shoulder, tell him a joke, and everyone would laugh. That happened all through my sermon. Then I started the call. We were singing, and a few began to come down front. I was terribly embarrassed, but we kept singing, and I would say, "We will sing one more hymn, and if no one comes, we will stop the call." Then someone else would come forward. So we would sing one more hymn, and then another person would come down front. I finally decided to shut up and just let them keep singing. People kept coming, just one or two at a time.

As I said, those were very hardened people. When we had been singing for something like two hours, two very well-dressed girls came in from the outside and stood at the back. They were probably close to eighteen years old. I could tell by their dresses that they were chief's daughters. Well, immediately the sub-chief got up, went over and shook their hands. "Welcome to the meeting," he said, and then he went back and sat down. The two girls stood there at the back near the doorway for about fifteen minutes, and then they came down front and gave their hearts to Christ. They had not even been there during the sermon. They just listened to the music for a while and came down front.

When they came down front, I watched that sub-chief. His face just went way down. He hung his head, and there were no more wisecracks, and no more jokes. I thanked the Lord for miracles. We stayed there and kept on singing, and people kept coming, just one or two at a time. And after another fifteen minutes, guess what happened? That's right. The sub-chief came down and finally gave his heart to Christ. I went and shook his hand and welcomed him. Then more people came down front. They kept on coming like that, but I finally stopped the call because the people had stayed there for so long, they were getting weary.

That afternoon the mission director had a meeting on tithing. When he finished, some of the people asked, "Aren't you going to make another call?" There were more people that wanted to be converted. The next morning I would be preaching my last sermon, and when the time came, I had another call and more people came down front. A man and his two daughters came down front.

We left the next day to hold another camp meeting down the road several miles. That was a very difficult place. After almost a week later, we left the mission station early one morning because we had to drive all day to the next hotel. You don't stop in the jungle at night. About 7:00 o'clock in the morning, we went by that church on our way back to Rwanda. We had left for the long trip three hours earlier. They were just letting out the baptismal class which the sub-chief was attending in order to learn more about our message. Some of the people saw the car and recognized us, and they came running like little children. The sub-chief, a grown man probably in his forties, was jumping up and down just like a little boy. I could hardly believe it. I kept looking at him. That fellow who had cracked all the jokes was like an eight-year-old boy—just jumping up and down. He came over and hugged and kissed us, and shook our hands. People swarmed around the car like flies. They were just thrilled to death, all excited about Jesus.

The Lord can convert anybody, and I have seen Him do it. When you know the tremendous power of Christ unto salvation—when you see how God can work for the hardest sinners and just melt their hearts and make them like little children—you say, "Oh, Lord, forgive me for not believing in Your mercy. Forgive me for not believing in Your grace." Friends, the devil been defeating us for too long a time. Do you know that? We do not understand the goodness of God to sinners. We don't understand how much we need Him, and how desperate He is to give Jesus and His grace to us. He will do things for us that we have never dreamed could be done, if we will just give our hearts to Him and trust Him. If we go to the throne of grace confessing our sins, He opens up His arms. Come boldly. He loves to forgive us. He rejoices to forgive the biggest of sinners. It makes Him happy. It's an honor and glory for Him to forgive us. He has earned the right by giving Christ to die on Calvary. Blessed is the soul who can say "I am … what?" "… Guilty before God, but Jesus is my advocate. I make the precious blood that is shed on Calvary all my plea."

Friends, it's like magic. Do you know that? There is no other help for guilt except Jesus and confession. No other help. All we can do about our sins is come to Jesus and bare our souls; we can't do anything else. We can't say we are going to do better because we are not. Except the Lord comes into our hearts, we are going to keep on falling and falling. The Bible says, "Now unto Him that is able to keep you from falling, and to present you faultless before the presence of His glory with exceeding joy." Jude verse 24. We can't keep ourselves, but He can keep us. He will hold us with His right hand. Oh, if we only knew how willing He is, and how much ability He has. All we can do with our sins is to come to Jesus.

Confession is a fantastic thing. It's a marvelous thing. Don't be afraid of it. If we are afraid of confession, we are afraid of God. We don't have to be afraid of Him. Our God is a marvelous, marvelous God Who loves us with everlasting love. He longs to bless His children because He is a marvelous Father. Trust Him, and all the guilt will be gone. We will have sweet peace, a gift of God's love.

Let me ask this prayer for us: Loving Father, we're thankful most of all for the sweet fellowship with Jesus and the holy angels. Surely they are with us when we contemplate the love of God, or else we could not have the peace that He offers. We're thankful for the fellowship of those of like precious faith. We're thankful for the marvelous hope in God's word. How good He is. Turn our eyes upon Jesus. May we look full in His wonderful face, and see the marvelous things He wants to do for us: take away all the despair, all the hopelessness; take away the looking at self and all our sins; and teach us to come boldly to the throne of grace because He is a God of grace. Show us how we can help each other by encouragement, by hope, by being companions, by sweet fellowship, by being a friend, by listening, by being close. And as we go through each day, may we in our souls be fed, and may Christ be preciously near. May we have a whole new experience, and know that we walk with the Lord, and that He abides in our hearts. May we have hope by knowing that Jesus is ours, and we are His. Take away all fear, all despair, all guilt, and give us that marvelous, wonderful peace. In Jesus' name I pray. Amen.

CHAPTER 3: NO PUNISHMENT FOR THE GUILTY

You may have trouble believing the title of this chapter. Don't forget that the guilty come confessing their sins before God. "Blessed is the soul who can say, 'I am guilty before God: but Jesus is my Advocate.'" *Sons and Daughters of God*, p. 120. Please remember that.

The guilty come boldly to the throne of grace because they trust Christ and His great mercy for sinners. You don't have to be afraid to be a sinner if you know Jesus. If you don't know Him, you had better be scared to death. And all you need to do is come to Christ. He is available all the time, isn't He? There is no problem. He has taken care of all guilt and all sin on the cross. He took our punishment upon Himself; therefore, there is no punishment for the guilty who make Jesus their Advocate and Substitute.

Now, all of this has to do with the resurrection. "And therefore it [Abraham's faith and trust in the promises of God for an offspring] was imputed to him for righteousness. Now it was not written for his sake alone, that it was imputed to him; But for us also, to whom it shall be imputed, if we believe on Him *that raised up Jesus our Lord from the dead* [the resurrection]." Romans 4:22-24.

It shall be imputed to us, if we believe on Him that raised up Jesus our Lord from the dead. Now, verse 25: "Who was delivered for our offences, and was raised again for our justification." We always talk about Jesus dying for our justification, but the Bible also talks about Jesus being resurrected for our justification. Have you ever heard a sermon on the resurrection of justification? The Bible says that Christ was raised for our justification. It means much more than the resurrection. All that was involved in the resurrection of Christ is a tremendous hope for every human being.

The worst thing to us about guilt and about sinning is the punishment. "The wages of sin is death" (Romans 6:23). Death! And that is everlasting death. Legally, there should be no resurrection. Legally, we should die and stay dead and never live again.

The Bible has some controversy about this. We seldom look in that little book just before Revelation for light on the resurrection, but there is something precious there. "Yet Michael the archangel, when contending with the devil he disputed about the body of Moses, durst not bring against him a railing accusation, but said, The Lord rebuke thee." Jude verse 9. Apparently Moses had died but had not been raised yet, and there was a contention between the devil and Michael. They argued, or disputed, about the body of Moses. The verse says that Michael did not bring a "railing accusation" against the devil, but rather said, "The Lord rebuke thee." And what did Michael do with Moses? He resurrected him and took him to heaven. It was Moses, one of the patriarchs, who appeared on the Mount of Transfiguration to bring encouragement to Jesus. Elijah was also there with Moses. Elijah had been translated straight to heaven without experiencing death.

There is a quotation concerning Moses at the time when the children of Israel were just about to enter the Promised Land. "Satan had exulted at his success in causing Moses to sin against God, and thus come under the dominion of death." *Patriarchs and Prophets*, p. 478. A dominion is a kingdom, by the way. So Satan exulted at his success in causing Moses to sin against God, and thus come under the dominion of death, which is part of Satan's kingdom. Moses died because he sinned, taking glory to himself that was due to God. The one who caused him to sin was Satan, and he just exulted (rejoiced exceedingly) at his success. Often our sins and our guilt are caused by the devil. I didn't say always, but more often than we realize. Much of our human weakness is taken advantage of by Satan, and then we blame ourselves.

Satan was able to cause even the great patriarch Moses to sin and come under the dominion of death. Now let's finish the quote started above: "The great adversary declared that the divine sentence—'Dust thou art, and unto dust shalt thou return' (Genesis 3:19)—gave him [Satan] possession of the dead. The power of the grave had never been broken, and all who were in the tomb he claimed as his captives, never to be released from his dark prison house."

So the contention was between Satan and Michael. The devil said that the dead were his. He referred to the decree made by God after Adam had sinned—that from dust he came, and to dust he would return when he died. Satan claimed that all who died should remain forever in the grave. And since Satan had conquered everyone up to that point (for all had sinned), he claimed that they were everlastingly his.

The Bible calls the grave a prison house. Did you know that? The grave is a prison, a jail, a penitentiary. When you read in the Bible about delivering the captives and the prisoners, God is talking about taking those captives out of the grave. Now notice one more passage as the quote continues: "In consequence of sin Moses had come under the power of Satan. In his own merits he was death's lawful captive, but he was raised to immortal life, holding his title in the name of the Redeemer" (p. 479). Moses was legally guilty, legally a criminal, and the punishment demanded by the law of God for being legally a criminal or a sinner is to die and stay dead. So the devil argued with Michael, saying that Michael could not have Moses. And what did Michael say? "The Lord rebuke thee." That is all He said. He said He would put Satan in the hands of God, and God would rebuke him for this, because the resurrection had not yet been confirmed in human existence. Jesus had not yet come out of the grave.

You must understand what this is all about. The Bible states that "of whom a man is overcome, of the same is he brought in bondage." 2 Peter 2:19. The bondage here is really slavery.

In the old wars, way back before the days of Jesus, when a king went out to fight against another king and kingdom, if he conquered the other kingdom, he enslaved all the persons in that kingdom. It was an automatic practice. Those who were conquered were led away in chains to the conqueror's city, passing through triumphal gates like those that can still be seen in Rome. All the people became slaves of the conquering king. So when the devil conquers you and me by causing us to sin, we become his slaves and his prisoners. We are his property because we have sinned.

As in olden times, once you have sinned, you come under the dominion of the one who has conquered you. When Adam sinned, the devil conquered the whole human family, legally and legitimately. All of Adam's offspring have been brought into bondage that way. And the devil claims that when we die, our punishment for sin should be that we must remain in the grave forever. Satan wants to destroy the idea of a resurrection. So there was an argument about the body of Moses. Satan made his legal claim, but the Lord resurrected Moses, anyway.

We need to study in greater depth about this captivity. Isaiah, the gospel prophet, wrote something that is found nowhere else in the Bible. He asks the question: "Shall the prey be taken from the mighty [Satan], or the lawful captive delivered?" Isaiah 49:24. What is the prey? It's like one of those little bunny rabbits out there in the ditch along the highway, and a hawk hovering overhead swoops down and takes the rabbit for lunch. The rabbit is the prey. "Shall the prey be taken from the mighty?" We are all the legal prey of the devil because we are all guilty of sin. But shall we be delivered?

"But thus saith the Lord, Even the captives of the mighty shall be taken away, and the prey of the terrible shall be delivered: for I will contend with him that contendeth with thee, and I will save thy children" (verse 25). He doesn't say, "I *may* contend with the devil." He says "I *shall* contend with him that contendeth with thee." If the devil contends with you about your sinful past, then just remind him of his future, which is eternal destruction. Satan is a defeated enemy.

God will contend with the devil on our behalf. He will fight the one that is fighting with us, and "the prey of the terrible shall be delivered." God will set us free from the bondage, the slavery, of the devil. He promises to do that for us. The one who is legally guilty, who has sinned and sinned and sinned, is going to be set free.

This is an assurance for those who have become legal, spiritual criminals. The big question is: "How can a just God set people free who are legally guilty? How can He do that, and still be just?" This is one of those questions we have yet to grapple with and resolve. How can God's justice be served, if He delivers those who are legally guilty?

In the State of Tennessee several years ago, the governor was soon going to leave his office. He began to allow great numbers of convicts in the state prisons to go free. Many citizens of the state were going to sue the governor, to try to stop him from releasing so many criminals onto the streets. They could not understand what strange reason motivated the governor. Many citizens did not consider that governor to be a just person.

And so it is that many ask, "How can God be just, yet set free those who are legally guilty?" The answer is found in a seemingly strange verse: "Because He hath appointed a day, in the which He will judge the world in righteousness by that Man whom He hath ordained; whereof He hath given assurance unto all men, in that He hath raised Him from the dead." Acts 17:31. Here again the Bible brings in the importance of the resurrection of Jesus.

The resurrection of Christ gives to all human beings assurance in the time of the judgment. Before I can reveal more about the judgment, though, I must try to straighten out some problems here. I must tell you that often we as pastors explain to you that the judgment is like a worldly court. It is like that in some respects, but please do not forget the differences. Always state the differences as well as the similarities, or the people will be misled.

Let me explain. In most courts, at least in North America, we are supposed to be considered innocent until proven guilty. The purpose of the court is to determine our innocence or our guilt. This is *not* the reason for the heavenly judgment. Are you with me? The heavenly judgment is not to determine our innocence or guilt. You will understand that quickly when you read in the Bible that "there is none righteous, no, not one." Romans 3:10. No innocent person other than Jesus has ever existed.

So the judgment is not trying to find out our innocence or our guilt. All are guilty, right? No exceptions; everyone has sinned. That makes us all guilty. If we sin only once, we're guilty, and the law condemns us. That is why the law cannot justify—because it has already condemned. How can it justify when it condemns? It can't do that; they are opposites. So the judgment is not to discover our innocence or our guilt. We're already guilty.

Those who realize that fact recognize there is only one hope for anyone who is guilty, and that is the mercy of God. Therefore, they come boldly to the throne of grace, confessing their sins and their guilt. Christ died for the guilty; the righteous don't need a savior. Christ would not have had to die if we were not guilty. When I believe in God's provision for my sin and my guilt, I come confessing my sins, laying them on Christ. Then what is the judgment for? The Bible teaches that the judgment is simply to find out who really believes in God's mercy, and that Christ has died for their sins. The judgment discovers who really believes in God's method of saving sinners. Do I really believe in Christ and His death on the cross for me personally? Do I really believe in God's mercy and love and grace, or don't I? My actions will prove what I believe.

The judgment is not looking for the innocent; we're all guilty. "Because He hath appointed a day, in the which He will judge the world in righteousness by that Man whom He hath ordained." Acts 17:31. Of what do we have assurance, then? Verse 31 goes on to say, "He hath given assurance unto all men, in that He hath raised Him from the dead." I would like to tell you that what comes before assurance is the resurrection—that in the judgment, we may have tremendous assurance. The reason we may have that assurance is that He has raised Jesus from the dead. When you understand that, it gives you a tremendous amount of hope. Our assurance is predicated on the resurrection.

Now the question that I have to answer here is: "Who raised Jesus from the dead? The Father? Or Jesus Himself?" To argue over this question will only bring about spiritual blindness. We usually try to establish our viewpoint, even though the other person may have more evidence than we do. In the case of our question, the Bible has strong evidence for both sides. That is, the Bible seems to say that the Father raised Jesus, and it also seems to say that Jesus raised Himself. Did you know that? You can't throw away some of the Bible and believe only part of it. That is ridiculous. You must believe all that the Bible says by harmonizing both sides to derive the wonderful truth.

Let's look at a couple of texts. "Therefore doth my Father love Me, because I lay down My life, that I might take it again. No man taketh it from Me, but I lay it down of Myself. I have power to lay it down, and I have power to take it again. This commandment have I received of My Father." John 10:17-18. The Father told Jesus that He could both die and resurrect Himself.

The text that many use is this: "Destroy this temple, and in three days I will raise it up." John 2:19. Not His Father, but Jesus Himself would raise up the temple of His body. Another text is "In Him [Jesus] was life; and the life was the light of men." John 1:4.

On the other side of the question are texts about the Father raising Jesus. "Be it known unto you all, and to all the people of Israel, that by the name of Jesus Christ of Nazareth, Whom ye crucified, Whom God raised from the dead, even by Him doth this man stand before you whole." Acts 4:10. Other similar texts include: "The God of our fathers raised up Jesus, whom ye slew and hanged on a tree" (Acts 5:30); "Him God raised up the third day, and shewed Him openly" (Acts 10:40); "But God raised Him from the dead" (Acts 13:30); and finally, "But for us also, to whom it shall be imputed, if we believe on Him that raised up Jesus our Lord from the dead" (Romans 4:24). And there are others. So the Bible says that Christ raised Himself from the dead, and the Bible also says that the Father raised Him from the dead. It says both.

"He who said, I lay down my life that I may take it again, came forth from the grave to life that was in Himself. Humanity died, divinity did not die. In His divinity, Christ possessed the power to break the bonds of death." *Selected Messages*, Book 1, p. 301. In other words, it was the divinity in Christ that raised Him from the dead.

Then why does the Bible state so emphatically that God raised Jesus from the dead, when there is so much evidence to the contrary? You must not say they contradict each other; they do not. They agree perfectly, and when you begin to study this, you will find out how they agree.

The answer is found in the work of the mighty angel that came down and rolled away the stone from the tomb on that resurrection morning. "And, behold, there was a great earthquake: for the angel of the Lord descended from heaven, and came and rolled back the stone from the door, and sat upon it. His countenance was like lightning, and his raiment white as snow: And for fear of him the keepers did shake, and became as dead men. And the angel answered and said unto the women, Fear not ye: for I know that ye seek Jesus, which was crucified. He is not here: for He is risen." Matthew 28:2-6.

The word *angel* is not an English word. It's really a Greek word, which is *angelos*. The best English translation for the word *angel* is *messenger*. So a messenger came down from heaven, and what was his message? He had a primary message that was separate from what he said to Mary. *He had a message for Jesus.* What did he say? What did he do? He came down, and he rolled away the stone from the tomb. Do you remember what Isaiah called the tomb? He called it a "prison house." The Bible calls the grave a prison, or a penitentiary, or a jail. The locked door to that jail was that huge stone, and the angel rolled it away easily. So now the prison house is no longer locked, right? It's unlocked.

Suppose you are in a state penitentiary, and the governor of the state comes to visit you. He sits there with you in your cell for half an hour; then he leaves the cell. Suppose that when he leaves, he leaves the door to your cell wide open. You look out down the hall, and every gate is wide open, all the way to the outside. What is the message of the governor to you? "You are not a prisoner anymore. All the doors are open. You may leave." That is what it means. An open grave means an open prison door. You are not locked up; come on out. That is the message.

"Brave soldiers [that were guarding the tomb where Jesus lay] that have never been afraid of human power are now as captives taken without sword or spear. The face they look upon is not the face of mortal warrior; it is the face of the mightiest of the Lord's host. This messenger is he who fills the position from which Satan fell. It is he who on the hills of Bethlehem proclaimed Christ's birth. The earth trembles at his approach, the hosts of darkness flee, and as he rolls away the stone, heaven seems to come down to the earth. The soldiers see him removing the stone as he would a pebble, and hear him cry, Son of God, come forth; Thy Father calls Thee. They see Jesus come forth from the grave, and hear Him proclaim over the rent sepulcher, 'I am the resurrection, and the life.' As He comes forth in majesty and glory, the angel host bow low in adoration before the Redeemer, and welcome Him with songs of praise." *Desire of Ages*, p. 779. The angel came from God the Father with a message: "The door is open. You don't have to stay there in the prison house any longer." And so Jesus resurrected Himself.

The Father raised Jesus through the fact that He sent the angel Gabriel to call Jesus forth from the tomb, but Jesus resurrected Himself. You must remember how Jesus arrived in the prison house: "All we like sheep have gone astray; we have turned every one to his own way; and the Lord hath laid on Him the iniquity of us all." Isaiah 53:6.

The Father laid upon Jesus the iniquity of us all. How did Jesus get into the grave? He died, of course. But why did He die? It all began in Gethsemane. He pleaded, "Let this cup pass from Me: nevertheless not as I will, but as Thou wilt." Matthew 26:39. The Father was trying to give Him that symbolic cup of all our sins. Three times Jesus asked if it were possible to let that cup pass from Him, but apparently the Father gave it to Him to drink. That cup contained all of our sins. He laid on Him the iniquity of us all, according to Isaiah. Jesus, the active Agent in the creation of the human race, took the blame. He took our sins upon Himself, and He knew it was the Father's will for Him to do so.

The Father willed that Jesus bear our sins to the cross, and Jesus willingly took them upon Himself. Those sins crushed out the life of Jesus, and He died. That's why He ended up in that grave—that prison house. The Father offered His own Son, and our sins killed Jesus. The Father separated Himself from Jesus because of our sins, and Christ ended up in the grave because of the Father's will. Jesus stayed in the grave for as long as His Father determined He should be there. That is exactly how it happened.

I want to pose a hypothetical question and then answer it. This is not the gospel, but only my guessing. Since Jesus was totally obedient, if the Father had never called Him, where would He be today? I believe that Jesus would still be in the grave. This is purely hypothetical, you know, but Jesus was that obedient, wasn't He? He arrived in the grave by obedience to His Father's will. What I am trying to say is stated quite well in *The Faith I Live by*, p. 50: "He who died for the sins of the world was to remain in the tomb the allotted time. He was in that stony prison house as a prisoner of divine justice. He was responsible to the Judge of the universe. He was bearing the sins of the world, and His Father only could release Him." So there was a specified time determined by the Father. Forget about the three days and nights and all the arguments about that. That is a study all by itself. The important fact is that Jesus was in that stony prison house as a prisoner of divine justice. He was responsible to the Judge of the universe. He was bearing the sins of the world, and only His Father could release Him. He who died for the sins of world would remain in the tomb the allotted time.

Was God the Father satisfied with all that was accomplished in the death, burial, and resurrection of Jesus? Was He satisfied? Would it take care of all of mankind's sins for all time? Only the Father could decide this. Was the punishment sufficient for all, for everyone, for all sin? Was it good enough? Only God would know the answer. So there Jesus was in the grave, which is called a prison house—a prisoner of God's justice, waiting for the Judge to decide. One of the worst things about being in jail is not knowing how long we are going to be in there. Only the Father could decide if and when it was satisfactory, so Jesus remained obedient and submissive to His Father, and awaited the decision of the great Judge. And the Father left Him there for the "allotted" length of time.

When the messenger came down from heaven, he had a message from the great Judge, the God of heaven. His message was that the prison door was now fully open, and Jesus could come on out; the Father is satisfied. That is what was meant when the angel proclaimed, "Son of God, come forth; Thy Father calls Thee."

This has been a lengthy explanation, so don't forget the problem—the big question—and that is: "How can a just God set people free who are legally guilty?" This question is related to what I previously quoted: "Satan had exulted at his success in causing Moses to sin against God, and thus come under the dominion of death." *Patriarchs and Prophets*, p. 478. Concerning Moses, Satan, the great adversary, had echoed the divine sentence pronounced against Adam after he sinned: "Dust thou art, and unto dust shalt thou return" (Genesis 3:19). Satan said that the dead are legally his. Up until the time of Moses' death, the power of the grave had never been broken. Therefore, all who were in the grave, Satan claimed as his captives, never to be released from his dark prison house. That was the devil's claim, and since man had sinned, man was legally guilty. And the devil seemed to have a good argument.

God somehow had to take care of that argument, so we must think about this. God's plan to counter the argument of Satan was that Christ must not only die for every person's sins, but He must also be raised in order for us to stand just before the Judge of the universe. In fact, the resurrection has more to do with justification than the death, because it has something to do with the Father calling forth His Son after the allotted time. The Father must make a decree. Jesus not only must conquer death for us, but He also must conquer the grave. The first Jesus did by dying in our place; the second Jesus did by resurrecting Himself after His Father sent the angel to call Him forth from the tomb.

These wonderful truths are taught at most funerals: "So when this corruptible shall have put on incorruption, and this mortal shall have put on immortality, then shall be brought to pass the saying that is written, Death is swallowed up in victory. O death, where is thy sting? O grave, where is thy victory? The sting of death is sin; and the strength of sin is the law. But thanks be to God, which giveth us the victory through our Lord Jesus Christ." 1 Corinthians 15:54-57.

You see, if Jesus had only died on Calvary but had never gone into the tomb, that would mean that all who had died would stay dead. They would stay in the grave. Had there been no burial of Christ in the prison house of Satan, had He never come under the dominion of Satan in his kingdom, which is the grave—had that never happened to Jesus, all who had died would stay in their graves and never be resurrected. Only the living could ever hope to go to heaven. There could be no hope of the dead going to heaven.

Jesus had to conquer not only death but the grave, and the resurrection accomplished that. He was tearing down the kingdom of Satan by destroying the victories of both death and the grave. So He did more than die for my sins. He came to destroy the kingdom of Satan, which is the kingdom of the dead and the grave. He accomplished that by going into the grave, and He gained the victory over the grave by resurrecting Himself and walking out of the grave after the time allotted by His Father.

The devil had tried to hold Jesus a prisoner, to keep Him in the grave. "When Jesus was laid in the grave, Satan triumphed. He had dared to hope that the Saviour would not take up His life again. He had claimed the Lord's body, and had set his guard about the tomb, seeking to hold Christ a prisoner. He was bitterly angry when his angels fled at the approach of the heavenly messenger.

When he saw Christ come forth in triumph, he knew that his kingdom would have an end, and that he must finally die." *Desire of Ages*, p. 782.

Satan had hoped that the Lord would be his prisoner. His presumption led him to believe that. He was bitterly angry when the mighty angel quoted the message that he was sent by the Father to deliver. Satan knew that his kingdom would be lost, and that he must ultimately die.

Now, if Christ resurrected Himself, as we read previously, only His humanity died, but not His divinity. Divinity cannot die. How can the death of one Human Being be enough to satisfy the punishment for all humanity and all our sins? I was asked that question back in college by a professor. I know one answer. It may not satisfy you, but here it is: "Justice demanded the sufferings of man; but Christ rendered the sufferings of a God." *SDA Bible Commentary*, Volume 7, p. 913. Death itself isn't bad. It's the suffering that came before the death of Jesus that was so terrible. The justice of God demanded the sufferings of a God, and Jesus is God.

If you were out driving and you came upon an auto accident and saw bodies on the road, you would run around to check their pulses and breathing to find out if they were dead or alive. If they were dead, you'd say, "Let them alone. No one can help them." If they were not dead, you would tell someone to call the police and an ambulance. If the person is dead, that's it. The dead don't know anything, but again, it's the dying that is bad.

And thus it wasn't the death of Jesus that was so terrible; it was the violent agony of His sufferings in the dying process. He provided the sufferings of a God. What is the capacity of God to suffer? I don't have any idea. I don't think any human could minutely comprehend the capacity of God to suffer. The only illustration I can think of is that when you punish your child, you tell them that it hurts you more. Why does it hurt Dad and Mother more than the child? It isn't the physical pain so much as the emotional pain you are causing your child. Imagine how the Father felt when He separated Himself from the One with Whom He had been close since eternity past.

As parents, we know where some of the rebellion and sin that we see in our children leads. Some of us have been down those roads ourselves, and we discovered that they were not very pleasant. If we see that our child persists in living a certain way, we know that his or her life will be miserable, both to the end of that road and back again. We can think of all the things that are going to happen to our child if he or she persists in that stubbornness and rebellion. We want to cry out and say, "Oh, why do you have to do that? Why do you want to suffer so much?" If we parents could only save our children from taking the wrong roads, it would give us peace, and life would be more wonderful. It's because we know where the road leads. And it's really true that Dad and Mother do suffer more than the child, because the parents think about the end of the road. It's the pain along the way that hurts so much.

God knows all about sin and its results—things that we don't know. All the sickness, all the wars, all the disasters—the accidents, the pestilences and plagues, the catastrophes—unbelievable things—all of them a result of sin. Today we are seeing more and more of the natural consequence of sin.

It isn't just humans involved in this. The devil and his fallen angels are involved in sin and all the corruption and crime and hatred and violence. Just every place you go, all over this world. There's the damage to the ecology, and the constant wars and rumors of war. In thousands and thousands of ways, sin is producing its natural consequences, and we think that somebody else is to blame. God knew all about the results of sin. It tears His great heart to pieces. It really does.

Imagine all of the pain from all of the sins of all of the people who will live on this earth—and all of that being placed upon Jesus. That's why justice required the sufferings of a God. What natural man could withstand that? The fact is, Jesus provided the sufferings of a God and took care of all people's sins for all time. But so many have not believed in what Jesus did for them. We must believe. Belief has always been a big part in man's problems with sin.

God the Father made the decision to transfer the sins of mankind onto His holy, spotless Son, and allow Him to suffer through Gethsemane, the scourging, the cross, and finally to become a prisoner in the grave. After all of that, the Father said that it was enough for all time. His justice was satisfied. After Jesus left the tomb, He wanted to make sure that He had really accomplished the task that He had been sent to do. That is why He told Mary not to touch Him (it really means not to "detain" Him), because He wanted to ascend to His Father to hear the approval from the Father Himself.

In the book *Desire of Ages,* page 790, we learn that "Jesus refused to receive the homage of His people until He had the assurance that His sacrifice was accepted by the Father. He ascended to the heavenly courts, and from God Himself heard the assurance that His atonement for the sins of men had been ample, that through His blood all might gain eternal life." What a marvelous thing to contemplate—that Christ's atonement for the sins of man had been ample; and that through His blood, all who would truly believe might gain eternal life.

The word *ample* means that the sacrifice was sufficient. It was enough. The Father called His Son out of the grave because His justice had been satisfied. That is why the Father sent the mighty angel to bear the message to Jesus that His Father called Him forth from the tomb. If that message had never been sent, then Jesus would have remained in the grave until the sin problem was all taken care of, no matter how long that took. The resurrection of Christ was God's decision that what Christ had accomplished was good for all people, for all sins, for all time, taking care of all punishment; and that through Him all might have access to eternal life.

For a short time after the resurrection, Jesus spent time with His disciples, and then He led to heaven some who had been prisoners of the grave. The Bible calls them *captives*. "And the graves were opened; and many bodies of the saints which slept arose, and came out of the graves after His resurrection, and went into the holy city, and appeared unto many." Matthew 27:52-53. This text tells about those who came out of their graves when Jesus resurrected Himself. They appeared to many in Jerusalem for a while, and then they ascended to heaven with Jesus. Here are people who had sinned, because the Bible says that all have sinned, and yet they have now been in heaven for many years. How could those guilty people get into heaven? Because Jesus took care of all their punishment for all their sins. The Father said that His justice was satisfied. They are accepted into heaven in the Beloved—in Jesus.

He went back to heaven the second time with those many prisoners He had delivered from the jail. He had said, "Father, I will that they also, whom Thou hast given Me, be with Me where I am." John 17:24. "The voice of God is heard proclaiming that justice is satisfied. Satan is vanquished." *Desire of Ages*, p. 834. "To the praise of the glory of His grace, wherein He hath made us accepted in the Beloved." Ephesians 1:6.

Thus God says, as Jesus ascends to heaven with the host of captives, that justice is satisfied. Satan is vanquished. The struggling ones on earth are accepted in the Beloved. The Father said to bring them on in.

Is it clear how those captives, all of whom had been guilty sinners, got into heaven? "What right had Christ to take the captives out of the enemy's hands? The right of having made a sacrifice that satisfies the principles of justice by which the kingdom of heaven is governed. He came to this earth as the Redeemer of the lost race, to conquer the wily foe, and, by His steadfast allegiance to right, to save all who accept Him as their Saviour. On the cross of Calvary He paid the redemption price of the race. And thus He gained the right to take the captives from the grasp of the great deceiver, who, by a lie framed against the government of God, caused the fall of man, and thus forfeited all claim to be called a loyal subject of God's glorious everlasting kingdom." *Selected Messages*, Book 1, p. 309.

"Justice demands that sin be not merely pardoned, but the death penalty must be executed. God, in the gift of His only-begotten Son, met both these requirements. By dying in man's stead, Christ exhausted the penalty and provided a pardon." Ibid., p. 340. If Jesus "exhausted the penalty," then how much is left? What does *exhausted* mean? If you say the bread is exhausted, do you have any bread left? If the potatoes are exhausted, they are all gone. If you exhaust the penalty, how much penalty is left? Do you really believe that? If, through my total devotion and dependence upon Christ, I can say that the penalty for my sins has been exhausted, then I have no reason to have hang-ups with guilt. By hang-ups, I mean prolonged guilt. The penalty is all gone. There is none left. There is no need, then, to live for years with feelings of guilt because of some terrible sin we committed before Jesus became our Master.

"When the enemy comes in like a flood, and seeks to overwhelm you with the thought of your sin, tell him: 'I know I am a sinner. If I were not, I could not go to the Saviour; for He says, "I came not to call the righteous, but sinners to repentance" (Mark 2:17). And because I am a sinner I am entitled to come to Christ. I am sinful and polluted, but He suffered humiliation and death, and exhausted the curse that belongs to me. I come. I believe. I claim His sure promise, "Whosoever believeth in him should not perish, but have everlasting life" (John 3:16).'" Ibid., p. 325.

Then there is the precious promise: "There is therefore now no condemnation to them which are in Christ Jesus." Romans 8:1. There is no condemnation if you now abide in Jesus and He abides in you. The condemnation is gone. The title of this chapter is exactly correct. There is no punishment for the guilty, as long as we have admitted our guilt. If we run around evading it and excusing it, then we have some problems. If the Father, the divine Judge, has made a determination that Christ suffered a penalty sufficient to take care of all people's sin for all time, there is no penalty left. Admit your guilt and the penalty for you is all gone. That is essentially the decree that the Father made when He called Jesus out of the grave. The Father said to Jesus that all He had done on Calvary and the time He spent in the grave took care of all sin and all penalties for all time.

I know that you have a lot of questions, and I'll try to answer a few of them. But do not deny what the Father has decreed. Don't argue with Him. Some people do argue with God; they want to quibble about this and that. They want to use their logic to out-argue God and all that He has done. They want to eliminate what Christ has done, or else depreciate it. So the Bible teaches assurance in the judgment: "Because He hath appointed a day, in the which He will judge the world in righteousness by that Man whom He hath ordained; whereof He hath given assurance unto all men, in that He hath raised Him from the dead." Acts 17:31. The Father, through the angel, called Jesus to come forth from the dead. That should give us tremendous assurance, because that means that God is satisfied that

Christ had taken care of all of the penalty. There is no penalty left for us; it's all gone. If you really believed that, you would be jumping for joy. You would shout out so loudly that the roof would cave in. We have a terrible time believing the good news of our salvation.

Let me ask you some difficult questions. Will the Father punish you for the same sins for which He has punished Jesus? If all of my sins have been laid upon Jesus, is He going to turn around and punish me again for the sins for which Jesus suffered and died? In legal parlance, that is called "double jeopardy." Human courts have decided that no one must be put in double jeopardy; a person cannot be punished twice for the same crime. So Jesus died for Bill Lehman's sins, and am I to think that I have to die for them, too? That would make God more sadistic and more horrible than any human being, because men won't even do that. The Bible says that God is love. He surely couldn't punish me for the same crimes or the same sins for which He has already punished Jesus.

Then you ask, "Why will some be punished? Why will the wicked die?" I'd like to suggest to you that the answer is found in the following verses: "For God sent not His Son into the world to condemn the world; but that the world through Him might be saved. He that believeth on Him is not condemned: but he that believeth not is condemned already, because he hath not believed in the name of the only begotten Son of God. And this is the condemnation, that light is come into the world, and men loved darkness rather than light, because their deeds were evil. For every one that doeth evil hateth the light, neither cometh to the light, lest his deeds should be reproved." John 3:17-20.

Never forget that part of the Scripture above that says, "For God sent not His Son into the world to condemn the world." You know that text very well now, don't you? If it were not for the Son of God, we could never be saved. "He that believeth on Him is not condemned: but he that believeth not is condemned already." The condemned ones are those who are unbelievers in what God has accomplished for man. A person is condemned "because he hath not believed in the name of the only begotten Son of God. And this is the condemnation…."

Light has come into the world, and Jesus said of Himself, "I am the light of the world." John 8:12. What did Jesus call Himself? The "light of the world." "This is the condemnation, that light has come into the world, and men loved darkness rather than light because their deeds were evil." They rejected Jesus. *That is a different kind of sin.* They rejected God's provision for taking care of man's guilt and penalty. They rejected the plan of salvation. It wasn't just that they had sinned by disobeying the law. They rejected the way out. They rejected the Person who is the way to truth and light; they wouldn't have Him to reign over them. They wouldn't believe that God is a God of love and mercy. They wanted their own way.

"The wrath of God is not declared against men merely because of the sins which they have committed, but for choosing to continue in a state of resistance, and, although they have light and knowledge, repeating their sins of the past. If they would submit, they would be pardoned; but they are determined not to yield. They defy God by their obstinacy. These souls have given themselves to Satan, and he controls them according to his will." *Testimonies to Ministers*, p. 74.

The Spirit of God persistently comes back and comes back—not to nag us, but to rescue us, to win us, to get us to yield and submit and love Him because He loves us. The Spirit and the holy angels try to win and to woo and to entice us, and over and over to lure us to Christ, but we will not. Over and over and over again, hundreds and thousands of times, we reject Christ and His love for us.

We turn away Jesus, the way of life, and that is why we are destroyed. We are not destroyed merely because of the sins that we commit, but because we will not accept God's way of life and His way of rescue for mankind. We reject Christ as the light of the world.

So God does not come to destroy us just because we have sinned. The Father has said that the penalty is all paid. He is satisfied; why aren't you? I know the problems I have with this, and I suspect you are sometimes just as bad as I am about this one area, at least. So many of us want to deserve salvation; so many of us want to be good enough; so many of us want to get some praise, some pats on the back. And somehow we have been so brainwashed on this idea of deserving approbation or acceptance in heaven that we want to do something to prove that we are worthy of it.

You can never be worthy of heaven, and neither can I. To simply accept Christ's grace and sacrifice as a gift of God sort of deflates our ego. We like a do-it-yourself religion; we like a pat on the back. And we seem to crave this so desperately that we will not accept the hard facts of what God has already done for us.

We're each like a little boy who needs a box for his bedroom. He has never used his daddy's hammer, and he doesn't know how to pound nails, but he decides he is going to put a box together. And so he goes out there on the back porch and finds Dad's hammer and some boards and nails and begins to make a box. Dad comes by and says, "Let me help you." And the boy says, "No, I want to do it myself." He begins to bend the nails and split the boards, and every time he pounds away, he bends more nails and splits more boards. Father comes by again and asks, "May I help you?" "No. I want to do it myself. Let me alone." The boy continues, still splitting boards and bending nails. Finally the dad comes by and the boy is crying and crying—what we call depression, or a guilt trip. Dad asks, "What's the matter?" "I can't have a box. All the nails are bent. All the boards are split. I need a box." The boy continues to cry and cry. He starts to admit that he can't build the box, so Dad sits down and straightens out a few nails and starts putting the boards together. In just a few minutes there is a beautiful box, exactly what the boy wanted. All the time the father was waiting to do it, but the boy kept saying, "I want to do it myself."

Believe me, that is what happens to us in the Christian life. "I want to do it myself"—and the gospel is almost meaningless to people like that. We want approval for *our* works, and we have problems accepting *His* works. It doesn't work that way. The Bible teaches that the judgment no longer condemns me. Instead, I can have tremendous assurance in the judgment. I can come boldly to the throne of grace without any fear whatsoever. Why? Because God called Jesus forth from the dead.

May I read it to you from the reasoning of Paul, who knew the Bible so well? I wish that I knew the Bible half as well as Paul did. This is from the New English Bible: "What then shall we say about these things? If God is for us, who can be against us? Indeed, He who did not spare His own Son, but gave Him up for us all—how will He not also, along with Him, freely give us all things? Who will bring any charge against God's elect? It is God who justifies. Who is the one who will condemn? Christ is the One who died (and more than that, He was raised), who is at the right hand of God, and Who also is interceding for us. Who will separate us from the love of Christ? Will trouble, or distress, or persecution, or famine, or nakedness, or danger, or sword? As it is written, *'For your sake we encounter death all day long; we were considered as sheep to be slaughtered.'* No, in all these things we have complete victory through Him who loved us! For I am convinced that neither death, nor life, nor angels, nor heavenly rulers, nor things that are present, nor things to come, nor powers, nor height, nor depth, nor anything else in creation will be able to separate us from the love of God in Christ Jesus our Lord." Romans 8:31-37.

There are an awful lot of people who don't know that God is on our team. "If God be for us, who can be against us?" Romans 8:31. If we have the greatest, the strongest, the mightiest One on our side, what are we afraid of? "He who did not spare His own Son, but gave Him up for us all." Romans 8:32. With the gift of Jesus, how can He fail to lavish upon us all that He has to give? If He has given the most precious thing He owns—the Lord Jesus—will He not give us everything else of lesser value? That includes everlasting life. Surely He will. That is Paul's argument, and it's a good one. Who will bring any charge against God's elect? It is God who justifies. Who is the one who will condemn? Because God called His

Son out of the grave, He says there is no more guilt and no more condemnation. That is acquittal. Who is going to find fault now, since God Himself has said it's okay? We are justified. Then who can condemn? Christ is the One who died (and more than that, He was raised), Who is at the right hand of God, and Who also is interceding for us. Who will separate us from the love of Christ?

Then, who or what can separate us from the love of Christ? Let me explain the reasoning here. If Jesus took all my sins—all of them, because the Father laid them on Jesus, and then He died, was put in the grave, and came out of the grave and ascended to heaven—then can I not go to heaven? All my sins are taken away from me. They were put on Jesus. He has all the stigma, all the guilt, all the punishment. If He is acceptable to the Father, then why not me? Get the idea? If the contaminated One was welcomed into heaven, then the ones from whom the sins were taken and who were cleansed by His blood, are they not welcome, also? Of course, they are welcome. That is Paul's reasoning.

We have been made clean by Jesus' washing our sins away with His blood; He is the dirty one because He has taken upon Himself all the sins of all who will live. The Bible puts it in such beautiful language when it says, "Neither death, nor life, nor angels, nor heavenly rulers, nor things that are present, nor things to come, nor powers, nor height, nor depth, nor anything else in creation will be able to separate us from the love of God in Christ Jesus our Lord." Romans 8:38. Nothing can separate us, not even past sins. Jesus took them all out of the way.

Again, I wish I had one of those big syringes I told you about so that I could just inject this into your brain, and from that time on, you would shout *hallelujah* and be a convinced believer with all your heart, without one shred of doubt. You have to be a serious agnostic, a quibbling doubter, a person who wants to trust your own logic rather than a "thus saith the Lord," in order to doubt this. The Bible is so filled with evidence that God has taken care of all the guilt and all the punishment. There is no reason to fear—not one reason under the sun except unbelief.

The Jews had problems with unbelief, Paul said. Today, the biggest hang-up of Christians is not guilt, but unbelief, just like with the Jews. We are no different than they, for we are all of the human family.

Friend, there is enormous reason to be joyful and happy, and to shout for joy and to praise God every day of your life. Enormous reason! There is tremendous reason to live a life of gratitude. How can we ever thank Him when He loved us so? The penalty is all gone. We even have assurance in the judgment. No more fear. No more condemnation. No more punishment. It's all gone. Jesus paid it all.

Here is my prayer for those who rejoice in what Christ has done for us: Loving Father, Lord, we believe; help Thou our unbelief. We surely do have trouble with good news. We've looked at our sins so long, and our human weakness and helplessness, and all the dark scenes of our memories, so that sometimes we can't even see the sun when it's shining in all its glory. We seem to have our minds so filled with darkness and gloom. Lord, open our hearts and open our minds. Help to us understand that God is true, and that these are words of truth—words of life and beauty. Beautiful words, wonderful words, wonderful words of life. Lord, come into our hearts. Convict us in our innermost souls of the truth and the glory of the resurrection. Convict us that all the sin is taken away, and all the penalty, so that we can rejoice in Christ. We are now accepted in Christ the Beloved. There is, therefore, now no condemnation. Lord, may we live a life of gratitude and joy, every day thanking Thee for such a marvelous, marvelous gift, for such a wonderful God, for such a tremendous Savior. May we sing Thy praises for all eternity. In Christ's name we pray. Amen.

CHAPTER 4: THE JUDGMENT AND THE GUILTY

I have learned from talking to many Christians that it is very easy to misunderstand how to get rid of guilt. If you have misunderstood me so far, or think you have misunderstood me, please keep reading. You can criticize me if you want to. It would be nice if we could just sit and talk together about some of these things so we could really comprehend each other.

This is another one of those controversial topics. If you are an average Christian with any habitual sins, the traditional teaching about the judgment can drive you up the wall. In fact, if you are suffering with guilt, it's probably one of the most detested teachings we have. The concept of the judgment makes some people cringe when they read that we are all going to be judged by every idle word that we speak and every deed that we do. How do you feel about that?

Actually, I think that the devil would like to distort every good teaching we have. I wish that you would look at the judgment with me, to review a few things that most people probably already know.

We understand that the judgment takes place in the most holy place of the heavenly sanctuary. In that second compartment of the sanctuary is the law—the law on stone tablets that reveals us to be sinners, and thus makes us feel guilty. The Bible says, "Thy way, O God, is in the sanctuary." Psalms 77:13. If you take a little tour and approach the most holy place, you will discover some amazing things that we usually leave out in our teaching about the law and about being judged by the law.

Let me take you on a guided tour. As we enter the courtyard, there is a huge altar—the altar of sacrifice, which symbolizes the death of Christ for your sins and mine. Just beyond it is the laver, symbolizing how the blood of Christ cleanses or washes us from all sins. Then we enter the holy place, and on our right is the table of showbread, pointing to Christ, the living Bread. John 6:32-33. The goblets of wine remind us of Christ's blood that was poured out during His scourging and crucifixion. On the left is the seven-branched brass candlestick with its seven lamps. Jesus said, "I am the light of the world." John 8:12. Jesus knew that we were destined to die because of our sins, but He came as the light of this world to give us life.

There is oil in the candlesticks that makes the lamps burn. The oil is derived from beaten olives, symbolizing the sufferings and beatings of Christ. "He was wounded for our transgressions, He was bruised for our iniquities: the chastisement of our peace was upon Him; and with His stripes we are healed." Isaiah 53:5.

As we progress further into the holy place, there is the altar of incense, that golden altar of His perfect righteousness. Oh, how we need the merits and righteousness of Christ, because we have no righteousness apart from Him. We enter into heaven by His righteousness alone. Then there is the glorious veil, behind which is the most holy place. In the earthly sanctuary, the veil was rent from top to bottom when Jesus died. Paul tells us that the torn veil symbolizes Christ's crucified flesh.

On our tour, the most holy place is next. The only way the priest could enter the most holy place, where the ark of the covenant is found, was with incense in one hand and blood in the other hand. The incense symbolizes Christ's righteousness mingled with the prayers of God's people, and the blood represents His death. As we enter the most holy place, we see the two golden cherubim standing at either end of the mercy seat that covers the ark of the covenant. Those cherubim represent the ministering spirits sent to intercede and work for human beings, to assist in their salvation. There is the mercy seat that represents the marvelous grace and mercy of our loving Lord. Mercy is the first attribute of God's character.

When we lift the mercy seat, inside we find the law nestled between two other objects—Aaron's rod that budded, symbolizing the resurrection power for those that die, and a golden pot of manna, representing God's provision that we might live.

It is only after encountering all that I have described of God's merciful provision for sinners that we finally find the law. If the sanctuary is presented in any other way, it is a perversion. Do you agree with me? If all that procession of mercy for sinners is left out, and the two tables of law at the end are all that is mentioned, then the law becomes a perversion of truth. And, unfortunately, we usually present only the law and leave out all the rest. That's what we do. We put the other items of the sanctuary that show mercy and love in studies so far removed from the law that we can't remember the mercy any longer. I contend that too many of God's people have taken the law out of context in the judgment, and doing that gives us all a very different idea about the judgment. One thing that we find very troubling is that the Bible teaches, "Behold, I come quickly; and My reward is with Me, to give every man according as his work shall be." Revelation 22:12. This worries us, and we begin to get concerned about our works, since we are judged and rewarded according to them.

I want you to look at some of the works and rewards in the judgment as taught by Jesus in some of His parables. The first parable concerns the prodigal son and his brother. I want you to listen to the argument of the prodigal's brother after his brother had come home to a great feast: "And he was angry, and would not go in: therefore came his father out, and intreated him, And he answering said to his father, Lo, these many years do I serve thee, neither transgressed I at any time thy commandment: and yet thou never gavest me a kid, that I might make merry with my friends: But as soon as this thy son was come, which hath devoured thy living with harlots, thou hast killed for him the fatted calf." Luke 15:28-30.

Notice his works. He never violated his father's law, "yet thou never gavest me a kid, that I might make merry with my friends: But as soon as this thy son was come, which hath devoured thy living with harlots, thou hast killed for him the fatted calf." Can you love a father like that?

Think carefully about this. The worthless, good-for-nothing son, who wasted all that his father had given him as an inheritance, comes home, and they make a joyful feast. The fellow who stayed home and did exactly what his father required of him all the time, who kept his nose to the grindstone and labored away all those years, never was given such a feast. He was so provoked by what he considered his father's unfairness that he wouldn't even go inside.

Do you think the father was fair? The prodigal's brother said in so many words. "Dad, you're not fair with me. You are cheating me. You are depriving me, and I don't like it. Why do you do these things for that worthless, guilty son? I am the one who has been so faithful and righteous, yet you did nothing for me. Why?"

Now, while you're mulling over this seeming inequality, let's look at another Bible parable: "So when even was come, the lord of the vineyard saith unto his steward, Call the labourers, and give them their hire, beginning from the last unto the first. And when they came that were hired about the eleventh hour, they received every man a penny. But when the first came, they supposed that they should have received more; and they likewise received every man a penny. And when they had received it, they murmured against the goodman of the house, Saying, These last have wrought but one hour, and thou hast made them equal unto us, which have borne the burden and heat of the day. But he answered one of them, and said, Friend, I do thee no wrong: didst not thou agree with me for a penny? Take that thine is, and go thy way: I will give unto this last, even as unto thee. Is it not lawful for me to do what I will with mine own? Is thine eye evil, because I am good?" Matthew 15:8-20.

This parable tells about the ones who were called the first hour of the morning and labored twelve hours, and those called the third hour and ninth hour and so on, working fewer hours, until finally some were called at the eleventh hour and worked only one hour. As they came to receive their wages, they all received one penny, which we understand was very good wages back then for twelve hours of work. But those who had worked a long time expected that they would receive more, since those who had worked only one hour received a penny. So they complained about that. The "goodman of the house" talked to them, saying, "Isn't this what you agreed to? May I not do with my own what I please? I haven't done you any wrong." Do you see anything wrong with that?

He told the ones who complained to take what was theirs and go their way, because it was lawful for him to do with his own money what he wanted to do. "Is thine eye evil, because I am good?" So although it seemed there was an inequality there, everyone had to agree that it was all legal. But let's leave out the legality of it, and talk about fairness. Was it fair? How would you like to have been the ones who worked twelve hours and received the very same wages as the ones who worked only one hour? How would you like that? In this world, there would be criticism and people would think that the whole thing was unfair. Many would not like one bit the way things were handled.

In these two parables, Christ is describing some things for us that we have difficulty understanding. These are illustrations of God's dealings with us, and we must perceive the deep meaning of these things, or we will misunderstand God. Now, add to these parables the idea that we are rewarded according to our works. Were the prodigal's brother and the twelfth-hour laborers rewarded according to their works? Was the prodigal rewarded according to his works? By the world's standards, it doesn't appear that way.

We are going to have to look at works a little longer than we have been looking in the past. When the Lord says we are rewarded according to works, He has a different meaning than most of us have thought. And the reason you feel so guilty sometimes about poor works is that you do not understand the kind of works He is talking about in these two parables, which are so important to us.

How can this dilemma between the prodigal and his brother, and the situation with the wage earners, be explained? The Jews said about the Lord, "The way of the LORD is not equal [or fair]." Ezekiel 18:25. They charged God with injustice. And the Lord answered them by saying, "Is not my way equal? are not your ways unequal?" (Same verse.) The Lord tells us that *we* are the unfair ones, and He is the fair One. It seems in these two parables that the Lord is unfair, but He really is not. If we study them carefully, we will understand why.

One more parable will help us understand: "But which of you, having a servant plowing or feeding cattle, will say unto him by and by, when he is come from the field, Go and sit down to meat? And will not rather say unto him, Make ready wherewith I may sup, and gird thyself, and serve me, till I have eaten and drunken; and afterward thou shalt eat and drink? Doth he thank that servant because he did the things that were commanded him? I trow not [I think not]. So likewise ye, when ye shall have done all those things which are commanded you, say, We are unprofitable servants: we have done that which was our duty to do." Luke 17:7-10.

Will the servant serve himself and eat first? Or will a servant take care of his master first and then, after his master has finished eating, take care of himself? Jesus in the parable said, "So likewise ye, when ye shall have done all those things which are commanded you, say, We are unprofitable servants: we have done that which was our duty to do." Remember the prodigal's brother? He said he had done all of his father's commandments. To put that in perspective, Jesus taught that when we have done all the things we are commanded to do, we do not deserve a pat on the back or special treatment. We are only "unprofitable servants." We have done only that which was our duty to do.

When you have kept all the law and all of the requirements of being a Christian, and there are many of them, you are to say that you are only an unprofitable servant. We have done only the things that it is our duty to do. Our obedience to the requirements does not earn us any special favors. That is, we deserve no special commendation. The Master has received His due from us, but nothing more worth mentioning. He is not profited by our service to the extent that He should feel obliged to show us special honor. We have our wages, and that is all we should expect. When we have done our best for God, we do not thereby place Him under any particular obligation to us. We have done no more than by right we should do.

This teaching is more than a little bit different from that held by those who believe God's favor can be earned. When we have done all the right things, we are simply to say, "I am an unprofitable servant; God is not obligated to me at all." If He were obligated, then we would be saved by our works. The big question in these parables is this: Is God indebted to us? Or are we indebted to Him? How about you? Do you serve God, expecting Him to pay you because He is obligated to you? Do you serve Him to make Him obligated to you? Or do you serve God because of your obligation to Him?

Is the judgment concerned about God's obligation to us—whether or not we are deserving—or is it concerned about whether we have shown our gratitude and paid our debt of grace to Him? It's a vastly different thing, depending on the way we look at it.

The bigger problem we have with this is accepting the idea that we are guilty, and that we are sinners. The problem is that "the wages of sin is death." Romans 6:23. The wage that sinners earn is death. All have sinned; all are guilty. If the Lord deals with us according to what we deserve, what have we all earned? We all would die. We should want to find a better way than to be paid the wages that we deserve.

What we deserve is bad; it's sour grapes for all of us. I don't want to be paid what I deserve, do you? I don't want the Lord to ever deal with me according to what I deserve—not ever! But I will never get good enough to deserve something better. So I really don't want to be dealt with according to wages or merit. I want to leave those two things out when it comes to the judgment.

I'm thankful that the Bible has some marvelous texts on this matter of how sinners do not get what they deserve. We need to get familiar with them, for we will need these texts at those times when we get very discouraged and depressed. Here is the first text: "He hath not dealt with us after our sins; nor rewarded us according to our iniquities." Psalms 103:10. There is a huge word in there, which is the word *not*. God has not dealt with us according to our sins, and He has not rewarded us according to our iniquities. This is talking about the way God deals with people. It is not according to our sins or iniquities—yet we are told that we will be awarded according to our works. How do we resolve the seeming contradiction?

If our works are sinful and God does not reward us according to our iniquities, what does this verse mean: "My reward is with Me, to give every man according as his work shall be"? Revelation 22:12. We must really confront ourselves with this apparent disagreement in the Bible, for if we do not harmonize the texts pertaining to judgment, we most likely will accept a falsehood.

This stretches our brain muscles a bit, so we don't like to sit down and labor mentally long enough to find out what the clash is all about. It's usually a misunderstanding in our thinking. Jesus said that He will "give to man according as his work shall be," but "He hath not dealt with us after our sins; nor rewarded us according to our iniquities." Is there a genuine contradiction?

Let's look at what Job had to say. He endured much, and had great wisdom. Job said that "God exacteth of thee less than thine iniquity deserveth." Job 11:6. We can be sure of that. God exacts from us less than our sins deserve.

In the New Testament there is another clarifying text: "… Who hath saved us, and called us with an holy calling, not according to our works, but according to His own purpose and grace." 2 Timothy 1:9. Not according to our works. If you put all of these texts together and think about them frequently, it would help you greatly. You must remember these things because we are talking about works. We are judged by our works and rewarded according to our works, but it also says we are not rewarded according to our works. Again, what is this all about?

It's not nearly as complicated as it sounds. Let's view salvation from the perspective of grace, accepting the fact that all have sinned. Everyone is guilty, and thus everyone needs grace. We dare not ask God to give us what we deserve.

If you look at all the parables about works from the perspective of grace, these will make great sense, and the lessons of Christ will become beautiful to you. If God deals with you according to grace, and not according to merit or works, then you have a debt to pay to grace, literally. Don't get too upset about this debt. Paul declared, "For sin shall not have dominion over you: for ye are not under the law, but under grace." Romans 6:14. This is the key text in resolving the seeming contradictions we have seen regarding how we are judged. We should focus upon the word *under*. That word really means *obligated to*, in one sense of the translation. Another meaning is *indebted to*.

What I'm trying to tell you is that when Jesus came and lived a righteous life in humanity, He provided righteousness for every human being, which was the righteousness inherent in the law. We cannot achieve righteousness by keeping the law, so Jesus lived a perfect life *for us*. Do you think that you can live a perfect life— obeying every commandment perfectly? "Can the Ethiopian change his skin, or the leopard his spots? then may ye also do good, that are accustomed to do evil." Jeremiah 13:23. Since I can't be good enough to be declared righteous by the Lord, and the Bible teaches that Jesus lived a perfect life and offers His righteousness to me, then I can be righteous only by faith in *His* righteousness. I'm not trying to quibble about righteousness, so please don't misunderstand me about that word. Jesus provides His perfect obedience for me because He knows that I can never live a perfect life. And I must appropriate Christ's righteousness for myself. I must live by faith in *His* right-doing, not in mine.

I am not judged by my own right-doing, because I can never achieve the degree of right-doing that will earn me a ticket to heaven. Therefore, I claim the right-doing of Jesus for myself, and He delights to give me His righteousness (right-doing) because He realizes how weak we all are, and because of His great love and mercy for sinners. It is Christ that works in me to will and to do of His good pleasure. And it is my cooperation and submission to Him that allows Jesus to accomplish right-doing in my life.

Now, as soon as Christ has done this for me, and I accept it by faith, does that leave me debt-free? Does that take away all of my obligation? It takes away my obligation to the law, because God knows that I can never perfectly obey the law, and therefore He has made free provision for me. But do I have another obligation?

In the Sermon on the Mount, Christ talked about the obligation of grace. In fact, our obligation to grace is discussed in many places throughout the Bible. Jesus taught: "For if ye forgive men their trespasses, your heavenly Father will also forgive you: But if ye forgive not men their trespasses, neither will your Father forgive your trespasses." Matthew 6:14, 15.

This is not as easy to understand as we might think. If I believe that God has forgiven me solely by His grace, with no merit on my part—and if I completely trust in that unmerited favor (called grace) toward me as a guilty person—and if I believe in His grace with all my heart, and believe I am saved because of it—then I will treat you the very same way that I believe God has treated me. If you wrong me, I probably will not know whether or not you will repent and seek forgiveness from God. Regardless, I will immediately forgive you, even before you ask—even if you don't ask—because I never want Him to treat me according to my merit. So I will never treat you according to your merit. If you are undeserving, that doesn't make any difference. I gladly forgive you because the Lord gladly forgives me when I am undeserving, and I am always undeserving. And because I believe in that undeserving favor manifested to me, I demonstrate this by my treatment of you. *I treat you with works of grace.*

You may not deserve being treated with grace, but I'll treat you that way anyhow, because I have tasted of the marvelous grace of God. My whole soul is dependent upon His grace. I love grace; I revel in it. It's my only hope of salvation. So when you wrong me, you get some of the grace that He has given to me. I show you grace quickly and spontaneously. I like it that way because I never want to be treated the opposite way by the Lord.

In the judgment, God is looking for works that reveal a character wholly dependent on God's grace. The judgment comes at the end of the kingdom of grace, which was instituted immediately after the fall of man, but not fully established until the death of Christ. The judgment has to do with the kingdom of grace that Jesus set up in Eden for fallen mankind, and in fact concludes that kingdom. Those who have been found citizens of the kingdom of grace are eligible for the kingdom of glory.

So if I live by His grace, and my works towards God and my fellow man are of grace because of His grace, it will be very evident in the judgment, and there is no problem with the judgment, then. There are works of merit, as well. If I try to merit heaven, I will be judged by my works of merit, not by grace. If I insist on trying to deserve it, He says, "I will give you what you deserve." And everyone knows what we all deserve. That's not too pleasant a thought.

Jesus says that He would rather treat us with grace, but if we insist on works of merit, we will be treated according to our merit. So in the judgment there are primarily two kinds of works that God looks for. Has He seen in our lives works of grace or works of merit? If He finds works of grace, we are saved by His precious grace. If He sees that we are depending on works of merit to be saved, we are rewarded according to our merit, and that does some disastrous things for us.

We've always thought that God has an electron microscope up there, scrutinizing every human being, and that the angels are writing down everything they find wrong in us. If we could only, somehow, make ourselves absolutely, flawlessly perfect so that He could find nothing wrong in us, then we would be deserving. But who thinks that they can perform flawlessly? Is it those persons who the Bible says are nothing but dust? Can it be any other? Why do people think they must try to perform flawlessly, anyway? It is for selfish reasons. I would like to suggest to you that God does not look for flawless performance. Flawless performance doesn't make us safe to be received into heaven.

I used to teach flying. Flying is a very difficult thing to learn quickly. In fact, flight students make repeated mistakes. After the longest process, they finally start doing things right. As an instructor, in my first class of six students, I had a fellow who could do the first time exactly what I showed him to do. I never saw such a flawless performer in flying as this fellow was. His name was Vince. I used tell the other instructors about this guy, because my other students were just abominable compared to Vince. They could do nothing right; they would bounce all the way down the runway. Vince would never do that. Every time, on about the first ten or fifteen feet of the runway, he would put it down right, and it would stick right there just like glue.

Every maneuver was just flawless. Instructors revel in students like that because they are so rare. I used to brag about Vince, saying that he was eligible for heaven right then because he did things so perfectly.

We had to write grade slips on their flights every day, and I could never find one thing wrong with Vince. One old veteran instructor said, "You better be careful of that fellow. Some day he will have an accident, and they'll blame you because you never put down the facts about him." But I did always put down the facts. The old-timer instructors thought I was crazy; they brushed off what I said about Vince because they thought I was really just a greenhorn instructor.

So when Vince would come in to land, sometimes I would kick the stick, bump the throttle, or kick a rudder so the airplane would just go skewing down the runway. Vince had never learned how to recover from a bad landing because he had never made one, until I would sort of gum things up while he was coming into land. I used to do all kinds of things, just to make it difficult for him to do things right. I felt like a stinker for doing it, but they told me that was the thing to do. I wasn't sure at that time that they were right.

Well, my students went on from our school to advanced school in Arkansas. The news came back after a month or two that out of all my students, five of them were horrible, but one was way up at the top. Out of those six students, though, only one had had an accident during the advanced training. Guess who it was. Vince! When I heard about Vince's accident, I said, "That's impossible!" Then suddenly I knew that the old instructors would be telling me, "I told you so."

At the advanced flight landing strip, the runway was built on top of the ground where three feet of concrete stuck up above the ground. They needed that to land some of the big planes. All of my other students besides Vince were lucky if the wheels on their aircraft hit the middle of the runway. Vince could hit the first ten or fifteen feet every time. But one day, for the first time in his life, he came in just a little bit low. His wheels hit the raised end of the runway, which caused the landing gear to fold up underneath the plane, which then went sliding down the runway on its belly. He was just a hair off; he made just a slight mistake in estimating where the wheels would touch down. No one was hurt, but there was some damage to the airplane.

You see, it was his constant attempts at perfection that got him into trouble. May I suggest to you that God cannot trust flawless performers in heaven. He cannot. They are still human; they are still prone to error. The ones that God trusts in heaven are those who *totally* distrust themselves and absolutely trust *Jesus* for everything. They don't take one step until they hear that still, small voice saying, "This is the way, walk ye in it." Isaiah 30:21. The ones who stumble and fall over and over again can finally learn to trust Christ and distrust self. When they do that, they are safe to save.

One night the worst student in my flight class had to make a forced landing onto a little runway in the dark from 5,000 feet. There was a spotlight shining down the runway about 300 feet. He had to hit the spotlight in order to tell how high he was. To gauge all the way from 5,000 feet, circle down, and come right down and land in that light is a tremendous skill, even for an old-time instructor. I went to work one morning, and there on the desk from my squadron commander was a note. It read, "Your student last night had a forced landing, and he landed right on the lights."

If only you had seen my grade slips for him. He failed on forced landings every day, and he had failed for six straight weeks! If someone had told me that he would have been able to make that forced landing, I would have said it was the biggest lie in the world. I was called in at lunchtime and was told, "Hey, you know, that guy is a sharp student." And I said, "It's the first time!" You just can't explain some of these things. He had made so many poor forced landings, yet in the emergency he performed well.

The prodigal and his brother are like that. The brother said he had done all of his father's commandments perfectly. The prodigal said he had done nothing right.

You must look at these things very hard and critically, or you will miss something. We are judged by our works. Will they be works of merit, or works of grace? We will be judged accordingly. Have we worked selflessly, trusting wholly in His grace, or have we worked for ourselves, hoping our own efforts would give us merit?

One final parable will illustrate works of grace versus works of merit. It's the parable of the two debtors, one who owed a huge sum of money, and the other who owed a very small amount. The king forgave the man who owed the very large debt. That debtor had pleaded for his king to have patience with him and that he would pay all he owed. In reality, he owed so much that he could not have paid his debt, even if he lived for two or three lifetimes. But the king, by his grace, gladly forgave him the whole amount. He told the debtor to forget about it.

Now remember, when we don't pay a debt, somebody has to pay it for us. In telling that huge debtor that his debt was forgiven, or written off, the king had to pay the debt himself. He took the loss, so the man could be free. It cost the King of heaven His dearly beloved Son in order to pay our debt as transgressors of His law. God the Father is very wealthy, but when it came to sons, He only had one. His only Son was the price He had to pay to forgive us. Our sins hit God where He was the poorest.

Well, the man who owed so much went out and met someone who owed him a few dollars. Just after being forgiven for a very huge debt, he couldn't find it in his heart to forgive his own debtor a few miserable dollars. He ordered his debtor to be thrown in jail, which was the punishment for debtors. Some of the neighbors and friends of the man who had been jailed heard about this. They went to the king and told him what happened. "Then his lord, after that he had called him, said unto him, O thou wicked servant, I forgave thee all that debt, because thou desiredst me: Shouldest not thou also have had compassion on thy fellowservant, even as I had pity on thee? And his lord was wroth, and delivered him to the tormentors, till he should pay all that was due unto him. So likewise shall My heavenly Father do also unto you, if ye from your hearts forgive not every one his brother their trespasses." Matthew 18:32-35.

Jesus is not trying to be severe here. He is asking, "How can you demand payment from others when I don't demand it from you? How can you be so dictatorial and so exacting and demanding, when I am so merciful and kind and gracious to you? Is your heart so hardened that you cannot forgive others a debt that is much less than the debt you owe to Me? Are you just a rock? Are you like a lion that wants to devour everything? What is *wrong* with you? Why doesn't love come out of your heart towards others?"

The Lord has no pleasure in the death of the wicked. It is not His will that we should die eternally. Therefore, He is long-suffering and manifests marvelous grace towards undeserving sinners. "But where sin abounded, grace did much more abound." Romans 5:20. "Much more," Paul wrote. Where there is sin, there is a tidal wave of grace. Friends, we will never finish God's work until we are a church with tidal waves of grace towards those who are undeserving. Never. Until then, we will frighten the world half sick until they all feel so guilty that they will hate our God. They know they are sinners, but they need to know about the grace of Christ. And His grace is not permissiveness, at all. Don't ever think that or give anyone that impression. Grace brings an *obligation*. Permissiveness has no obligation. God is so gracious to us, and He tells us that we now have a debt to pay that we are able to pay. We can pay our debt to grace *if we know Jesus*. Our debt is to grace and not to the law (Romans 6:14). We couldn't pay the debt we owe to the law if we lived a thousand lifetimes. Jesus paid our debt to the law by perfectly keeping the law. But now, we have a debt of grace to pay. What is that debt? To be gracious unto others who are wholly undeserving, just as we are. That is what God expects.

Can't we love people? Can't we be kind to them when they wrongfully use us, realizing that the Lord has been so kind to us? Can't we understand why people are so prone to sin? Why do we say evil things? Why do we lose our tempers? Can't we understand? Aren't we sinners, too? The God who never sins understands us; why do we sinners not understand each other? Why are we so critical and so nasty about bad things that people do to us? Why do we make life so unbearable by our exactions and our demands? Why do we do that? The Lord doesn't do it.

In His marvelous judgment, the Lord is looking at our works to see how much we believe in His grace. Jesus is looking to see if He finds our kindness to others when they are not deserving, and patience for those who do not deserve patience. He is looking to see who is helping the fatherless, the widows, the hungry, and those in prison. He is looking to see who has compassion for the downtrodden. He is looking for those whose hearts are melted with love and grace for other sinners, because they are just like we are. When He finds those people, He says, "Come, ye blessed of my Father, inherit the kingdom prepared for you from the foundation of the world." Matthew 25:34. Those in whom He doesn't find those types of works, He says, "Depart from me, ye that work iniquity." Matthew 7:23. Those people thought that they could deserve heaven, but Christ says that we can never deserve it.

Let's go back now to the prodigal's brother. Recall that he told his father that he had always done that which was commanded of him. He worked all those years trying to earn his father's love, and he got upset to discover that his brother had been given a feast after squandering his inheritance on fast living. The prodigal's brother complained that his father never did anything special for him. What was he really saying? He was saying, "Treat me according to what I deserve." And his father did just that. That son who kept his nose to the grindstone would get his wages, but he will have no feast. He knew nothing of the grace that motivated the father to give a feast to the son who had wandered away but returned in repentance.

I say that the guilty are blessed because of what the prodigal son said. "Father, I have sinned against heaven, and in thy sight, and am no more worthy to be called thy son." Luke 15:21. What a marvelous verse. The prodigal asked for mercy, and his father threw his own robe around him so no that one could see him in that filthy condition. He took him home and gave him a bath, shaved him, cleaned him all up, fixed up his hair. When he looked spotless, the son realized that his father had done those things for him out of a heart filled with love for his son who had returned home.

Then the father called in all his friends, and He said, "Come and make merry with me, for my son who was dead in trespass and sins is now alive. Rejoice with me; be happy. He has come back from the dead." Doesn't that make you happy? When I come home to Jesus, and confess that I am a sinner, asking for His forgiveness, He says to me, "I'm so happy you are home. I'm so happy." And He throws His robe of righteousness around me, and He cleans me all up, and He presents me spotless before His Father as though I had never sinned. And He says to all of heaven, "Rejoice with me. The one who was lost is found." But to those who say, "Father, I have kept all your commandments. I worked all these years, but you never did anything special for me," He says, "Depart from me; I never knew you."

I pray that you will get these things straightened out in your mind. The judgment is a marvelous thing. It's the climax of the whole kingdom of grace. As God looks at all the candidates of grace, and He sees how they love souls out of response to a God of love, Christ will say to them, "Well done, thou good and faithful servant, …enter thou into the joy of thy Lord." Matthew 25:21. May God grant every one of us to understand the difference between works of merit and works of grace.

CHAPTER 5: THE GREATEST SINNER

A friend of mine who had retired from the Navy loaned me the diary of his father. In it, I read of an incident that happened during World War I—a story that reveals some of the terrible things that happen in wars. The sailor was on an American gunboat. Somehow an engine went bad, so they had to beach the boat on an island near the Azores in the Atlantic Ocean, a few hundred miles west of Portugal. While they were there repairing the engine, a German U-boat surfaced not far from the island.

The German U-boat aimed its biggest gun at the American gunboat. But then the U-boat put off a small boat, and the captain and another officer paddled to shore, where a most unusual incident took place. It turned out that the chief of the American gunboat and the captain of the German submarine were brothers! They had not seen each other for many years. Both of them were originally from Denmark, but when they were children, one was sent to America and the other to Germany. These two enemies renewed their old acquaintance, talking for a long time about what had transpired with each of them since they parted as children.

The time grew close when the two men there on the island had to part. As they shook hands, they reminded each other that they were now enemies, and that the next time they met, it would not be on such friendly terms. The two German officers paddled the little boat back out to the submarine. That evening the submarine left, out to open sea. In another few days, the American gunboat had been repaired, so as the tide came in, the boat went out to sea, also.

A couple of days later, someone on the Navy gunboat, which was actually outfitted for anti-submarine warfare, noticed a submarine off in the distance. Using binoculars, they noticed that the identification number on the sub was the same number that was on the submarine that had surfaced while the gunboat was on shore being repaired. The men on the gunboat were called to battle stations, and they prepared to do something about the submarine that had been spotted some distance away.

The Navy chief was the man who pulled the lanyard to fire the five-inch gun that sank that submarine. He killed his own brother—and, by the way, all in the name of patriotism. I read that story in the diary and had some mixed feelings; I still have those same mixed feelings today.

What is the greatest sin? Is it to kill your own brother shortly after having had a pleasant reunion with him just two days before? That Navy chief no doubt carried feelings of guilt—possibly for the rest of his life. Is murder the greatest sin?

Or perhaps rape is the greatest sin. That particular sin happens both in war and in peaceful times. Or is idolatry the worst sin?

I would like to give you a definition of sin that we almost never think about, and I believe that the definition identifies the greatest of all sins. The Bible teaches that "sin is the transgression of the law." 1 John 3:4. Therefore, it is only logical to conclude that the greatest sin is the transgression of the greatest law. But which is the greatest law? "Then one of them, which was a lawyer, asked Him a question, tempting Him, and saying, Master, which is the *great commandment* in the law?" Matthew 22:35-36. What was the answer of the Lawgiver Himself? "Jesus said unto him, Thou shalt love the Lord thy God with all thy heart, and with all thy soul, and with all thy mind. This is the first and great commandment. And the second is like unto it, Thou shalt love thy neighbour as thyself." (Verses 37-39.)

Based on what Jesus said was the greatest commandment, we may conclude that the greatest sin is to *not* love the Lord with all the heart, soul, and mind. Have you ever felt guilty about that? We feel guilty about all kinds of things, but we don't feel guilty about not loving God with all our hearts, do we? In fact, it is rare that any person ever confesses that sin. When I do not love the Lord with all my heart because He has done so much for me, then there is something wrong with me. That sin is more than a wrong act or a wrong thought. It's something way down deep inside.

I'd like to relate a Bible story about a man who didn't understand this. He didn't understand it at all, even though he was religious. The story is found in the book of Luke; it's about Simon the Pharisee. "And one of the Pharisees desired Him that He would eat with him. And He went into the Pharisee's house, and sat down to meat." Luke 7:36. That same incident is found in three of the gospel accounts, so I will put together those three chapters to get the full picture.

In Matthew's account of this story, we find out something interesting about Simon. "Now when Jesus was in Bethany, in the house of Simon the leper...." Matthew 26:6. Simon, the man who had invited Jesus and His disciples to dine with him, was a Pharisee and had been a leper. Jesus had healed him of that disease that has been called a living death.

Have you ever seen a leper? In the station in Rwanda where I was a missionary, there was a girl who came who was in her early twenties. I wish I could take a photograph of your face if you could see her for the first time. Half of her nose was gone. One cheek was gone all the way down to the jaw. On one side of her face, there were only bones and teeth hanging out. You'd grimace to look at her. She looked like she was half skeleton and half human. As I looked at her one day, I thought that she must have been a very pretty girl at one time; but by then half of the flesh was missing from her face. How would you like to be like that? How would you like to come for treatment and watch people as they wince at you? Wouldn't that make you feel wonderful? Sometimes our actions show that we almost detest people, and it takes us an awful long time to catch on—that this is a very lovely person. Do I look only at the skin? Can't I look at the heart? Am I so dense that I cannot see beyond the face? We are very ugly, sometimes, in our reactions. The medicine doesn't do much good for people if the one giving the treatments is sitting there grimacing at them all the time. The lepers would like to have some tender loving care (TLC) along with the injections. It would help an awful lot.

What was it personally like to be a leper in Christ's day? I do not know. We are told that they walked through the streets shouting, "Unclean! Unclean! Unclean!"—advertising how bad they were. The Jews called leprosy "the finger of God," which meant that God had put a curse on them because they were so evil and sinful. Everyone looked upon them as though they were totally condemned, just as though they were already dead. The lepers' practice of shouting, "Unclean! Unclean!" and people's avoidance of the lepers because they did not want to catch leprosy were very phony ideas, but that's what they thought back then.

Simon the Pharisee had been saved from a living death. He was apparently a wealthy man, for he made a large feast. So Simon was going to have a feast and invite all his neighbors and friends to honor Christ, to thank Him for saving him from leprosy. That was the whole purpose of the banquet. Please don't forget that.

There was another person there. "Then Jesus six days before the Passover came to Bethany, where Lazarus was, which had been dead, whom he raised from the dead. There they made Him a supper; and Martha served: but Lazarus was one of them that sat at the table with Him." John 12:1-2. Simon also lived in the town of Bethany where Lazarus, who had been raised from the dead, lived. If you continue reading in that chapter, you will see that there were many who came to the feast just to see Lazarus. They wanted to find out what Lazarus had to say about what it was like to be dead, but Lazarus said nothing about it because "the dead know not anything." Ecclesiastes 9:5.

"At the table the Saviour sat with Simon, whom He had cured of a loathsome disease, on one side, and Lazarus, whom He had raised from the dead, on the other." *Desire of Ages*, p. 558. You must think about that: Lazarus raised from the dead, and Simon saved from a living death. So here is the Life-Giver between two who had come back from the dead—one from the grave, and one from the living death of leprosy.

It was a jovial occasion until a very strange fragrance filled the whole room. "Then took Mary a pound of ointment of spikenard, very costly, and anointed the feet of Jesus, and wiped His feet with her hair: and the house was filled with the odour of the ointment." John 12:3. This was an unusual thing. Where did Mary come from, anyway? It tells us that Martha was serving, that Lazarus was an honored guest along with Jesus, but Mary was not invited. "And, behold, a woman in the city, which was a sinner, when she knew that Jesus sat at meat in the Pharisee's house, brought an alabaster box of ointment, and stood at His feet behind Him weeping, and began to wash His feet with tears, and did wipe them with the hairs of her head, and kissed His feet, and anointed them with the ointment." Luke 7:37-38. Mary had not been invited because she "was a sinner." Bethany was a small town, about a two-hour walk from Jerusalem. Mary was not invited because the whole town knew that she was a sinner. If you were a Jew, you must never invite a sinner to your house, for that would defile you. So she wasn't invited.

How did she get in there, then? How would you get into places where you are not invited? She sneaked in. Have you ever sneaked into something? When I was a boy and poor, we sneaked into everything—ballgames, races, and everything else. We never paid. If you haven't sneaked in, you don't know what it's like. If you haven't sneaked into something, you have a new experience coming. There's also a bad aspect to sneaking in: you don't have a ticket stub. If anyone ever comes asking, you have no reason for being there. You always have the idea that there's someone around looking for you. You're never quite completely comfortable. You just keep looking around like someone is looking for you.

I remember when I was a boy trying to sneak into a football game, and finally the guard *let* me in over the fence. I sat down in the reserved section. After a while the same guard came over and found me sitting there in the reserved seats. He said to me, "You certainly have your gall. I let you in for nothing, and you sit in a reserved seat." I didn't know there was a price difference between regular and reserved seats; I had never paid to get into a ballgame in my life. We didn't have the money to pay. I didn't want to tell him how stupid I was, that I didn't know any better. So it's uncomfortable to sneak in. You never know if you're welcome or not. Mary sneaked in, anyway.

When I pastored in Texas years ago, there was a huge man who used to sneak into church. It's awfully hard to sneak in when you're big. He must have been six feet three or four inches tall—a very distinguished-looking man, but not slim or skinny. About the time I would start to preach, he would come in the back door and find a vacant seat way in the back. It was a fairly good-sized church. He would always find a seat and sit down. Then during the closing hymn…*poof!* He was gone. My, he used to arouse my curiosity. He came to church for three months like that, and he was always gone before I could get back there. Who was he? (You have no curiosity at all, do you?) By the way, I'm delighted when people sneak into church. I hope that thousands sneak into church; I really do—and I hope you'll let them sneak in. If they come in and you never know who they are, that's fine, so long as they come. All that is important is that they come back. Don't try to put brands on people; don't try to expose them. They sneak in because they don't want to be noticed. Let them sneak in, correct? That's being kind and sensitive and respectful. Anything else is not Christian. If they want to sneak in, let them sneak in. I'm just glad they are coming, aren't you? I just want them to keep on coming to church.

A member of that church who owned a large service station told me, "You sure do have some very special people coming to your church." I asked, "*Who is he? Who is that big fellow who sneaks in?*" He asked me if I read the papers, and I told him that I did. It seems that the big man had started a huge development outside of town. He was a millionaire many times over. When he came under litigation because of that big development, he started coming back to church. I don't know why he stopped in the first place. I can still remember his name, although I had never met him personally. He always sneaked out before I could meet him.

Mary sneaked in. Remember the feelings you had when you sneaked in? Sort of a queasy and not-quite-settled feeling? She managed to get in and somehow had not been exposed—except for her love. She came to honor Jesus and to express her affection and thanksgiving for all He had done for her. So she came with that very special gift. We learn more about that gift in *Bible Commentary*, Volume 5, p. 1137: "*Pure, sanctified love*, expressed by Christ's lifework, is as sacred perfume. Like an opened bottle of perfume, it fills the whole house with fragrance. Eloquence, an extended knowledge of the truth, outward devotion, rare talents, if mingled with sacred, humble love, will become as fragrant as the opened box of ointment. But gifts alone, ability alone, the choicest endowments alone, cannot take the place of love."

If we have some of these things mingled with pure love, it touches just everybody. It has a way of permeating the whole environment until everyone is affected by it. In other words, love finds a way into people's minds when talents cannot succeed, right? It just worms its way in. So when Mary applied that gift of love, it just wafted throughout the whole room. Then an amazing thing happened. The most selfish person there was the first one to complain. "Then saith one of His disciples, Judas Iscariot, Simon's son, which should betray Him, Why was not this ointment sold for three hundred pence, and given to the poor?" John 12:4-5.

"This he said, not that he cared for the poor; but because he was a thief, and had the bag, and bare what was put therein." John 12:6. Judas didn't care for the poor. He was the treasurer who kept charge of the meager funds off which Jesus and the disciples lived, and he would have liked to use that money for himself. So the most selfish man present was upset by the unselfish love of this woman. Isn't that amazing? When someone is sacrificial, there is always someone to gripe; have you ever noticed that? They're always complaining, because the sacrificial example hits them in their own pocketbook. The most *unselfish* one, this woman who sneaked in, immediately affected the most selfish one there. He began to criticize her, asking why the expensive perfume had not been sold and the money given to the poor.

As a result, all the other disciples also started criticizing. This was supposed to be a banquet, with everyone happy, honoring Jesus. The host was upset when Judas and the others began to complain about the misapplied money. The woman, who had been a well-known sinner, was exposed, and Simon was embarrassed that she was even there. She was contaminating the whole place. The guests were griping, and the host was embarrassed, so what does he do? "Now when the Pharisee which had bidden Him saw it, he spake within himself, saying, This man, if He were a prophet, would have known who and what manner of woman this is that toucheth Him: for she is a sinner." Luke 7:39. Note that Simon "spake within himself." He did not say anything out loud. This man, whom Jesus saved from a living death, is now doubting that Jesus is even a prophet, much less the Messiah. In his mind, he is criticizing Jesus, whom he outwardly claims to be honoring. Do you see the dilemma and the confusion here?

How did Simon know that Mary was a sinner? "Simon had led into sin the woman he now despised. She had been deeply wronged by him." *Desire of Ages*, p. 566. This was Mary Magdalene, the former prostitute. She had been caught in the very act of adultery and dragged before Jesus by the Pharisees. Simon himself had committed adultery with her, but, forgetting his own guilt, he branded Mary to be a sinner, and was actually criticizing Christ and doubting if He was a prophet, because He had allowed her to come and touch Him. Isn't that interesting? By the way, fellows, we have to be very careful that we don't act like the Jews when it comes to adultery. There is evidence to suggest that men still think like that, to some extent.

So Simon is criticizing Jesus. He feels very innocent, and considers himself a very righteous man. Simon had led Mary into sin, but in his mind, he is guiltless. The Jews believed that any man who had leprosy was the worst kind of sinner, but Simon didn't feel very badly; he thought he was okay. He was a real Pharisee. By the way, it's easy to be a Pharisee. You don't even have to try. Just be yourself. It's as natural as breathing. We all can be very good Pharisees, and we don't need an education to accomplish it. This man thought very highly of himself.

As a result of all this, Jesus presented a parable. Remember that Simon was thinking in his heart that the woman was a great sinner. "And Jesus answering said unto him, Simon, I have somewhat to say unto thee. And he saith, Master, say on." Luke 7:40. Simon had not been talking out loud, but Christ answered him, anyway. That should have shocked him. Then Jesus went into the parable: "There was a certain creditor which had two debtors: the one owed five hundred pence, and the other fifty. And when they had nothing to pay, he frankly forgave them both. Tell me therefore, which of them will love him most? Simon answered and said, I suppose that he, to whom he forgave most. And He said unto him, Thou hast rightly judged. And He turned to the woman, and said unto Simon, Seest thou this woman? [Note that Jesus turned to the woman, but he was talking to Simon.] I entered into thine house, thou gavest Me no water for My feet: but she hath washed My feet with tears, and wiped them with the hairs of her head." Verses 41-44.

It was a common courtesy to wash visitors' feet when they arrived at the host home. It was an absolute social necessity for an honored guest, but Simon had not had Jesus' feet washed. One reason people had their feet washed upon entering someone's house was that they wore open sandals and had been walking along dusty, dirty roads. It's not very comfortable to sit down with sand between the toes. Some would sit there and pick their toes. Washing the guests' feet made them comfortable. Washing the feet was also a mark of honor and respect, and it was practiced by almost all Jews. Simon's intention was to honor Christ, but he didn't even wash His feet—so there was something wrong with Simon. Jesus continued, "Thou gavest Me no kiss: but this woman since the time I came in hath not ceased to kiss My feet." Verse 45. (She wouldn't presume to kiss His cheek.)

I remember seeing a figure-skating program out of Vienna. The girls who won the championships—all the medal winners—were kissed on both cheeks by all the judges. It's a mark of respect that is practiced in many countries. In many countries, dignitaries are kissed on the cheek. This practice of washing the feet, then, was not something new. Jesus commented to Simon that he had not kissed Jesus on the cheek, but Mary had not stopped kissing His feet since He came in. His point was that He was a guest at *Simon's* house, not Mary's.

Jesus continued, "My head with oil thou didst not anoint: but this woman hath anointed My feet with ointment." Verse 46. (Guests often had been sweating; ointment helped them to smell fresh and fragrant.) All of the acts of common courtesy and honor were omitted when Jesus visited Simon's house. Jesus did not come right out and ask, "Why didn't you do these things?" That would have been too harsh for Simon to bear. Christ just reminded him of those things in a very kind way.

Verse 47 contains the key point that Jesus wanted to make: "Wherefore I say unto thee, Her sins, which are many, are forgiven; for she loved much: but to whom little is forgiven, the same loveth little." Now I need to ask you a question. Who was in debt the most—Simon or Mary? Who *thought* they were the deepest in debt? Mary was sure that she was the greatest sinner. That's why she was so grateful. She just could not thank Jesus enough, because she regarded herself as a terrible, terrible sinner. That the Lord could forgive her was so wonderful, she was ecstatic. Therefore, she found a most beautiful thing and brought it to Jesus. She was thrilled to do it, and did not feel it to be even a small sacrifice. She was just so satisfied that she could do something to show her gratitude. She felt pure, real, sanctified love, and she wanted to express it. You cannot hide love; it must be expressed. One way or another, it has to come out. She was expressing it the best way she knew, and the Lord *knew* that.

Simon *omitted* all the things that would honor Jesus. Why did he leave them out? Here is a very strange contradiction. Now, who was the greatest sinner? It was really Simon, but he didn't think so. Mary was sure that she was; and she wasn't even welcome, so everybody knew she was a great sinner. Publicly she had been branded as a sinner. But Simon was considered a fine, upstanding fellow, and probably one reason was that he had a lot of money. Sometimes money seems to cover a multitude of sins, but not in God's mind. So Jesus, in a very delicate way, exposed Simon, hoping to help him understand his own heart.

Without knowing it, Simon branded himself. It's as if he was waving a large flag saying, "I'm a tremendous Christian," but in reality he was branding himself a skunk. Everybody could see it; it was as plain as could be. He didn't wash Jesus' feet; he didn't kiss him on the cheek or anoint him with a fragrant oil—all the common courtesies of that day. He left them all out, and yet he thought he looked good. Do you know that we can be just as deceived as Simon was, if not more?

When I read about the Israelites in the Bible, I used to think, "What a bunch of poor, deceived people they were." I felt so comfortable because I wasn't that way. But the older I get, the more I find out that I am like those people. We can't tell when we are deceived. Others can tell it, but we don't know it. Isn't that true? We keep saying things and acting out things as if everything is all right, but our spouses and children and neighbors and friends know that there is something pretty bad inside us. Somehow it's being revealed by the little things we neglect to do. If we really had the love and gratitude in our hearts that Mary had, we'd do differently; but since we don't do these things, we must be missing something inside, as Simon was. Love will always expose itself, and lack of love always reveals itself, too. Mary couldn't hide her love, and Simon could not hide his lack of love. We are always witnessing. We don't have to go out and preach, to witness. I'm not saying that we should judge people superficially, but we advertise about these things.

This man who had continually violated the greatest commandment—"Thou shalt love the LORD thy God with all thine heart, and with all thy soul, and with all thy might" (Deuteronomy 6:5)—felt that he was the best Christian. He didn't think that he was a big debtor like the man in Christ's parable of the two debtors. He was smug and complacent. This is frightening to me, especially when I read the message to the church of Laodicea. They think they are "rich and increased with goods and have need of nothing," and don't know that they are "wretched, and miserable, and poor, and blind, and naked." Revelation 3:17. They don't even know it. That message tells me not to look at you, but to look at me and see how I really am, spiritually. The incident at Simon's home comes home to roost right there in the message to Laodicea. Was Simon that deceived? Am I that deceived? It's easy to be deceived and never know it.

Mary was unafraid to be a sinner. When we really know Jesus, when we really know the love of God for sinners, we'll not be proud that we're sinners, but we'll not be afraid to be sinners. I think that many of us are afraid to be sinners. Most are scared half to death. We are eternally trying to be righteous, but we can't be righteous by trying. The Bible says righteousness is a gift, freely given by Jesus. We talk about Christ our righteousness, and that means we don't have any righteousness of our own. It means that *He* must be our righteousness. We're always trying to be good enough to get through the judgment. The only ones who get through the judgment are sinners who trust in Jesus entirely.

All these guilt trips about not being good enough are total unbelief in the Bible; they really are. Sure, we are all sinners. No one is righteous—no, not one. Can you go to bed tonight without confessing that you're a sinner? Then what do we get worried about? Do you understand what I am trying to tell you? *We are sinners.* But Jesus "came not to call the righteous, but sinners to repentance," right? Mark 2:17. He came not to call those who are whole, but the sick. Jesus came and died for the sinners, not for the righteous, because the righteous don't *need* Him to die for them. Who needs Jesus? The sinners do! Will I need Him tomorrow and the day after that and so on, right up until He returns or until I die? All sinners always need Jesus. I dare not walk alone; I cannot walk alone. Sometimes we think we get so righteous that we can live without Him. That's ridiculous; there is no way I can live without Jesus. "Without Me ye can do nothing." John 15:5. It will always be that way, until we are resurrected or translated. Then we'll follow the Lamb whithersoever He goeth.

Mary loved Him so much because He had forgiven her so much. The following verses enlarge upon this: "Wherefore I say unto thee, Her sins, which are many, are forgiven; for she loved much: but to whom little is forgiven, the same loveth little. And He said unto her, Thy sins are forgiven. And they that sat at meat with Him began to say within themselves, Who is this that forgiveth sins also? And He said to the woman, Thy faith hath saved thee; go in peace." John 7:47-50. No more anxiety, no more guilt trips, no more worry—just peace. What Jesus pronounces *takes place*. We can sleep well tonight and tomorrow night. Isn't that fantastic? If you're a real Pharisee, it doesn't mean much to you. When you feel like a sinner, and Jesus says to you, "Go in peace," it's the sweetest thing in all the world. Peace is the most marvelous thing. All the guilt is gone; all the worry is gone; all the anxiety is gone; all the concerns are gone. There is nothing to worry about. Peace is just a fantastic thing.

Do you know that in this book I just fulfilled a prophecy? "Verily I say unto you, Wheresoever this gospel shall be preached in the whole world, there shall also this, that this woman hath done, be told for a memorial of her." Matthew 26:13. This is about the experience of Mary, who sneaked into the house of Simon. Wheresoever the gospel shall be preached, the story of Mary, the sinner who was forgiven much, will be told—everywhere in the world! Christ predicted it, and I did it in this book, along with all the others who have preached the gospel. Jesus established a memorial for the marvelous love that Mary had for Him. The story is not to be a memorial for Simon.

They don't love very much, to whom little is forgiven. "Those to whom He has forgiven most will love Him most, and will stand nearest to His throne to praise Him for His great love and infinite sacrifice." *Steps to Christ*, p. 36. In the front row in heaven will be the greatest sinners—in their own estimation. Do you realize that perhaps the most sinful follower that Jesus had was Mary? But she was the only one of His followers who did not, at some point, forsake Him. The rest were all *chicken*. The Bible tells that all the apostles and disciples fled on the night of His trial. One did not, and that was Mary. The one whom everyone had branded as the worst of all was still there. These things were written for our admonition today. Mary would rather have died than leave Jesus. She could sing, "No one ever cared for me like Jesus." She had no other reason to live, except for Him. She'd rather die than forsake Him; she stuck to Him like glue. If she lived today, we probably would not grant her church membership. Seven times she had devils cast out of her. And I'm afraid that we would look down the ends of our noses at her and say, "You're not eligible; you're not qualified." The Lord looks on the heart, but man looks on the outside.

The Bible says that "though your sins be as scarlet, they shall be as white as snow." Isaiah 1:18. Mary thought that her sins were all scarlet, but Jesus told her that her sins were all forgiven. "Have peace. Go in peace; no more problems." You know, I think that sometimes we get it all backwards. "Jesus saith unto them, Verily I say unto you, that the publicans and the harlots go into the kingdom of God before you." Matthew 21:31. Why is this true? Because they look upon themselves as sinners in tremendous need. Have you noticed how those who have been in deep sin love the Lord so very much? They just can't stop thanking Him publically. And those who come out of fine, upstanding neighborhoods—highly qualified citizens of the community—have almost nothing to say.

You may have heard about Albion Ballinger, who wrote a fine book called *The Power of Witnessing*. The book doesn't have much on theology; it's mostly on Christian experience. Ballinger was a minister. He tells a story of when he was suffering greatly because of a lack of an experience with the Lord. He prayed and went searching for it many times. He finally went to an old mission house on Skid Row in some unnamed city; he was looking for Jesus. He sat way in the back in a small gathering of people. They began to testify that night, along with a song service, and they praised the Lord. The man who was in charge said, "Three years ago, I was an alcoholic and a gambler," and he named all his sins. He said that the Lord found him and rescued him and took all his sins away. All those three years Jesus had saved him from the sins that once held him captive. He said, "I praise His holy name!" and the crowd shouted, "*Amen!*"

Then a lady stood up and said, "Five years ago I was luring your daughters into prostitution, and I was an alcoholic. The Lord found me and rescued me and turned me back. All these years He has been saving me from those things, and I haven't gone back to them. Now I'm trying to lead your daughters to Jesus. I praise His name that He has been so good to me!" And the crowd shouted, "*Amen!*"

All around the room, stories kept being told of how Jesus rescued them. And there in the back, Ballinger said, "AMEN!" too loudly, and everyone looked at him. That's why most people don't say "Amen," by the way. He was a bit embarrassed, but he was quite desperate. He stood up and said, "I'm a minister, and I don't have an experience like yours, and I can't praise the Lord like you do. Won't you pray for me?" And they all said, "Amen," and then he sat down.

According to Ballinger's testimony, he went back to his hotel room and there, weeping, he began to pour out his heart to the Lord, trying to seek an experience with Christ. He said he decided that he had to become like they were—an alcoholic, a gambler, or something like that, in order to love the Lord enough. He'd have to go out and sin and sin and sin. As he kept praying and worrying about this, the Holy Spirit began to talk to his heart, showing him that he was already the chiefest of sinners, but that he just didn't recognize it. In all his pride and complacency and jealousy, his envy, his materialism, his seeking the highest place—all sins that the world no longer condemns—he began to find out how selfish he was, and how vile and corrupt and rotten he was on the inside. As the Bible says in Ezekiel, he began to loathe himself as the Spirit revealed to him how corrupt he was. He wasn't on a guilt trip. As he realized how he really was, he realized how much the Lord had already forgiven him. He began to get happy and excited, no longer morbid and depressed, because now he was a great sinner.

He went back to that mission a few nights later and sat down in that same little hall, and that time he told his testimony. And he said, "Now I praise the Lord with all my heart." And everybody said, "*Amen!*" They really did. It was a discovery; it was a revelation that only the great sinners love Jesus. We shall never finish God's work until we become much worse sinners. We're just too righteous to finish God's work. We're too saintly to finish God's work. People don't love God very much until they become sinners, and we're scared to death of being sinners, aren't we? Frightened to death.

What I am trying to tell you is that the things we are worried about the most are the very things that can bless us. We're worried about being sinners; Jesus loves sinners! Paul said he was the chiefest of sinners; he became the greatest of witnesses. He loved very much and couldn't stop going for Jesus—because he had so much forgiven. Mary loved Him so very much and stuck to Him like glue when everyone else forsook Him. Why? *Because she had so much forgiven!* If we make ourselves little sinners, we won't love Him very much, and we won't *do* very much. When Christ becomes so marvelous in His grace, where grace does much more abound than our sins—when we see His grace sweeping like a tidal wave over our souls, taking care of every last sin—we'll have a reason to shout for joy, and not be afraid of sin anymore. That doesn't make us want to sin; it makes us want to *stop*. How can you hurt the One who loves you so much and forgives you so much? Now we really have a reason to stop. Before, we just tried to stop to make ourselves look good. That's rotten. That's not good. The Lord wants to change our hearts by leading us to love Him very, very much, after we first discover how bad we are. And we think that's the wrong road, don't we? We fight like everything to avoid seeing ourselves as sinners.

For some time I have been saying that my God has been growing. I served a midget god for a long time. He isn't that small, but to my understanding He was. I didn't know any better. Some of you don't know any better, either. My God has grown so big now, that it doesn't frighten me anymore for Him to see the inside of me. I'm more satisfied with Jesus than I've ever been. I'm not satisfied with *me* one bit, but I'm satisfied with Jesus. I've become much more comfortable with Him. It's not a fearful thing to have Him see me—to be exposed to Him—because I know that whatever He finds in me, He can quickly forgive and take care of, and still accept me. That's precious. I don't have to fight anymore trying to look good. I don't. He knows I'm not, and He still loves me, and He still accepts me, and He still wants me. My only problem is in believing this with all my heart until I praise Him all the day long, and cannot stop serving Him. Sacrifice comes happily, delightedly, joyously when I know how much He forgives me and how much He still wants me and how much He accepts me. We're always going the wrong direction in our fight against sin. I must come boldly to the throne of grace, not boasting, but thanking Him for how much He loves and forgives sinners. You'll be amazed at the peace He gives you, and how much blessing He gives you, how much hope, and how much He makes the Christian life entirely different.

How big is your debt? Fifty pence? Five hundred pence? We have a very difficult time saying that our debt is five hundred pence. We somehow just can't believe that being a big sinner puts us on the right road. But Christ made it very plain, it's the *only* road.

There's a quotation in *Selected Messages*, Book 1, p. 316: "We can learn the depths of our transgression only by the length of the chain let down to draw us up." How far down did Jesus come to get you and get me? Some of us He has had to chase halfway around the world. I believe He did that with me during the war. He chased me over to India and China and all the way back home. There were many experiences which He brought me through alive, and I couldn't figure out why. I had some deep convictions in my heart that I couldn't understand at all, but He brought me home alive. I used to ask, "Why me?" when so many had died out there. He chased me home, even though I had something else in mind than serving Him. In fact, I didn't have any interest at all in serving Him. I went to church and still had no interest in serving Him. He doesn't stop pursuing us, but He doesn't pursue us to find fault. I call Him the persistent Suitor. That's the old-fashioned word for someone who comes to court you, to woo you. He never gives up.

Mrs. Lehman and I know a woman who courted a man for seven years before he would say "Yes." His first wife died, and that woman had never been married. She courted him for seven years, never giving up. Now they are very happily married. Christ doesn't give up on you and me, either. Do you know that? He came a long, long way from heaven; He knew already that we were sinners, but He came, anyway. He still comes down, courting us, seeking us, loving us. Which is the great commandment? "Thou shalt love the LORD thy God with all thine heart, and with all thy soul, and with all thy might." Deuteronomy 6:5. Not to love Him that way is the greatest sin. How can I help but love Him when He first loved me? Do you realize how much He has loved you?

Friends, you don't have to be afraid of Jesus. He came not to condemn, but to save. Don't be afraid of Him. And don't be afraid of being a sinner in front of Jesus. He already knows that you are. He never points the finger, and He never looks down the end of His nose at you. He said, "Come unto Me, all ye that labour and are heavy laden, and I will give you rest." Matthew 11:28. "I'll take away all the burdens of sin, all the guilt, all the depression, all the despair, all the hopelessness. I'll take it all away. Come unto Me. Why do you struggle with such a load? It will kill you. Come to Me," "for My yoke is easy, and My burden is light." Matthew 11:30. "I will give you peace."

This is my prayer for all of you: Loving Father, thank You so much for Jesus—precious Jesus. Help us to understand how much our God is a God of love. How precious we are to Him. How He longs to have us as His very, very own; how much He comes to love us and demonstrate His love by gladly forgiving us of everything, even before we ask Him. Take away our fear of being sinners. Take away our fear of guilt, of condemnation, of all these things. May we look into the face of Jesus and see nothing but mercy and grace and love and kindness. No condemnation. And may we be so free and open with Him that we'll gladly come, exposing all our souls to Him, and ask Him to forgive us and to cleanse us, and to keep us day by day. May our hearts be so filled with love and rejoicing, so ecstatic, that we will constantly seek to thank Him and praise Him because He is so good to us. May we never be afraid to share the fragrance of His marvelous love in all we do and say, so that every soul around about us might be permeated with the beautiful, sweet fragrance of His amazing grace and love. Bless us, I pray in Jesus' name. Amen.

CHAPTER 6: FREEDOM FOR THE GUILTY

Freedom is a special thing in the Bible that sometimes we don't think about. The guilty always worry about forgiveness, and not too often about freedom. I want to talk about freedom. There are some questions or problems in Christianity that I think we often bypass and almost never answer or address. I would like to state them as best I can.

When you know what is right, and you know what is wrong, can you stop doing the wrong and do the right? When you are highly educated as to what is right and wrong, can you stop the wrong and do the right? When someone has come along and told you about all the evil effects of certain bad habits and how you are killing yourself, can you stop the wrong and do the right? No? Why not? You can even desperately want to stop the wrong, whatever it is, but still keep on doing the wrong thing. Has this been your experience? You can have a great knowledge about it; you know all the evil side effects, but education does not give you victory.

One more step. We can not only know the terrible effects of something, and we can pray and pray and pray, but yet still keep right on doing the wrong thing. The question is: Why? After we understand all the evils of doing wrong, and we have prayed and we desire very strongly to stop, we still keep on doing the wrong. At that point, some of us jump the track mentally. We freak out. We get on a continual guilt trip, and we just can't see clearly from then on. We get all kinds of peculiar ideas about this, because the guilt blinds us. We get rather hopeless and despairing. We say to ourselves that nobody is perfect. Have you never said that? We sometimes think that when we get old enough, then we will do the right; but you know, age doesn't help a bit.

Of course, there are those who conclude that they are hopeless cases. "There is no sense trying. I might as well quit." Or "maybe I haven't interpreted the Bible correctly." We have hundreds of explanations for continuing to do the wrong, mostly because we are confused and feel terrible. Now, why is that?

Recall the Bible text by Paul that states: "Know ye not, that to whom ye yield yourselves servants to obey, his servants ye are to whom ye obey; whether of sin unto death, or of obedience unto righteousness?" Romans 6:16. First, notice that it reads "to *whom*" we yield ourselves to obey. We, at any moment in time, are either yielded to Satan and self, or to Christ. Next, that word *servants* is an old-fashioned word that is more correctly translated as *slave*. The Greek word is *dulos*, and that means *slave*; it doesn't really mean *servant*. So that verse is really asking us if we understand that "to whom we yield ourselves *slaves* to obey," we become their slave. We are slaves either to Satan and self, which cause us to sin, and in turn that leads unto death; or we are slaves to Christ, which leads us to obedience, and in turn that leads to life everlasting. A proper understanding of that verse answers a tremendous number of questions for us about our bad habits, why we're so helpless in fighting them, and why we sometimes get on guilt trips that never seem to end.

Christ talked about slavery to sin, so let's look at that text: "Jesus answered them, Verily, verily, I say unto you, whosoever committeth sin is the servant of sin." John 8:34. That word *servant* again really means *slave*. Christ talked about slavery to sin. Also, Paul described his very frustrating experience in Romans 7, a text that is sometimes misused, but let's look at it: "For that which I do I allow not: for what I would, that do I not; but what I hate, that do I.... For the good that I would I do not: but the evil which I would not, that I do." Romans 7:15, 19. So Paul talks about this knowing, desiring, and praying to do what is right, but he still keeps doing the wrong. Most people do not realize that the Bible says that since we have all sinned, we've all become slaves to sin. We don't understand slavery well, anymore. Maybe that is good in some ways. But what it is saying is that I am ruled by sin; I am controlled by it. It becomes a master, a tyrant that dominates my life.

In Romans 6, some of the language of the domination of sin is described. I am trying to help you understand that there is a different aspect of guilt trips than sometimes we realize. "Let not sin therefore reign in your mortal body, that ye should obey it in the lusts thereof. Neither yield ye your members as instruments of unrighteousness unto sin: but yield yourselves unto God, as those that are alive from the dead, and your members as instruments of righteousness unto God. For sin shall not have dominion over you: for ye are not under the law, but under grace.... But God be thanked, that ye were the servants of sin, but ye have obeyed from the heart that form of doctrine which was delivered you." Romans 6:12-14, 17.

This is marvelous language, and very hopeful, if you understand it correctly. The great problem with stopping sinning or doing right is not how to stop some bad habit. I think most of us have prayed for the wrong thing for too long a time. The problem is not how to stop some bad habit. The problem is, "How do I escape from slavery?" Do you understand me? Have you ever prayed, "Lord, how do I get out of slavery?"

By the way, this Bible concept of getting out of slavery is not all bad. It's very good, actually, for when we begin to see it this way, there is a whole other aspect to the problem that gives a lot of hope. It really helps to solve many problems about guilt. How can I escape the mastery of sin—this dominance in my life? What can I do about something that controls me—that just leads me around like a bull with a ring in his nose? How can I control something like that? What can I do about it? You see, *bad habits are only symptoms. Don't treat the bad habits.* It's like a physician putting alcohol on smallpox marks. That is treating the symptoms. Then the doctor says, "That will be one hundred dollars, please." That is not the way disease should be treated. The pox marks are not the disease; they are the symptoms. My bad habits are symptoms of my problems; they are not the cause of my problems. They are the results of my problems, and the Lord wants to come into my life and treat the cause.

What do I do about the problem? I'm talking about the deeper problem—the cause. What do I do about that? What can a slave do to no longer be a slave? Here is the deep-seated problem: "Can the Ethiopian change his skin, or the leopard his spots? then may ye also do good, that are accustomed to do evil." Jeremiah 13:23. In our Bible studies, we too often omit this verse; but I think that we should use it in every Bible study because if we leave it out, we are frustrating people terribly.

This Bible text says that we are all accustomed to sinning. It's as impossible for us to do good as it is for us to change the colors of our skin. Invariably, we teach people all the wrongs and rights concerning what they must do and what they shouldn't do. We tell them that if they don't do the right things, then look out. We leave out this verse which tells them what they cannot do. The Bible says that they cannot do the right and avoid the wrong. It is as impossible for them to do the right and avoid the wrong as it is to change the color of their skin. If you don't believe that, then please rip that page out of your Bible. There are a lot of other passages that go with it, by the way. It seems to me that we always are satisfied with educating people about right and wrong, and then we stop there. We leave them pulling their hair out and climbing the walls in frustration, because they can't do the right and avoid the wrong. Our lives are testimony every day that this is true. We cannot. The Bible says that we cannot. We must tell people after we educate them about right or wrong that they cannot stop doing the wrong and do the right. I realize that all this makes some people nervous, but keep on reading, because there is an answer to our dilemma.

We must answer some of these very difficult problems and, unfortunately, people don't tell us about them after we are baptized. So when I'm teaching someone else, I must not frustrate them with just an education on right and wrong. If I stop there, I'm really causing a lot of problems. We've done this for years, haven't we, and we wonder why people are not performing better. "Okay, so I know what right things I should do. So what? What difference does that make?" You can tell an alcoholic he is killing himself, and he still goes out and gets drunk. You can tell people that it has been proven from science that tobacco is going to give them lung cancer, and they still go out and get lung cancer. I know those who have had surgery from lung cancer and they still keep smoking. Education does not stop people from doing the wrong things.

The Lord told us to go forth and teach all nations; however, He didn't say that teaching them would stop them, right? Education does not always prevent people from doing the wrong. So do not be satisfied with simply giving people knowledge, thinking that the knowledge will stop them from doing wrong. It doesn't accomplish the task. And that is another dimension of the problem. The strong-willed do stop some bad habits. Unfortunately, they still crave them inwardly, and often they still have secret bad habits that they hide, which means they are still slaves. The strong-willed are no better off than the weak-willed, by the way. Some strong-willed people don't believe that there are weak-willed people. They just think we are soft on ourselves. But they are hiding from their own weak will, as well. They have a lot of problems, too. I know, because for a long time I thought I was strong-willed, and I have watched others who thought they were. In reality, they just can't see their problems. They were not as strong as they thought they were.

How, then, can I obey? And to be sure, God requires that we obey. Yet the Bible says that we cannot. What a dilemma! Until you resolve the dilemma, you are not giving much Christianity to the people. Many people try all kinds of methods, and they are still failing. They wonder what's wrong.

Let me put all this in a little different way. What can a person who is a slave to sin do to stop sinning and to start obeying? There is a strange thing in a verse that we already saw: "Know ye not, that to whom ye yield yourselves servants to obey, his servants ye are to whom ye obey; whether of sin unto death, or of obedience unto righteousness?" Romans 6:16. This verse has to do with obedience. The fact is, we all obey someone—either God or Satan. In fact, everybody is *totally* obedient—no exceptions. Little boys and girls, grandpas and grandmas, young and old, married and single. Everyone is totally obedient to some master. Really, we are.

Did you notice that the verse says to *whom*, and not to *what*, we yield ourselves slaves to obey? If we leave the *whom* out of Christianity, we have left out everything. We must have the right Man on our side. Christianity is all about a Person, not just right principles and right things and wrong things. Christianity centers on a Person. If we have habitual sins, then we know to whom we are slaves. Therefore, all obedience has to do with the person whose slaves we are. Obedience isn't just doing right things and avoiding wrong things. It has to do with a person. Obedience has always been like that.

If you look up the word *obey* in the dictionary, you'll be shocked to find out that you probably never understood that word. For years and years I thought I understood it. I went and dug out the dictionary when I got intrigued about this subject, and I could hardly believe it. I had never understood the word *obey*! Even with a college education, I still didn't understand it. If you think you understand it, listen to this definition: "*Obey* means to be ruled or controlled." *Webster's Collegiate Dictionary*. It doesn't say a single word about doing right or wrong. The definition for the word *obedience* is "submission to control, restraint or command." It implies due and willing submission to control of some authority. That is obedience. Again, it doesn't say a thing about what is right or wrong. To be ruled or controlled, and to submit to control or restraint or command, implies a willing submission to authority or control. Obedience is unconditional surrender. That means unconditional surrender to a person.

"The essence of all righteousness is loyalty to our Redeemer. This will lead us to do right because it is right—because right-doing is pleasing to God." *Christ's Object Lessons*, p. 97. The essence of all righteousness is loyalty to our Redeemer. Everything regarding obedience includes a relationship to either the wrong person or the right Person. It is a willing submission to authority and control; that is obedience. So what comes automatically when I yield to another person's authority? What comes automatically? It's not trying to do what is right. It is simply yielding and submitting to another authority. That's all it is.

Christ described the Jews, saying that they would not have God rule over them. "The Jewish rulers did not love God; therefore they cut themselves away from Him, and rejected all His overtures for a just settlement. Christ, the Beloved of God, came to assert the claims of the Owner of the vineyard; but the husbandmen treated Him with marked contempt, saying, We will not have this man to rule over us." Ibid., p. 293. "We won't let this Man tell us what to do." Jesus said that their attitude regarding God's control of them was their problem. Obedience, then, has entirely to do with a Person, with divine authority; the law is merely the expression of His authority—of what He wants us to do. His authority is the important thing. So it's my right relationship to Him that leads me to obedience. The relationship itself is not obedience, nor is it righteousness, but a right relationship does lead to obedience and righteousness. If I am submissive to Christ and He reigns in my life, righteousness is the result. If I do not become submissive to the sovereignty of God's love, sin is the result. It all has to do with to whom I yield myself a servant to obey. In obedience to Christ, I become His slave or His servant. It's that simple; it's not complicated. Sin, then, has a new definition that many have not discovered. Sin is obedience to the wrong master. Righteousness will be obedience to the right Master.

Righteous is obedience to the right Person. No problems understanding that; that is what it is. It gives me a whole different view of obedience. We can never do right unless we have a new Master. If I find myself having problems with my sinful habits, and I find myself sinning over and over again, not doing the things I know I ought to do, my problem is that I still have the wrong master, the wrong leader, the wrong king of my life. That is my problem. When I have the new King in my life and He rules, I'll have no trouble.

We are all born in subjection to Satan, with a propensity to do what is wrong. That's why Satan so easily dominates in our lives. We are in harmony with him, and not at odds. Instead, we begin at odds with Jesus, and not in harmony with Him. Jesus came to get us to serve the right Master. So it doesn't matter how hard I try, or how hard I pray, or how hard I study. The only way I can get out of that dilemma is to have a new Master. I cannot do righteousness until I have Him to be the ruler of my life. It is important to note that even when I have Jesus ruling over me, my carnal nature will crave for attention every day, but that doesn't mean that I have to answer the call of self. When self calls and wants to be indulged, God's grace will enable me to not answer the call.

How do I obtain a new Master? This is such an important question, so I will go very slowly. I hope you can race ahead of me—those of you whom I am talking about. Question: How does a slave get a new master? Think back to the days of slavery in America. Did that slave pray and pray and pray? Did he try harder to not be a slave? Did he go to another slave and ask, "Have you found a new gimmick to get out of slavery?" He might hear the answer, "Oh, yeah, I heard a preacher down the road last week, and he has a new gimmick on how I can get out of slavery." That doesn't work.

How do slaves get out of slavery? They have to be *bought*. Where slavery is legal in the eyes of the law, slaves are the property of some master, just like cows, horses, sheep, goats, cars, and houses. Slaves are property and may legally be dominated and ruled by somebody. The owner can do anything he wants with his property. What he does with his property is his business, and not somebody else's. Therefore, he controls all his slaves just the way he wants to, because they belong to him. He owns them; the law says he owns them. They are his property. He can do what he wants to with them. The devil plays with his slaves like a cat with a mouse, because they are his property.

Some sins are the result of yielding to unexpected or undiscerned temptation, and the sinner may find peace with God by immediately fleeing to Him for forgiveness. However, once we fall into habitual sin, the Bible says we become slaves of sin. Satan dominates our lives, and we can't do what we desperately want to do. In so many words, Paul wrote in Romans 7 that there was something wrong with him because he couldn't do what he wanted to do. But no, there was nothing wrong with Paul, or with any of us who desire to be released from slavery to sin. The Bible simply tells us that we have the wrong master. The master is the one who is controlling us. When we really understand this, and we talk to people with some really severe problems, we will find out they are not able to do what they want to do.

I've met many alcoholics that don't want to be alcoholics, but they can't seem to control themselves. Somebody else besides them is in control; that is just the way it is. They seem to be *compelled*. Have you ever felt compelled to do what you do not want to do? Therefore, we must be bought from a bad master by a good Master. That is the only way; there is no other way. We must be purchased by the right Master. What does the Bible call that transaction? It is called *redemption*. Redemption is buying us from terrible slavery to sin. Every time you sing about being redeemed, you are saying, "When I was a slave, Someone paid the price and bought me." You are confessing that you have been a slave. We hardly know what we're singing. "I was bought when I was a slave, and I am now the property of another Person. He is a marvelous new Master."

The Bible says that we must be redeemed, and it tells us how: "Forasmuch as ye know that ye were not redeemed with corruptible things, as silver and gold, from your vain conversation received by tradition from your fathers; But with the precious blood of Christ, as of a lamb without blemish and without spot." 1 Peter 1:18-19. Also, "What? know ye not that your body is the temple of the Holy Ghost which is in you, which ye have of God, and ye are not your own? For ye are bought with a price: therefore glorify God in your body, and in your spirit, which are God's." 1 Corinthians 6:19-20. The Bible says we are redeemed, or purchased, by the precious blood of Jesus. Christ came to buy us because the only way that He or anyone else can get a slave is to buy him or her. There is no other legal way. Christ came to buy us with the price that was required, which was the shedding of His own blood. So Jesus is our new Master; sin and the devil are the old masters. Christ came to be our new Master, and those who walked with Him often called Him *Master*, which also meant *teacher* in His time. But Jesus also came to declare Himself King, which means to be the ruler of our lives.

Jesus had some interesting titles in the Bible. I'd like to make it very clear about one of His titles found in Hebrews 7:2. It's discussing Melchizedek, who was a type of Christ. I'm not going to tell you who Melchizedek was, because I don't know. The Bible is not very clear on that. Melchizedek means *King of righteousness*. What does that mean? You must let your thoughts roll that around for a while, because it won't click right away, but I can try to explain it.

Jesus is the only human being who ever lived in human flesh, who totally ruled and controlled His body and mind for all of His life. He never sinned, not even by a thought. He had absolute reign and control over His whole life. He ruled His own body in righteousness during the entire time He lived on this earth in human flesh. Is that correct? The Bible confirms that; therefore, He is the ruler or the King of righteousness. He is able to control His humanity, totally and completely. If He becomes the King of my life, literally, can He then control my humanity in righteousness?

There can be a problem here. Sometimes we choose a different master to rule us. Sometimes we choose Christ, but sometimes we choose self or Satan to rule us. Jesus taught that no man can serve two masters; we will hate the one and love the other. Therefore, Christ's rulership over us must be singular in our lives. "And thou shalt love the Lord thy God with all thy heart, and with all thy soul, and with all thy mind, and with all thy strength." Mark 12:30. Our love for Christ must be total. In the Bible Christ is called "The Lord Our Righteousness." Jeremiah 23:6. Whenever you talk about justification by faith in Christ, please do not omit the text, "The Lord Our Righteousness." There is no justification by faith without the Lord, Who is our righteousness. Too many people, in discussing that topic, leave out the Lord, and all that the word *Lord* means.

If you had to translate the Bible today into modern street language, how would you translate the word *Lord*? Do each of you ladies, when your husband comes home after work, say that your lord has arrived? Is that what you say, like they did a few hundred years ago? Or do you say, "Here is the master of my house?" Does anybody say that anymore? Not at all. What do we use in place of *lord* and *master* today? It might sound irrelevant at first, but the only word we have that I know about is *boss*. "The boss is home." Try not to think of the derogatory connotations of that word; the boss is simply the one who gives the directions. The boss is in charge—the one who tells others what to do and where to go and when to do it. Jesus is the Boss. In modern language, Jesus is "the Boss our righteousness." That is what it means, especially because we don't understand the words *lord* or *master* anymore. Those words have lost most of their real meaning.

Jesus is the Boss of righteousness. And He must become the Boss of my righteousness, the One who can control me and lead me in paths of righteousness for His name's sake. As the Bible says, "He leadeth me in the paths of righteousness for His name's sake." Psalms 23:3. He is the One who is able to lead me to do the right things. I am not of myself able to do right things. When He is the right Man by my side, when I am intimately related to Him and connected with Him, when I follow Him all the way, He leads me in paths of righteousness. He is able to do that. He knows the way through the wilderness. I don't know the way; I must follow Him all the time. It makes a difference. Too often we walk alone, and He doesn't want us to do that. So He is the King of righteousness; He is the Master; He is the Boss. And He wants to come and rule my life in a very kind, loving way.

Have you made Jesus also your Lord, and not just your Savior? If you become engrossed with your guilt and your sins, you will want Jesus only as your Savior—the One Who can rescue you and forgive you. I think sometimes there may be too much emphasis on Jesus only as our Savior. I know that your needs are great, and mine are, too. I would never take those needs away or diminish them; don't misunderstand me. But if you emphasize Christ *only* as Savior, you'll never have Him as Lord. I think that in some of our problems, we need Him more as Lord than Savior. We're a little confused about His functions. I really need Him to dominate me sometimes, rather than to just forgive me. Sometimes the problem I'm having is not forgiveness. The guilt I have for my problems is something that I cannot take care of myself. I need Someone to control me properly. I'm kind of a runaway, maverick horse; I need Somebody to take the reins and lead me down the straight path. I just can't do it myself, so I need Him as Lord, or Boss. I think it's beneficial for those who have problems with guilt to say, "Jesus, be my Lord. Boss my life; rule me in righteousness. I cannot. Don't let Satan do it." Only Christ can rule me the right way. I need the new King—the new Master.

Since Christ has already redeemed us, already purchased us that we might be free from the old master and have the new Master, how can we have this new Master dominate us? That's a key question. How can we have Him rule our lives? I'm being as simplistic as I know how. "And if it seem evil unto you to serve the Lord, choose you this day whom ye will serve; whether the gods which your fathers served that were on the other side of the flood, or the gods of the Amorites, in whose land ye dwell: but as for me and my house, we will serve the Lord." Joshua 24:15. "And if it seem evil unto you to serve the Lord...." Don't forget the word *Lord* here. Then, "choose you this day whom ye will serve." There are the words *choose* and *will*. These words are synonymous.

The verse is saying that we must choose, or decide, whom we will serve. For Joshua, his choice was to "serve the Lord." To make a choice means we must use our *wills;* we enact the power of choice. Note that the choice is *not* whether to do right or do wrong; it doesn't say that. Rather, the choice is to whom we will submit. Whom will we choose? To what person will we choose to submit? I will choose the Lord, and I will serve Him. Again, it is important for me and you to realize that I am not saying, "I will, or choose, to stop sinning." I'm not saying that at all. I'm saying that I choose to serve Christ the Lord. Do you see the difference? I give my will to Christ.

"Know ye not, that to *whom* ye yield yourselves servants to obey, his servants ye are to whom ye obey; whether of sin unto death, or of obedience unto righteousness?" Romans 6:16. That's a verse that we read earlier. So our choice is in submitting to a power, to a person, to an authority. We will serve the Lord; we choose Him.

Jesus made an emotional proclamation when He said, "O Jerusalem, Jerusalem, thou that killest the prophets, and stonest them which are sent unto thee, how often would I have gathered thy children together, even as a hen gathereth her chickens under her wings, and ye would not!" Matthew 23:37. Did Jesus say that they *could* not? Or was it that they *would* not? They could have chosen Jesus, but that is not the choice they made. He would have gathered them like a hen gathers her chicks, but they *would* not choose Christ. There are some things we can do, and there are some things we cannot do. The Lord makes the distinction quite plain. Joshua says, "*Choose* you this day whom ye will serve." We can choose to serve the right Master or the wrong master. We have that power of choice. We can yield ourselves to, or choose, the right Master.

To some people, all of this can be confusing. Every day I hear it being misunderstood or misquoted. The following quotes should help our understanding: "Many are inquiring, '*How* am I to make the surrender of myself to God?'" *Steps to Christ*, p. 47. Now notice what we can do, and what we cannot do. Some have had these mixed up for years. First, notice from the first part of the quote above that we are submitting to, or surrendering to, or choosing, God. And now the quote continues: "You desire to give yourself to Him, but you are weak in moral power, in slavery to doubt, and controlled by the habits of your life of sin. Your promises and resolutions are like ropes of sand." We are in *slavery* to doubt. We cannot even give ourselves to God because we are so morally weak. "Your promises and resolutions are like ropes of sand." Imagine trying to climb a rope made of sand.

And here is another thing that we cannot do: "You cannot control your thoughts, your impulses, your affections." We can't control those things. Also, "the knowledge of your broken promises and forfeited pledges weakens your confidence in your own sincerity, and causes you to feel that God cannot accept you; but you need not despair." How many times have we promised or resolved to stop doing what is wrong and start doing what is right? We have broken promises like that for years.

It is because we have not been able to keep our promises to obey that we come to think that there must be something bad about us, but we are told to not despair. In other words, our failure to perform by trying to perform is not the problem, so we need not despair. Instead, we should discover what we *can* do. And then the quote begins to tell us what we can do. "What you need to understand is the true force of the will. This is the governing power in the nature of man, the power of decision, or of choice. Everything depends on the right action of the will. The power of choice God has given to men; it is theirs to exercise."

The power of decision or of choice is also called "the true force of the will." It seems that everything in being able to perform what is right depends on the right action of the will, which is the power of choice that God has given to all of us. It is ours to exercise, and even the devil cannot take that power away from us. That is something we can do.

Now, here are more things that we cannot do: "You cannot change your heart, you cannot of yourself give to God its affections." We cannot do those two things—change our own hearts, or even give the affections of our hearts to God. However, "you *can choose* to serve Him. You *can* give Him your will [your power of choice]; He will then work in you to will and to do according to His good pleasure. Thus your whole nature will be brought under the control of the Spirit of Christ; your affections will be centered upon Him, your thoughts will be in harmony with Him." The main point is that we can choose to serve God. If we do, "He will then work in you to will and to do according to His good pleasure," and our "whole nature will be brought under the control of the spirit of Christ."

Our affections will be centered upon Him. Our thoughts will be in harmony with His thoughts. But please realize that we cannot choose to stop sinning, because we cannot change our hearts. The carnal human heart—or self— is bent towards sinning, and we have no power to empty ourselves of self. We will naturally choose what self desires. However, we can give our wills, or our power of choice, to Jesus; and then He will work out in us whatever His will is, because we have given our wills to Him.

Jesus prayed, "Father, not my will, but…". But what? "Thy will be done." He gave His will to His Father. Then I am not to say that I choose to stop smoking, or swearing, or lusting, or whatever. It won't work. I'm sorry, folks, but it will not work. But I *can* say that I give my will to Jesus, and when I do, He controls my life. *He* takes away the smoking, the swearing, the lusting, or whatever. He works out His will in my life.

Paul wrote about all this at great length—about how it is God who wills in us to do of His good pleasure. So our choice is in whom we will choose to serve, and not in choosing to stop sinning. Most of have thought for years that we can choose to stop sinning. We have been taught that for years. Then when we see no victory, we think there is something wrong with us and we won't make it. We must come to discover that we can choose only to give our wills to the new Master. We have that privilege. We have that ability. We have that right. The Lord will do what we cannot do, but He will not do what we *can* do. What we *can* do is daily choose to give our wills to Him—but to do this requires a struggle.

"The battle which we have to fight—the greatest battle that was ever fought by man—is the surrender of self to the will of God, the yielding of the heart to the sovereignty of love." *Mount of Blessing*, p. 141. That struggle, which is "the greatest battle ever fought by man," "is the surrender of self to the will of God." We think that our struggle is in gaining victory over our sins, yet the secret to victory is not in a struggle with sin, but in surrendering our wills to Christ. We can ask for victory, or we can surrender to Jesus. We pray, "Lord, give me the victory," but we continue to meet with defeat. The Lord says, "You must surrender to Me. I am the only One who can give you success."

So in Christianity, just praying for victory ends in failure, but in surrendering, there is success. If we pray simply for victory, and we get victory, we are likely to end up as Pharisees. Therefore, if I understand this correctly, we must stop praying for victory and start praying for surrender. The big battles are not for victory; the big battles are for surrender. That's a tough thing for some people, especially men, to do—to surrender. We guys have a "Take that hill, men!" mentality. The bigger and tougher men are, the more pride we have and the more difficult it is to learn to surrender. We feel that to surrender is defeat, but in reality, when we surrender, then victory comes our way. Victory comes only after surrender. When I find myself failing and failing and failing, I don't need victory; I need surrender to Christ. That doesn't sound natural, and can be confusing. We all have difficulty with it, so don't point the finger at somebody else.

When doubting Thomas, whom I think we criticize too severely, said, "My Lord and my God," he really said a mouthful. Not too many people say what Thomas essentially said. He said, "Lord, dominate me. Rule me. Boss me. Show me what to do, and I'll do anything you say. Control my whole life, my Lord and my God." That is a marvelous confession, isn't it? Please don't knock Thomas too much; we need to do what he did. I call this the greatest problem in Christianity that we have with sin. We say we want a new Master. We say we want to stop sinning. We think we're sincere. We pray to stop sinning, but we do not stop. Why not? What is wrong? The question is: Is Christ controlling us? He can't control us until we submit to Him, until we surrender to Him. As long as we keep trying to run the show ourselves, He is not the Lord of our lives. We keep crowding Him off the throne time after time.

"Desires for goodness and holiness are right as far as they go; but if you stop here, they will avail nothing. Many will be lost while hoping and desiring to be Christians. They do not come to the point of yielding the will to God. They do not now *choose* to be Christians." *Steps to Christ*, p. 47. "They desire the good, they make some effort to obtain it; but they do not choose it; they have not a settled purpose to secure it at the cost of all things." *Mount of Blessing*, p. 143. And we have problems with this.

Paul teaches that choosing Christ as a new Master is like dying. "How shall we, that are dead to sin, live any longer therein?" Romans 6:2. He wrote about being baptized into Christ's death. "Know ye not that so many of us as were baptized unto Jesus Christ were baptized into His death?" Verse 3. It is about being baptized into His death. Don't you just love to die? We hate it. Our sins are close to our hearts. I can't stand yours, but I love mine; you can't stand mine, but you love yours, right? It's the truth. We do like sin. Sin is a very intimate thing; it becomes part and parcel of us. It's enjoyable. Watch people as they enjoy going over to the bar for a drink. Don't say that they don't enjoy it. It doesn't matter what the sin is; they like it. Why does a man take a puff on a cigarette, and dreamily watch the smoke go up into the air? He's enjoying it. Sin becomes a part of us. So when you try to take away something that is a part of me, you're killing me. I say, "Get out of here. I enjoy this. I don't want you to take away what I enjoy." Some people would rather die than stop their sinning. We don't realize that when we ask people to follow Christ, we're asking them to die. They want to fight that. We ask, "What's wrong with you?" and they answer, "I want to live, and I can't survive without my darling sins."

Our children sometimes don't realize that their sins are foolish. They don't want anyone to come along and take away what they enjoy so much. Well, then, the question is: "How can I ever stop sinning? Sin has been so precious and so dear to my heart; how can I get it out of my life?" The answer is in this quote: "The kingdom of God's grace is now being established, as day by day hearts that have been full of sin and rebellion yield to the sovereignty of His love." *Mount of Blessing*, p. 108. That is the key—this yielding to God's love.

Suppose there is a teenage boy, thirteen years old. His mother has been after him for a long time because when he goes to school, he wears an old dirty pair of jeans, the worst he has. Ragged, torn, and a real mess. His tennis shoes have big holes in them. The shoestrings hardly hold the shoes on his feet. He wears a shirt with a couple of buttons missing, and it looks as if he slept in it all night. His hair looks the same. His mother is just exasperated. She finally asks, "When are you ever going to clean up your act and dress like a human being?" She starts to nag him all the time. She tries to train him; she tries to educate him. She does that for years, yet he is still a slob. He has better clothes, but he won't wear them.

One day after years of education and nagging and training, he is in the bathroom getting ready to go to school. All the other family members are waiting to get into the bathroom. He has been in there for forty-five minutes, the longest he has spent in there for the last ten years. Family members keep knocking at the door, asking, "When are you going to get out of there? We all have to go to work and to school. When are you going to open up and let us get into the bathroom?" After the longest time, he suddenly emerges with his hair just immaculate, and he asks his mother, "Don't I have a better pair of jeans than these? There's a spot on them. And don't I have a better shirt than this?" Mother looks at him with her mouth wide open and asks, "What has happened to you? I have tried for years to get you to look better, but you were happy looking terrible. What is wrong with you today?"

Well, if you follow him to school, you will find that some young lady is now in the picture. You realize that he has been preening himself like a peacock in breeding season, showing his feathers. He is in love. That young girl never tried to train and nag and educate the boy for years to look better, but his mother thought that nagging and educating her son would change him. All it took to change that teenage boy was for him to fall in love with that young girl.

That happens to boys and also to girls. I had six sisters. I used to walk to high school with my future brother-in-law. I didn't know that he was in love with one of my sisters. I didn't have enough sense to know what that was all about in those days. But suddenly I noticed that he just sparkled all over. He'd come out of his house wearing a snazzy jacket. I remember one time on the way to school, I wondered what was wrong with him. His hair just looked great. He was in love, and love changes everything. We must yield to the sovereignty of God's love, and just like that our whole lives are changed. The things we couldn't stand to get rid of are gone, and sometime we wonder why.

A new love evicts an old love by displacement. When I was in the Air Force, they asked to check my teeth. The military had a lot of money invested in their pilots, and they said that they didn't want to lose us. I went to the dentist, who said that my wisdom teeth were crowding my front teeth, so the wisdom teeth had to come out. I had heard terrible stories about people who had had their wisdom teeth removed, such as the horrors of the dentist having to drill into the jaw bone, and how people had ended up in the hospital. I just knew that I would be in the hospital for a week. The dentist scheduled the surgery for an early afternoon. I was teaching flying in those days, but I took a day to go to the dentist's office. He was an old-fashioned farmer-turned-dentist. He deadened my gums and my tongue. After a while, I thought he stuck his whole fist in my mouth. He also had something in his fist that I couldn't see. After a few minutes he said, "Spit it out." I asked, "What?" And he said, "The tooth, you idiot. Spit out the tooth." I did what he said, and out came a big tooth into the sink. I asked him, "How'd you get it out so fast?" He said, "It was easy," and he held up a chisel. It had a big handle on it, with a tip on it about as big as my finger, flat on one side and round on the other. He said, "Where this thing is, the tooth can't be." I told you he was an old farmer. That's called displacement.

Where the love of Jesus is, the love of other things cannot be. That is a fact. When Christ gets hold of our hearts, when we yield to the sovereignty of His love, He evicts all other lovers, all other rulers, all other masters, and becomes the King of our lives. I crown Him as ruler of my heart. And when He is in command, He leads me in paths of righteousness for His name's sake.

This terrible problem we have with sin and masters was solved a long time ago. Christ has purchased you and me because we are so dear to Him. It cost Him an extremely precious, invaluable price, didn't it? It cost the Father, also. Christ became a human being for eternity. He is still the Son of God, but He will live for eternity in human form. The Father gave us something uniquely special when He gave us Jesus, and the Son gave us the ultimate gift of His life. The high price Jesus paid for us advertises to the whole universe how valuable we are to Him. He wants us, and He asks each of us, "Do you want Me? Will you choose to love and honor and obey Me, until death us do part?" *Do you?* Will you have Jesus to be your spiritual husband? Will you let Him reign over you in all His great love? When you do, you will find complete freedom from slavery to sin. The slavery to Satan will be gone. The Bible says that the Son shall make you free.

I need that freedom, don't you? I need a freedom where all the guilt is gone. Our big problem is more than making Christ our Savior and getting forgiveness. We need Him every day to rule over our lives. I ask Him, "Lord, what do we do today? Where would you have me to go? What shall I say? Where shall I work? What do you want to happen today? Lord, lead me. I don't know how or where to go. Show me the way." When Jesus becomes our King of love, He never forces us. Never. He comes to reign over us in love. It's marvelous to yield to someone when he or she loves you; it's terrible to yield to someone who doesn't love you. When we submit to His love, we have a new Master. Freedom is ours, because Jesus is ours.

Here is my prayer for us: Loving Father, King of our lives, how often we have walked all by ourselves down life's way, and wondered why we have stumbled and fallen so frequently. We have wondered why we are so helpless, and cannot do what we want to do. How seldom we have realized that Jesus is right there to take us by the hand, to strengthen us, to rule over our lives, to take us down life's pathway hand-in-hand, so we might be able to stand. Somehow, by Your marvelous grace and by the Spirit of the living God, show us Your tremendous love—how precious we are to You, how much You long for us, how much You long to lift us up above sin, how much You long to encourage us, how much You long to just be with us, hand-in-hand, side-by-side, filling our hearts with Your marvelous love. Lord, come into our hearts just now. Forgive us for trusting so much in self, for believing we can do it. Forgive us for failing to surrender to You all these years when You have loved us so much. Forgive us for failing to say "I do" and "I will." Lord, we give our wills to Thee. We choose Jesus above all others. Come and reign over us in Your magnificent love, and lead us all the way to the kingdom. We will never stop praising You throughout all the ages, for Thou art a wonderful God. In Jesus' name we pray. Amen.

CHAPTER 7: THE GUILTY AND THE LAW

As we continue our thoughts on God's love affair with the guilty, I want to emphasize the *love* more and more as we continue. Our thoughts here will center on guilt and the law. The first few ideas might depress you for a moment or two, but please bear with me. In order to correctly understand guilt, we must understand the law, for sin is transgression of the law. It's sin that causes guilt. So the more we preach only the law, the more we feel guilty. Is that correct? Don't get too depressed. Paul wrote, "But sin, that it might appear sin, working death in me by that which is good; that sin by the commandment might become exceeding sinful." Romans 7:13.

In other words, if you really preach with strong emphasis on the law, you make people cringe with guilt. The stronger we preach the law, the stronger the guilt. Paul said that the commandments make sin appear "*exceeding*" sinful; therefore, the sinner will feel *exceedingly* guilty. Is that what we want to happen to people? We need to come to terms with a statement made many decades ago that, "as a people, we have preached the law until we are as dry as the hills of Gilboa that had neither dew nor rain." *Review and Herald*, March 11, 1890. If we preach only the law, our preaching is awfully dry. In your estimation, have things changed since that statement was first published?

Some Christian people have preached the law until they're just dry as can be. Directly following the above statement, however, is found the remedy for our dry preaching: "We must preach Christ in the law, and there will be sap and nourishment in the preaching that will be as food to the famishing flock of God." If we preach the law, all we get is guilt. The people are starving for the real nourishment that is found in preaching *Christ in the law*. Do we preach Christ in the law today?

Think about this new concept of preaching Christ in the law. What is the law like when Christ is put into it? We may also phrase it in reverse and say that when the law is put into Christ, the people will be nourished. In other words, if you preach Christ without the law, that preaching is dry, also.

The law in Christ, or Christ in the law, is described by Jesus when He said, "Thou shalt love the Lord thy God with all thy heart, and with all thy soul, and with all thy mind. This is the first and great commandment. And the second is like unto it, Thou shalt love thy neighbour as thyself. On these two commandments hang all the law and the prophets." Matthew 22:37-40. I believe this is what Christ is saying happens to the law when He is put into it. If this is the law, as Christ has taught it, then obedience to the law is supreme love for God and loving our neighbors as ourselves. That is genuine righteousness, or obedience. It is supreme love for God and loving our fellow men as ourselves. Along with what Christ said, we may also bring in a text by Paul that reads, "Love worketh no ill to his neighbour: therefore love is the fulfilling of the law." Romans 13:10.

Love always does good to its neighbor, and therefore it accomplishes the law. If obedience is supreme love for God and unselfish love for our fellow men, then what is transgression? Don't run away from me, will you? Obedience is that kind of love, but what is transgression? It's vastly different than we have been thinking for years. Transgression or disobedience is an unloving attitude towards God or towards our fellow men. That is much different, and we'll amplify this as we go along. Now, if an unloving attitude towards another person is transgression of the law, what is true guilt? Do you see it? Genuine guilt comes only from violation of the law of love. True guilt causes ill feelings because we have wronged someone. It isn't because we lied to that person. It isn't the lie that is so bad; it's our attitude towards that person—our treatment of him or her. If we're experiencing true guilt, we don't say, "Lord, forgive me because I lied." Instead, we say, "Lord, forgive me because I hurt a person I should have loved." But in our attempt for perfection, we always put it the other way, thinking that if we could just abstain from lying, we would be qualified to go to heaven. We say, "Lord, make me flawlessly perfect so I never lie." No. "… Make me *loving* so I never want to lie."

Motivation has much to do with our subject of feeling guilty, in terms of transgressing the law. If we are properly motivated with the right spirit, right actions will come. However, we can try, and strive, all our lives, and live long lives, and still not attain to anything right if the attitude is wrong. Jesus came, a gift of God to motivate us. The spirit of the law is self-renouncing love. Some people get concerned with the letter of the law, but never consider the spirit of the law. That spirit of the law leads us to say, "I'm sorry I've wronged you; I want to show love to you, not cause you hurt." All true guilt centers around that relationship of love. All other guilt, I'm afraid, is only an ego trip, trying to make ourselves look good enough for heaven.

The devil always capitalizes on false guilt, false concepts of God, and false concepts of love and obedience. We must learn that God is love, and His law is the spilling out of that love. True guilt, therefore, is a vastly different thing than we may have thought. Most of the guilt we suffer is not in this realm at all. We are always worried that we are not good enough, when really we are unloving. The main thing to be concerned about in transgressing the law is that we are not loving. This places guilt and sin and law-keeping and righteousness on a completely different stratum of living.

Unfortunately, we Christians are sometimes not known as the best lovers in the world, and I say that in a spiritual sense. Our own fellow church members do not feel the most loved of all people on the face of the earth, do they? We suffer with much lonesomeness right in our churches because of the lack of consideration and love for one another. Those in high positions also feel unloved, because somehow there is a remoteness and distance about a high position; and that doesn't qualify anyone for love, either. So we go on and on, thinking and hoping that something will someday make us loved by others, but it doesn't.

It is the spirit of the law that is sometimes missing from our whole work. Obedience is a love affair, one of relationships with God and man, rather than an ongoing attempt to satisfy an exacting code of behavior. That is so cold and so lifeless; it's so sterile. There is no feeling there. There is nothing. Heaven is not a sterile place, without feeling or emotions. It's not like that at all. For us, heaven is going to be a warm, affectionate place where we'll greet one another with a holy kiss, and that kiss will be truly holy and meaningful. There will be none of these little love pecks between husbands and wives that are meaningless. Everything will be meaningful, and we will embrace one another, and it will be most meaningful—right out of the depths of our souls. We begin here in this life in that kind of activity—within proper moral boundaries, of course. So it's not an attempt to be flawlessly perfect; it's a heart motivation to be loving and to demonstrate that loving action in all my life for others and for God.

Therefore, the love of Christ constrains us from doing harm or thinking evil towards others. Nothing else constrains us. It isn't fear that we're going to be lost, or because we're worried about ridicule or something like that. It's the love of Christ constraining us to treat others right, and it hurts us when we do not treat them right. I'm trying to help you to find this kind of love in your activity, whether it is at home, in a Christian school, at work, or wherever you may be. So don't consider the law to be a negative. The law is a positive action of loving others in sincerity, earnestness, and love for Christ that brings a blessing to them. This places the law, the Lawgiver, the Judge and the judgment on an entirely different basis. If God is love, the Judge is love. If we are judged by the law, and the law is love, then the judgment is love. It can't be anything else. You have a Judge sitting there on the throne, and that Judge is love; and there is the law by which we are judged, and that law is love. The whole judgment is an activity of love to see if we have responded to His great love. God so loved the world that He gave, and He continues to give. Is there any response in our hearts? Do we love Him supremely and others as ourselves? That is what He is looking for in the judgment.

The law will condemn us only when we are unloving and hateful and rejecting of His tremendous grace. Loving God and others is not so difficult an obligation; it's an indebtedness to grace, to God's great love for us. God Himself is the exponent of love, the great Advocate of love, and unwittingly, we have done so many things in our teachings and concepts to damage His character. Our groveling and depression and discouragement and striving to please Him are all denying that He is love. And too often we preach, by our own frame of mind and by our treatment of others, that God is not love.

Let us look at the law from still another perspective. "He that loveth not knoweth not God; for God is love." 1 John 4:8. "Philip saith unto Him, Lord, show us the Father, and it sufficeth us. Jesus saith unto him, Have I been so long time with you, and yet hast thou not known Me, Philip? He that hath seen Me hath seen the Father; and how sayest thou then, show us the Father? Believest thou not that I am in the Father, and the Father in Me? The words that I speak unto you I speak not of Myself: but the Father that dwelleth in Me, He doeth the works." John 14:8-10.

Jesus was not just a description of the Father's character, which is what the ten commandment law is. Jesus *showed* the Father; He *lived* the Father. He told Philip that if he had seen Him (as Philip had), then he had seen the Father. Take the language literally, and you will learn something different about Jesus and the gift of heaven. If God is love, and Jesus came to show us the Father, what do we see when we see Jesus? We see Love. That's obvious.

Now, go just one step beyond that, and remember that we are talking about the life of Jesus and the concept that God is love. "Think not that I am come to destroy the law, or the prophets: I am not come to destroy, but to fulfill." Matthew 5:17. The very life of Jesus—all His words and actions—were the fulfilling of the law. So if God is love—if, when you see Jesus, you see the Father—then the life of Jesus that fulfilled the law was... what? It was love. Therefore, the law must be love. Do you understand? If His life was the fulfilling of the law, and His life was the law, then His life is love, and His law is love. It doesn't matter how we approach the law in Christ. We always come back to the fact that the law is love. We cannot escape it, and the Bible teaches this in many ways. When we preach Christ in the law, we preach love in the law.

Paul described the life of Jesus in a most unusual way. "For God, who commanded the light to shine out of darkness, hath shined in our hearts, to give the light of the knowledge of the glory of God in the face of Jesus Christ." 2 Corinthians 4:6. Let's examine Paul's difficult language. He said that the "light of the knowledge of the glory of God" was seen "in the face of Jesus Christ."

On page one and in the first paragraph of *The Desire of Ages*, Jesus is called the "outshining of the Father's glory." If you study this in the Bible, you will discover some unusual things, such as what happened when Moses asked to see God's glory (see Exodus 33:18). In Exodus 34:5-7, the Lord passed before Moses and declared His character: "And the Lord descended in the cloud, and stood with him there, and proclaimed the name of the Lord. And the Lord passed by before him, and proclaimed, The Lord, The Lord God, merciful and gracious, longsuffering, and abundant in goodness and truth, keeping mercy for thousands, forgiving iniquity and transgression and sin, and that will by no means clear the guilty; visiting the iniquity of the fathers upon the children, and upon the children's children, unto the third and to the fourth generation." Exodus 34:5-7.

God's glory is in being merciful and gracious, longsuffering, and abundant in goodness and truth. His glory is His character. "The light of His glory—His character—is to shine forth in His followers." *Christ's Object Lessons*, p. 414. Since God is love, His character is love. Now, Jesus was the outshining of that glory. The thing that made Him radiant, that made Him beam for His Father, was the character of God revealed in Jesus—and that character was love. This is a most unusual concept about Him. When Jesus came to this earth and lived a life that was the fulfilling of the law, what happened to the law? It was glorified. Jesus showed us the Father; the law was a transcript of the Father's character; the Father's character is love; Jesus showed us love. So the law is love, and Jesus glorified the law as He showed the character of God in the law. That is what He was doing, and glorious things were happening to the law as Jesus lived that perfect life.

There is yet another quality to the life of Jesus and the law. The law was written on tables of stone. When we put Christ in the law, and the law in Christ, we have a new dimension, for Jesus was a human being who took our flesh after four thousand years of sin's degeneracy. He took weak human flesh. He was not a sinner, but He was tempted in all ways of life as we are, yet without sin. And in that weak human body after four thousand years of sin, He lived a life in perfect fulfillment of that law.

I can relate to the law in the humanity of Christ better than I can to the law on stone, can't you? I can love a human; I can love a person. People have difficulty loving rocks, even if they might be rockhounds. I love *Him*. I can grasp the keeping of the law in humanity after all those years of sin. That is meaningful to me; that is also effective in humanity. He put into effect the law that was in stone. He did no damage to the law whatsoever, and so when you see Him, you see the fulfilling of that law in weakened humanity.

When we talk about Christ our righteousness, we are literally talking about that perfect life in a human being—in Christ Jesus. Isn't that what we are talking about? Christ our righteousness—that Person in weak, human flesh. He was able to be tempted; He was hungry; He was weary; He needed sleep; He could succumb to temptation. That Person was the fulfilling of the law, and that is so meaningful. It helps us a great deal. At the very least, a new dimension was added to the law when it was put into the humanity of Christ, as compared to being on stone. Put into Christ, it then became most effective.

"For what the law could not do, in that it was weak through the flesh, God sending His own Son in the likeness of sinful flesh, and for sin, condemned sin in the flesh: That the righteousness of the law might be fulfilled in us, who walk not after the flesh, but after the Spirit." Romans 8:3-4. The law that Paul referred to that was weak in humanity was the law in stone. But when God sent His own Son in the likeness of sinful flesh, in weak humanity as we are, He lived that perfect life of the righteousness of the law. He did it so that the law could be fulfilled in us. It was fulfilled in Him, so He became the law in humanity, so that it might also be fulfilled in you and me. There was an ineffectiveness, a weakness, in the law in stone that was not found in the law in Christ. In fact, that weakness was all taken away, and the law in Christ becomes strong. It becomes effectual. It begins to function in us when we receive it in Christ. It's a new thing. Christ magnified the law when He perfectly lived out every precept in human flesh.

Isaiah prophesied that that is what Christ would do to the law: "He will magnify the law, and make it honourable." Isaiah 42:21. Jesus came to magnify the law. He came to make it honorable. *Magnify* means to "cause to be seen as greater or more important." That's what Jesus did, by living the spirit and letter of the law perfectly. Something glorious happened to the law on stone when Jesus walked in human flesh and totally fulfilled it.

I frighten many of you out of your skins when I talk this way about any possible change in the way we perceive the law, but I am not the first person who ever talked about this. In fact, this understanding—that Jesus' life gave greater importance, honor and effectiveness to the law given at Sinai than the law had before His incarnation—has been around for a long time, and it's time we came back to why the understanding came into Christianity, and why it has been forgotten.

There is a Bible text that is controversial amongst Christians. That text tells what happened to the law when Jesus came in humanity and lived the law perfectly. "Forasmuch as ye are manifestly declared to be the epistle of Christ ministered by us, written not with ink, but with the Spirit of the living God; not in tables of stone, but in fleshly tables of the heart." 2 Corinthians 3:3. Paul is here talking about the law written not on stone, but in hearts. He is saying there is something better about the law being written in hearts than on stone.

More light is shed from verses 7 to 11: "But if the ministration of death, written and engraven in stones, was glorious, so that the children of Israel could not stedfastly behold the face of Moses for the glory of his countenance; which glory was to be done away: How shall not the ministration of the Spirit be rather glorious? For if the ministration of condemnation be glory, much more doth the ministration of righteousness exceed in glory. For even that which was made glorious had no glory in this respect, by reason of the glory that excelleth. For if that which is done away was glorious, much more that which remaineth is glorious."

This is talking about the ten commandment law, because that was the only law "written and engraven in stones." Remember that the glory of the law is the character of God. "How shall not the ministration of the Spirit be rather glorious?" Or "… more glorious?" "For if the ministration of condemnation be glory, much more doth the ministration of righteousness exceed in glory." The law in stone was glorious, but the law as revealed in the life of Jesus was "rather glorious"—or "more glorious." Now, here is where some people who love the law get nervous. They resist the idea that the glory of the law in stone "is done away," but it doesn't say that the law in stone was done away with. It says that the glory of the law in stone was done away with.

How can the glory of the law in stone be done away? This is something that those who defend the law of God almost never bring up—that the glory of the law in stone was done away with. Some people go into a frenzy and declare that Paul was talking only about the ceremonial law, but that law was not written and engraved on stone tablets. I say it again: the text does not say that the law in stone was done away with, as some Protestant groups claim. It says that the law in stone was glorious. "For if the ministration of condemnation be glory…." Even here, some people get nervous, for how could the ten commandment law be the "ministration of condemnation"? Well, if a sinner looks into the law in stone, he feels condemned; isn't that right? That's one reason the law in stone was given—to make people realize their sinful condition. But some people get concerned when it is declared that the glory of the law in stone has been "done away." They don't realize that something happened that made the glory in the law even brighter. The glory in the law became greater when the law was revealed in the life, character, and teachings of Christ.

A simple illustration will help us see this. Suppose you are in a large building at night, and suddenly the lights go off. You pull out a box of matches and light one. The light from that match helps you see your way down the hallways and towards the exit. Suppose that the walls of the building are made mostly of glass. The fire department shows up and aims a ten-million-candlepower search light at the building. As soon as they flip the switch and that powerful search light comes on, the whole inside of the building lights up like it was noon on a cloudless day. There you are standing with a lit match. What happened to the light from the match when the searchlight was turned on? For all practical purposes, the light from the match was "done away" with. It was doing its job—helping you find your way out of the dark building; but when the search light was turned on, the light from the search light was far brighter than the light from the match. It is in that way that the glory of the law in stone was done away. When Jesus lived and demonstrated the glory of the law, it was far more glorious that the glory of the law in stone.

That illustration not only helps us understand how the glory of the law in stone was done away with when Christ came and revealed the glory of the law in His life. The illustration also helps us to understand what Paul meant when he wrote in Galatians 3:24 about the law in stone being the schoolmaster: "Wherefore the law was our schoolmaster to bring us unto Christ, that we might be justified by faith. But after that faith is come, we are no longer under a schoolmaster." The schoolmaster includes the moral law of ten commandments. The schoolmaster's job is to help us to see how dark our former lives of sin were. But when that schoolmaster has taken us in faith to Christ, then the law in Christ, as revealed to us by the Holy Spirit, is so much greater than the law in stone had been to us. We, then, are not obligated to the schoolmaster any more than we needed to keep holding a lit match once the powerful search light was turned on. If, after coming to Christ, we backslide, the schoolmaster—or the law in stone—is still there to bring us back to Christ. Is that not a good thing?

Jesus said that if He would be "lifted up from the earth," He would "draw all men unto" Him. John 12:32. It doesn't say, "If the ten commandments on stone be lifted up…." Christ is in no way opposed to the law in stone. It was Christ, the Jehovah of the Old Testament, Who wrote those commandments in stone and gave them to Moses. There is a divine purpose for the law to be written in stone. But Christ incarnated magnifies that law. He makes it more glorious than it was when only written on stone. Jesus enhanced the Father's character, but His life did not detract one bit from the Father's character. The law in stone condemns the sinner as a transgressor and deserving of death, but the law in Christ draws the sinner with an undying love. The law in Christ is the law living, breathing, loving, and forgiving. Therefore, the law in Christ makes the law a marvelous blessing to sinners who seek for pardon and power to obey. It was in making the law *more glorious* that Jesus magnified the law. The law in stone has no power to enable us to obey it; the law in Christ includes a power from above that enables us to obey the law. It is the law and the gospel united. Therefore, all my righteousness is found in having the law written not on stone, but on the fleshly tables of my heart. The law is written in my heart when I fall in love with Christ. It is impossible to get the law in stone into the heart, but we can fall in love with Jesus, who is the personification of the law.

It is time that Christians who defend God's law come to grips with the matter of how much more glorious is the law in Christ, than was the glory of the law in stone. The law plus the gospel of Jesus surpasses the law alone. As we mentioned earlier, some have preached the law in stone until their law-preaching has become as dry as the hills of Gilboa. If we preach Christ in the law, we preach that the law is love, and actions motivated by love are never dry.

The schoolmaster in Galatians chapter 3 included both the ceremonial law and the moral law of ten commandments. The ceremonial law was not a bad law; all of the mercy of God was symbolized in the ceremonial law. In the moral law, God's justice was revealed. When we hold up nothing but the moral law, where is the mercy that was found in the ceremonial law? We would depict that God is a just God, but omit that He is also a merciful God. In Christ, both laws were perfectly fulfilled.

In the ceremonial law, we see Christ as the sacrifice. Before the cross, if a man sinned (transgressed the moral law), he had to go find a lamb without spot or blemish and sacrifice it, thus transferring his sin to the animal. When Christ came, His perfect character did a better job than the law in stone ever did in revealing to us our sinful condition. The more clearly we see His perfect character, the more vile we see ourselves to be. In Jesus, our sins were transferred to the Lamb of God when He was sacrificed on the cross. Thus, Jesus was the perfect fulfillment of both the ceremonial and moral laws.

Jesus personified the law. Isn't that nice? Side-by-side in the Person of Christ were both laws—and thus both the justice and the mercy of God. So when I see one law, I see the other law right there in Him. Both laws are wrapped up in Jesus. I don't have to go somewhere else to find a sacrifice when I have come under the condemnation of transgressing one of the commandments. The sacrifice is right there in the same Person whose perfect character revealed to me my sinful deformity. And thus it is that the glory of the law is made more glorious when it is revealed in the life of one precious Being—our Lord and Savior Jesus.

When we put the law in Christ, and Christ in the law, there is no diminishing of the law. The principles remain the same. But the law is magnified and made honorable. No damage is done at all to the law. The law is still everlasting.

What about guilt? When Christ is put in the law (and remember that the title of this chapter is "The Guilty and the Law"), this makes guilt another thing altogether—totally different and very unusual. Guilt no longer is the result of transgressing some written code. Guilt is a rejection of God's unconditional love for the sinner. It is a failure to give our highest affections to Christ. It is a failure to respond to God the Father, in giving His spotless Son to die in our place.

The first three verses of Isaiah 6 relate the experience of the gospel prophet as he saw the glory of the Lord. Again, what is the glory of God? It is His character. And His character is what? Love, if you want to put it in one word. So here is Isaiah's experience as he sees the glory of God—His character: "In the year that king Uzziah died I saw also the LORD sitting upon a throne, high and lifted up, and His train filled the temple. Above it stood the seraphims: each one had six wings; with twain he covered his face, and with twain he covered his feet, and with twain he did fly. And one cried unto another, and said, Holy, holy, holy, is the LORD of hosts: the whole earth is full of His glory." Isaiah 6:1-3.

"Then said I, Woe is me! for I am undone; because I am a man of unclean lips, and I dwell in the midst of a people of unclean lips: for mine eyes have seen the King, the Lord of hosts. Then flew one of the seraphims unto me, having a live coal in his hand, which he had taken with the tongs from off the altar: And he laid it upon my mouth, and said, Lo, this hath touched thy lips; and thine iniquity is taken away, and thy sin purged." (Verses 5-7.) As Isaiah viewed the character, or the glory, of God, he felt unclean.

The apostle Peter experienced something similar when, at the command of Jesus, a net was let down into the clear water. "Now when He had left speaking, He said unto Simon, launch out into the deep, and let down your nets for a draught. And Simon answering said unto Him, Master, we have toiled all the night, and have taken nothing: nevertheless at thy word I will let down the net. And when they had this done, they inclosed a great multitude of fishes: and their net brake. And they beckoned unto their partners, which were in the other ship, that they should come and help them. And they came, and filled both the ships, so that they began to sink. When Simon Peter saw it, he fell down at Jesus' knees, saying, Depart from me; for I am a sinful man, O Lord." Luke 5:4-8.

What kind of a person was Peter? He was a proud fellow who thought that he never did anything wrong; but in witnessing the miracle of the fishes, Peter said, "Depart from me; for I am a sinful man." This is a true concept of guilt, the only kind of guilt that could be called good or right.

Here is a quote that describes the scene quite well: "The presence of divinity revealed his [Peter's] own unholiness. Love for his Master, shame for his own unbelief, gratitude for the condescension of Christ, above all, the sense of his uncleanness in the presence of infinite purity, overwhelmed him. While his companions were securing the contents of the net, Peter fell at the Saviour's feet, exclaiming, 'Depart from me; for I am a sinful man, O Lord.'" *Desire of Ages*, p. 246. Note these most important words: "shame for his own unbelief" and "gratitude for the condescension of Christ." Above all was Peter's sense of his uncleanness in the presence of infinite purity.

Peter asked his Lord to depart from him, yet he held Jesus by the ankles so that Jesus would not leave him. Does that scene remind you of Jacob wrestling with the Lord? Peter was overwhelmed with his sinfulness, but also with the enormous love of Christ. We, too, may experience seeing our sinfulness as we behold the unspotted glory, love, and life's miracles wrought by God; and yet while feeling our own uncleanness and unworthiness to go boldly into the presence of God, we wish to hold fast to that love of God that makes us never want Him to leave us.

Oh, to experience that love that will not let us go. It makes us want to embrace Him and cling to Him. When this is our constant experience, then all our hope is found in Him. This is the only true guilt that God would have us experience. Wrong guilt comes from trying and failing to be good enough to please Him, or thinking that our sins have been too great or continued for too long for Him to forgive us. We must learn that He already loves us, and we please Him by letting Him rule our lives as our Sovereign King. Jesus wants to take all other guilt away. He wants His perfect love to cast out all fear. You don't have to be worried about guilt when you are in love with Jesus. Jesus does a much better job of making us see our deficiencies and sinful selves than the law in stone does; and as the law in Christ makes us feel our vileness and corruption, our inadequacies and failures, yet at the same time we just bubble over with hope in His magnificent love, and we cling with all our might to Him.

This is the tremendous hope we have in Christ. The law in Jesus is a marvelous law, and we, along with David, can say, "I delight to do Thy will, O my God: yea, Thy law is within my heart." Psalm 40:8. May God help us to see the law in all its beauty in Jesus, and not remain so constantly focused on a law without mercy that we've held up for so many years—a law engraved in stone that has made our preaching as dry as the hills of Gilboa. Let us recognize the purpose of the law in stone; but once that purpose has been fulfilled, let us move on to dwell on the law as revealed in the life, character, and teachings of Jesus.

I offer this prayer for us all: Loving Father, we have often taught the things that we believed to be true. We did not want to damage the law. We did not want anyone to despise it or to be deceived about it. But forgive us if we have caused thousands or millions to feel guilty, who do not know the love and mercy of Jesus. Help us to understand the Lord our righteousness as He lived that beautiful life in weak humanity, perfectly fulfilling that marvelous law of love. When we find that both the justice and the mercy of God are embodied in Jesus, that magnificent Person, the gift of heaven, and as we receive Him by loving Him and responding to His love, the fullness of the character of God will come into our lives. Keep our eyes fixed on Him. By beholding Him, may we be transformed into His likeness so that the beauty of Jesus, the glory of God, might be seen in us. Take away all of our false feelings of guilt. May we understand this great love affair that Christ wants to have with each of us, and may we always be in love with the One who first loved us. We ask in Jesus' name. Amen.

Chapter 8: God's Love Affair with the Guilty

Too often we have missed the real heart of all obedience and law-keeping, the reason for being Christian, and the reason why Jesus came. We take the words so lightly, and do not realize that almost everything in the Bible is a love affair. Let's examine some more things about this love affair.

Christ pictures Christianity and the gospel work as a love affair involving marriage. We are going beyond the love affair into a marriage affair with Christ, and we hope that you have noticed that.

In Matthew chapter 22, we find this parable: "The kingdom of heaven is like unto a certain king, which made a marriage for his son, And sent forth his servants to call them that were bidden to the wedding: and they would not come…. And when the king came in to see the guests, he saw there a man which had not on a wedding garment." Matthew 22:2-3, 11.

You probably know the parable very well. Here is a comment that helps us to better understand it: "The parable of the wedding garment opens before us a lesson of the highest consequence. By the marriage is represented the union of humanity with divinity; the wedding garment represents the character which all must possess who shall be accounted fit guests for the wedding." *Christ's Object Lessons*, p. 307. A key point is that the marriage represents "the union of humanity with divinity." I wish I understood all that those words mean. When Christ, the God-Man, took human flesh, He made it possible for God to live in us. This is really at the core of the gospel story—God in man, and the two becoming one. That union makes the Christian life a possibility.

In marriage, two cannot become one except when love is the motivation and the cause. Now we are getting right down to the heart of why we should be Christians, and what it's all about. Jesus not only wants us to be united to Him; He wants a more intimate relationship with us. He described that relationship in His last prayer: "… That they all may be one; as Thou, Father, art in Me, and I in thee, that they also may be one in Us: that the world may believe that Thou hast sent Me. … I in them, and Thou in Me, that they may be made perfect in one; and that the world may know that Thou hast sent Me, and hast loved them, as Thou hast loved Me. … And I have declared unto them Thy name, and will declare it: that the love wherewith Thou hast loved Me may be in them, and I in them." John 17:21, 23, 26.

Jesus wants us to be with Him in the future as well as the present. He talks about this in verse 24, which I skipped. "Father, I will that they also, whom Thou hast given Me, be with Me where I am; that they may behold My glory, which Thou hast given Me: for Thou lovedst Me before the foundation of the world." Jesus said that He did not want to be away from those whom His Father had given Him. Like any man, He wants to live together with His bride. That is His desire and His plan for mankind.

This love story is all throughout the Bible, and so we'll be going back and forth quickly to quote a few texts. "The LORD hath appeared of old unto me, saying, Yea, I have loved thee with an everlasting love: therefore with lovingkindness have I drawn thee." Jeremiah 31:3. The love affair God had with Israel is a symbol of our love affair with Him. The gospel work is a wooing work; we are enticing people to come to Christ and give Him their hearts, which is a love term. You give your heart to the young man or woman you're in love with; you do not give your heart to anyone you do not love. And so He loves us and woos us with loving kindness. This is what it's all about.

The Book of Hosea is a book that we do not read much because it is sometimes misunderstood, and yet that Bible book is filled with God speaking words of love to His people whom He had chosen. "And I will betroth thee unto Me forever; yea, I will betroth thee unto Me in righteousness, and in judgment, and in lovingkindness, and in mercies." Hosea 2:19. God was saying, "I want you. I want to be engaged (betrothed) to you. I want to marry you." We often misunderstand the kind of persons that He will marry, though. We are quite selective in our own choices, and we think that perhaps He should be even more selective. But if He were, we would all be left out.

"The beginning of the word of the LORD by Hosea. And the LORD said to Hosea, Go, take unto thee a wife of whoredoms and children of whoredoms: for the land hath committed great whoredom, departing from the LORD." Hosea 1:2. Right in the first chapter of Hosea, God describes in symbolic terms the kind of people He is willing to marry. "Plead with your mother, plead: for she is not My wife, neither am I her Husband: let her therefore put away her whoredoms out of her sight, and her adulteries from between her breasts." Hosea 2:2. Here the Lord describes what we call spiritual adultery. God's beloved people went off to worship other Gods, yet He loved them still.

What will the Lord do about people like this? What will He do about them? As we continue reading the story, we see that God has a plan for wooing back His people who have gone after other gods. "Therefore, behold, I will allure her, and bring her into the wilderness, and speak comfortably unto her." Hosea

2:14. Those are nice words. It continues: "And I will betroth thee unto Me for ever; yea, I will betroth thee unto Me in righteousness, and in judgment, and in lovingkindness, and in mercies." (Verse 19.) And then finally, in verse 23: "And I will sow her unto Me in the earth; and I will have mercy upon her that had not obtained mercy; and I will say to them which were not My people, Thou art My people; and they shall say, Thou art my God."

The Lord said that He wanted to be joined with His people, even though they had done all those terrible things. He wanted them back. Then the Lord spoke to His prophet and had him tell the people: "Then said the LORD unto me, Go yet, love a woman beloved of her friend, yet an adulteress, according to the love of the LORD toward the children of Israel, who look to other gods, and love flagons of wine." Hosea 3:1. He told Hosea to go love an adulterous woman as a symbol of what His people had done to Him. The Lord doesn't give up on us because we go off to others. He doesn't turn His back on us, and He doesn't divorce us. He allows us to be separate, if we choose to be separate, but at the same time, He woos us to win us back. So He allured them. He went after them. He wanted them back. This is a very strange kind of love affair to most of us.

When you talk about guilt in this context, it's so different. He doesn't hold our guilt against us—our transgressions of going away and doing terrible things. Instead, He says He wants to win us back.

The whole of Jeremiah chapter 3 is filled with this kind of language. "And I saw, when for all the causes whereby backsliding Israel committed adultery I had put her away, and given her a bill of divorce; yet her treacherous sister Judah feared not, but went and played the harlot also." Jeremiah 3:8. The Lord put away Israel for adultery and now, He said, Judah went to do the very same thing. Now, don't stop there, or you won't like what the Bible says. God then tells what He is going to do to His wandering people: "Go and proclaim these words toward the north, and say, Return, thou backsliding Israel, saith the LORD; and I will not cause Mine anger to fall upon you: for I am merciful, saith the LORD, and I will not keep anger for ever. Only acknowledge thine iniquity, that thou hast transgressed against the LORD thy God, and hast scattered thy ways to the strangers under every green tree, and ye have not obeyed My voice, saith the LORD. Turn, O backsliding children, saith the LORD; for I am married unto you: and I will take you one of a city, and two of a family, and I will bring you to Zion" (Verses 12-14). God would not be angry with them, but would have mercy. All they had to do was to acknowledge their iniquity. "Come back to Me, after you have done all these things, for I am married to you, and I don't want to leave you."

"For thy Maker is thine Husband; the LORD of hosts is His name; and thy Redeemer the Holy One of Israel; the God of the whole earth shall He be called." Isaiah 54:5. God is our spiritual husband. He uses all the love symbolism to describe the intimate relationship He desires to have with us. He desires to have us as close to Him as a husband and a wife are in a very ideal marriage.

The marriage with Israel had taken place many years before, even centuries before, at the time the Lord led Israel out of Egypt. You can find just brief parts of the story where God literally proposed to His people at that time: "And I will take you to Me for a people, and I will be to you a God: and ye shall know that I am the LORD your God, which bringeth you out from under the burdens of the Egyptians." Exodus 6:7.

If we will study the language of marriage vows, and we go to a church to be married, the minister will ask, "Do you take this man…?" and "Do you take this woman…?" God says, "I will take you…." That is what the Lord says. The Bible has the same language as used today in weddings. God directed the high priest's choice of a wife, using the same verb *take*: "And he shall take a wife in her virginity. A widow, or a divorced woman, or profane, or an harlot, these shall he not take: but he shall take a virgin of his own people to wife." Leviticus 21:13-14. Just as a man takes a wife, so the Lord said, "I will take you unto Me." If He left out "unto Me," it would be different. "I will take you unto Me for My people. And I will be to you a God." This is marriage language of ancient history in the Bible, and in society today, as well.

The story of God's marriage to His people continues in Deuteronomy: "For thou art an holy people unto the LORD thy God: the LORD thy God hath chosen thee to be a special people unto Himself, above all people that are upon the face of the earth. The LORD did not set His love upon you, nor choose you, because ye were more in number than any people; for ye were the fewest of all people: But because the LORD loved you, and because He would keep the oath which He had sworn unto your fathers, hath the LORD brought you out with a mighty hand, and redeemed you out of the house of bondmen, from the hand of Pharaoh king of Egypt. Know therefore that the LORD thy God, He is God, the faithful God, which keepeth covenant and mercy with them that love Him and keep His commandments to a thousand generations." Deuteronomy 7:6-9.

"For thou art a holy people unto the LORD…." The word *holy* means *separated*. "You have left the others and joined yourself to Me. I have selected you to be Mine." Those who love Him will keep His commandments. He has mercy for them; He wants them.

And finally verse 13 of that chapter: "And He will love thee, and bless thee, and multiply thee: He will also bless the fruit of thy womb, and the fruit of thy land, thy corn, and thy wine, and thine oil, the increase of thy kine [cattle], and the flocks of thy sheep, in the land which He sware unto thy fathers to give thee." He would do all those nice things for them. As set forth in the Bible, this is literally a marriage situation that comes about because of God's love for us and our response to His love.

"Now when I passed by thee, and looked upon thee, behold, thy time was the time of love; and I spread My skirt over thee, and covered thy nakedness: yea, I sware unto thee, and entered into a covenant with thee, saith the Lord God, and thou becamest Mine." Ezekiel 16:8. Note the wording that "thy time was the time of love." "I took you as My possession; I included you in My circle. We had a wedding ceremony, a covenant. We entered into a holy covenant, and you became Mine. It was a time of love, and I took you in as My very own."

Dwelling on these thoughts will help us greatly. The covenant that God's people entered into was a marriage contract or marriage vows, which is what the ten commandments really are. In the previous chapter we talked about the law, and this chapter is an extension of that. The ten commandments are literally a marriage contract, in many ways. The Bible teaches this, and I wish we had more time to study it. This should not seem unusual. It probably does seem strange to you, but if God's character is love, and the law is the transcript of His character, then the law is love; and Jesus said that. So if the law is love, it's not unusual that it's a contract of marriage, is it? Not at all. The law is a contract of marriage.

Let's read from the law the first two commandments. Read them from the perspective of a marriage contract, or of marriage vows. They may sound old-fashioned, but see what they are actually saying: "I am the Lord thy God, which have brought thee out of the land of Egypt, out of the house of bondage. Thou shalt have no other gods before me…. Thou shalt not bow down thyself to them, nor serve them: for I the Lord thy God am a jealous God." Exodus 20:2-3, 5.

This is the language of love. "I want to be exclusive in your affections. I will not share your love with any other god. Love Me as your only God, the Lord thy God. I'm a very jealous God. I don't want you having eyes for another lover. I have loved you so much, I rescued you from Egypt. Be Mine and Mine alone." Love is like that, is it not? Marriage love is exclusive. I do not wish to share the one I love with anyone else; she must be all mine, and I must be only hers. The law is talking about a relationship in that kind of sense, and we must keep it exactly as it is.

In a later chapter in Exodus, this matter of being a jealous God is shown in stronger language. "For thou shalt worship no other god: for the Lord, whose name is Jealous, is a jealous God." Exodus 34:14. There is a jealousy that is legitimate in the Bible. He said, "My name is Jealous, and you are married to Me. Don't shop around. Our love is very isolated, very exclusive. You're all Mine. I am a jealous God."

This is discussed also in the New Testament: "For I am jealous over you with godly jealousy: for I have espoused you to one husband, that I may present you as a chaste virgin to Christ." 2 Corinthians 11:2. God's jealousy over His people was demonstrated when they crossed the line and forgot their God: "And I saw, when for all the causes whereby backsliding Israel committed adultery I had put her away, and given her a bill of divorce; yet her treacherous sister Judah feared not, but went and played the harlot also. And it came to pass through the lightness of her whoredom, that she defiled the land, and committed adultery with stones and with stocks." Jeremiah 3:8-9. This demonstrates that He wants us to be exclusively His, and why He requires a certain kind of obedience.

When you place the law in the context of marriage vows, the law is no longer just a written list of *thou shalt not's*. What they really mean is that if you really love God, there are certain things you never do. Is that true? If you don't believe it, try it in marriage and see what happens. If you break the marriage vows, you are advertising, "I don't love you." You are a living contradiction. If you say you love a person exclusively, you don't have eyes for any others. As soon as you look at others, you are saying to the one you vowed to love exclusively, "I don't love you anymore," or "I'm losing interest in you." At that point, love is not involved anymore.

The ten commandments are simply God asking us, "Do you love Me? If you love Me, this is the way you will live; otherwise, you don't love Me." Viewed in that light, the law is no longer just a list of restrictions. Keeping the law is simply demonstrating that you have come to love a Person, and you have confined yourself to that Person by the promises you make and the vows you take. It's a willing, voluntary thing; it's not extracted or demanded of you. This Person has wooed you until you love Him, and you say you want Him and Him only. You will not think of being joined to the gods of this world.

So the ten commandments simply exclude all other gods. I cling only unto Him, and that is exactly what it's talking about. If you are not joined unto Him, then, of course, there is no reason for keeping the commandments. That's why Jesus said, "If ye love Me, keep My commandments." John 14:15. If you don't love Jesus, don't bother trying to keep His commandments. It's impossible to keep His commandments until you are in love with Him. Far too many Christians are attempting to obey Him when they do not love Him. We ask people to obey the law before we have taught them how to love Him, or why they should love Him. We have punished people (especially children) because they don't obey, when we should have taught them how to love and why they should love Jesus. We should motivate people correctly, so that they will want to love Jesus. We get the cart before the horse many times. We are all guilty of that.

Law-breaking, or sin, or transgression—whatever you want to call it—is unfaithfulness to marriage vows. That is a different sort of transgression than we usually think about. All law-breaking in the context of love is transgression of marriage vows. I'm unfaithful to my Spouse. True guilt, then, comes from an entirely different cause than just breaking the laws in the ten commandments, and the guilt that most of us have experienced has missed that point. If I am unfaithful to my wife, that means I don't love her. Why don't I love her, when she loves me so greatly? If I am unfaithful to Jesus, it means that I don't love Him, my God, my Christ. Why don't I love Him when He has done so much for me? How can I think of forsaking Him to spend time with somebody else? No one else loves me like Jesus; no one ever cared for me like Jesus. How can I show interest in others when Christ is so all-loving to me?

You should now be familiar with how Jesus understood the law. He was asked, "Master, which is the great commandment in the law? Jesus said unto him, Thou shalt love the Lord thy God with all thy heart, and with all thy soul, and with all thy mind. This is the first and great commandment." Matthew 22:36-38.

What does that mean? There is no love like that except in marriage. We give ourselves completely unto the other, cleaving only unto that person, forsaking all others. Isn't that what it says in the marriage covenant? We embrace that person under all circumstances, and we give them our hearts completely, without reservation. That is what marriage is all about. He says that, and then He adds, "And the second is like unto it, Thou shalt love thy neighbour as thyself." (Verse 39.) So this law is a covenant of marriage.

There is another commandment that, if taken out of context, doesn't make too much sense. "Thou shalt not take the name of the Lord thy God in vain; for the Lord will not hold him guiltless that taketh His name in vain." Exodus 20:7. In marriage, the wife takes the husband's name. We should not take God's name without meaning. The margin in the King James Version of the Bible says that *vain* means *vanity* or *falsehood*. In the Common English Bible it reads, "Do not use the Lord your God's name as if it were of no significance; the Lord won't forgive anyone who uses His name that way." In other words, "do not take God's name to make a wrong use of it. Holy and sacred is His name, and you must keep it that way. You are in a marriage relationship with Him. Do not bring disgrace upon His holy name. It's an exalted privilege to have His name."

In Isaiah is an example of using God's name in vain: "And in that day seven women [in prophecy, women represent churches] shall take hold of one Man, saying, We will eat our own bread, and wear our own apparel: only let us be called by Thy name, to take away our reproach." Isaiah 4:1. The seven women (or majority of churches) want superficial legitimacy, an appearance of a real relationship with Christ. "Let us be called Christians." However, they have no true interest in a faithful spiritual relationship with Him. They want His name, but they prefer their own ways, rather than His. We must never use His name for spiritual adultery.

"Ye adulterers and adulteresses, know ye not that the friendship of the world is enmity with God? Whosoever therefore will be a friend of the world is the enemy of God." James 4:4. God says that friendship with the world is using His name in vain. Don't do that.

In the second commandment (Exodus 20:5), God talks about "visiting the iniquity of the fathers upon the children unto the third and fourth generation." For example, when the wife commits adultery and leaves her husband to marry another, any children born of the illicit relationship are not the husband's children. They are the children of the adulterer, and the children have no claim on the wife's first husband. They weren't born to Him; they were born to an adulterous wife with a different husband. Sometimes the situation is more confusing; sometimes no one knows who fathered the child or children born to the adulterous woman. All that is known is that they are not the children of the original husband. That makes the statement about visiting the iniquity of the father upon the children a vastly different thing. Children born of adultery have a terrible time, and God is not criticizing the children. He is just saying to the wife that if you play the adulteress, you bring great trouble on your children.

When God's people persist in their desire for other lovers, He must let them go, because love cannot be forced. Love cannot be commanded or exacted. He must let them go. If they want to have other lovers, if they prefer sin to marriage to the Lord, He can try to keep them, but if they insist, He will let them go. Love is always in response to love. If we wander after the gods of this world, God will still love us and try to win us back. That was the whole meaning of why Hosea the prophet was told to marry a harlot. It was an object lesson that God will take back even repentant spiritual adulterers.

Let's begin to apply all this to our Christianity and personal lives. "In this was manifested the love of God toward us, because that God sent His only begotten Son into the world, that we might live through Him. Herein is love, not that we loved God, but that He loved us, and sent His Son to be the propitiation for our sins." 1 John 4:9-10. *Propitiation* is that complete, overall work that Christ accomplished by His life, death, burial and resurrection. By His becoming our substitute and assuming our obligation—our debt to the law—He expiated (took away) our guilt by the vicarious punishment which He endured. Now verse 19: "We love Him, because He first loved us." All the motivation to remain loyal to God is the fact that He loved us first.

The love that God manifested through Christ to us and for us will accomplish amazing things. The apostle John shed a little light on what it accomplishes: "And I, if I be lifted up from the earth, will draw all men unto Me. This He said, signifying what death He should die." John 12:32-33. There is a drawing power in the love of the dying Christ. He took our sins, so that we might be His.

"Love is power. Intellectual and moral strength are involved in this principle, and cannot be separated from it. The power of wealth has a tendency to corrupt and destroy; the power of force is strong to do hurt; but the excellence and value of pure love consist in its efficiency to do good, and to do nothing else than good. Whatsoever is done out of pure love, be it ever so little or contemptible in the sight of men, is wholly fruitful; for God regards more with how much love one worketh than the amount he doeth. Love is of God. The unconverted heart cannot originate nor produce this plant of heavenly growth, which lives and flourishes only where Christ reigns." *Testimonies for the Church*, Volume 2, p. 135.

That love comes only from Him; we cannot manufacture it. He is the origin of it. Love is power; it always accomplishes good and nothing other than good. All other powers have byproducts or after-effects that are detrimental and not so good. We need that power because man is weak, powerless to perfectly obey the law. "For what the law could not do, in that it was weak through the flesh, God sending his own Son in the likeness of sinful flesh, and for sin, condemned sin in the flesh." Romans 8:3. We must *receive* power to do good, and that power is in love. God so loved that He literally gave us power as He loved mankind in the person of Jesus.

This power of love has come down as God has loved us, and it is an enabling power. As I read His word, beholding His love and responding to it and partaking of it, then I find myself loving Jesus and loving you and others. It has the power to create good in me, and nothing but good. *It always creates good*. Love does good to its neighbor.

"We love Him, because He first loved us." 1 John 4:19. Also, "Beloved, let us love one another: for love is of God; and every one that loveth is born of God, and knoweth God" (Verses 7-8). I come into an awareness of this as I behold His love.

Whenever we find poor obedience in our lives, we shouldn't get angry at ourselves (but we all do) and say, "I've got to do better. I've been doing this for years." Getting angry and chastising ourselves is not the answer. If obedience is a result of loving Him, and if loving Him is a result of beholding His love—His first loving me—then beholding His love is what we must do until our hearts are melted in response to the immeasurable depth and height and breadth of His selfless love for sinners like us. When I find myself disobedient, I must say, "Somehow I don't comprehend His great love for me." When I behold more of His love, I will love Him more. When I love Him more, I will be more obedient.

We are always trying to line ourselves up and say to ourselves that we *must obey* more. No, we must *love* more, and we cannot love more until we partake more of His love. Obedience comes because of love, and love comes because He first loved us. That's what God is telling us in all those verses in 1 John. Then this love from God coming into my heart produces love for you and others. God's love in you can produce love for your wife, even when are you ready to leave her; love for your husband, whom you might hate; love for your children when you cannot stand them; love for school; love for teachers; love for students. All kinds of things are encompassed in this love.

"Love cannot live without action, and every act increases, strengthens, and extends it. Love will gain the victory when argument and authority are powerless. Love works not for profit nor reward; yet God has ordained that great gain shall be the certain result of every labor of love. It is diffusive in its nature and quiet in its operation, yet strong and mighty in its purpose to overcome great evils." *Testimonies for the Church*, Volume 2, pp. 135-136. Love cannot live without action; it does something. And as love functions, it becomes greater; it increases. Love will gain the victory when argument and authority are powerless. That's mainly talking about evangelistic and missionary work.

Love overcomes evil and sin in our lives. The quote continues: "It is melting and transforming in its influence, and will take hold of the lives of the sinful and affect their hearts when every other means has proved unsuccessful. Wherever the power of intellect, of authority, or of force are employed, and love is not manifestly present, the affections and will of those whom we seek to reach assumes a defensive, repelling position, and their strength of resistance is increased. Jesus was the Prince of Peace. He came into the world to bring resistance and authority into subjection to Himself. Wisdom and strength He could command, but the means He employed with which to overcome evil were the wisdom and strength of love...." Love is power.

Notice that Jesus employed the wisdom and the strength of love. We do not use this kind of strength, this kind of effective agency. In fact, we do everything *but* love to transform lives and to win people and to give them victory. God so loved the world that He gave the most valuable thing that He had—His only Son. And Jesus gave His life. This is the kind of love that doesn't think of itself at all.

This love accomplishes miracles for us and miracles for those around us. Love, then, is the fulfilling of the law. Also: "For the love of Christ constraineth us." 2 Corinthians 5:14. Love restricts us, but how nicely it does that. My wife's love restricts me, but I haven't yet complained about it; and I don't imagine that I ever will gripe about it. Wives are restrictive; and husbands are restrictive of their wives. In fact, if my wife weren't restrictive, I would think that she didn't love me. Love is also possessive—not in a demanding way, but in a very nice way. It entices you.

When I started dating my wife, her father and mother thought I was a pest at their house. I would stay as long as I possibly could. I just wouldn't leave until it was late at night, and I would be down there every night if they would permit me there. We stayed together so much of the time, and I never got tired or bored. We could just sit and hold hands, even though there were folks around all the time. We weren't rich people in the days of the Great Depression. I didn't have a car, so we walked everyplace. It was nice just to be together, and I never thought of being apart; but when we were apart, I couldn't forget her. When I went to bed at night, I was thinking about her; and she was on my mind when I awoke in the morning. When I went to work, I was thinking about her. At school, I was thinking about her. I forgot about my buddies, and I forgot sports, and because I forgot school work, my grades went down.

After we had been married several years, I was in the Air Force in flying school. When she wasn't able to be with me where I was stationed, I did poorly as a pilot. I saw her only once a week, but all during the week, I just couldn't forget about her. She just occupied me. Isn't that nice? That "occupation" is what the Lord wants from us, too, and He doesn't want it any other way. He wants it by that method and by that motivation. He wants to consume us by His love for us until we love Him so much that we just can't think of anybody else.

The Bible talks about our first love. If you have never had it, you can't fully understand what I'm talking about. When I found Rose, my first love, I wasn't a Christian yet. We used to go to socials with some of her Christian friends. I usually was the only one talking about the Bible; the others were playing games. They were afraid to talk to a non-Christian about the Bible, but I wanted to talk about it. After working in the field sixteen hours a day, I would come in and read my Bible for a whole hour. And yet there were days before that when I couldn't stand the Bible. I would try and try to read it, but it was like pulling all my teeth out at one time. After I met Rose, though, I couldn't put the Bible down. There were other authors that Rose would read, and at first I hated to read them. I started to read one of those books to prove that the author was wrong, and suddenly I fell in love with the book *The Desire of Ages*. I couldn't put it down once I started to read it. When I would go home for lunch, I would sit there and read the book while eating my lunch. And I still hadn't been baptized.

What happens to people who hate the things of God, but come to the place where they cannot put those things away? What makes people compulsive talkers about inspiration? Before I got married, I always talked about my girlfriend, and I guess she talked a lot about me, too. Being with her had been fun all the time— just all the time. The Lord tells us that we have left our first love. "How can you forget Me?" He asks. "How can you leave Me? I can't forget you. Your name is right here on the palms of My hands. My love was there for you when I died on the Cross, and those scars will always be there because I never will forget you. I was so willing to sacrifice for you—how can you forget Me? I can't forget you. Don't you love me?"

Somehow, you know, we have just turned our religion upside down until it's almost a horrible thing. We begin to demand that people obey, but there is no love in that. We tell people they are going to burn if they don't obey. God doesn't constantly tell us that. He wants to understand how we can do anything else but love Him. There is no greater power than love. People can turn down our invitations to accept Christ whenever we use fear and threats and all these things, but let me tell you, when you heap the love of Christ upon them, it's very difficult for them to say no.

I already mentioned to you about a young lady who pursued a certain man for seven years. They are married now and attend church together. He is delighted that she never gave up on him. He wasn't ready to get married, but she was, and she just kept hanging around. She was very sweet about it. I could tell you many stories like this. This kind of love is discussed by the apostle Paul: "Love suffers long and is kind; love does not envy; love does not parade itself, is not puffed up." 1 Corinthians 13:4. Love doesn't behave itself improperly or unseemly. Love doesn't seek for its own good. Love is not easily provoked. Love thinks no evil of his or her spouse. Love rejoices in the truth, and believes all truths; it hopes in all good things, endures all things, and never fails. Other things will fail, but not love. Self-renouncing love endures and endures and endures. It's as eternal as the God of love. The promise is given us that God's love shall never fail.

This not only produces a righteous life; it produces everlasting life. In love, there is life. "In the light from Calvary it will be seen that the law of self-renouncing love is the law of life for earth and heaven; that the love which 'seeketh not her own' has its source in the heart of God; and that in the meek and lowly

One is manifested the character of Him who dwelleth in the light which no man can approach unto." *Desire of Ages*, p. 20.

On pages 20-21, the quote goes on to describe how everything in nature serves by love: "There is no leaf of the forest, or lowly blade of grass, but has its ministry. Every tree and shrub and leaf pours forth that element of life without which neither man nor animal could live; and man and animal, in turn, minister to the life of tree and shrub and leaf. The flowers breathe fragrance and unfold their beauty in blessing to the world. The sun sheds its light to gladden a thousand worlds. The ocean, itself the source of all our springs and fountains, receives the streams from every land, but takes to give." Even the angels of heaven are motivated by love: "The angels of glory find their joy in giving,—giving love and tireless watchcare to souls that are fallen and unholy. Heavenly beings woo the hearts of men; they bring to this dark world light from the courts above; by gentle and patient ministry they move upon the human spirit, to bring the lost into a fellowship with Christ which is even closer than they themselves can know."

And then: "But turning from all lesser representations, we behold God in Jesus. Looking unto Jesus we see that it is the glory of our God to give. 'I do nothing of Myself,' said Christ; 'the living Father hath sent Me, and I live by the Father.' 'I seek not Mine own glory,' but the glory of Him that sent Me. John 8:28; 6:57; 8:50; 7:18. In these words is set forth the great principle which is the law of life for the universe. All things Christ received from God, but He took to give. So in the heavenly courts, in His ministry for all created beings: through the beloved Son, the Father's life flows out to all; through the Son it returns, in praise and joyous service, a tide of love, to the great Source of all. And thus through Christ the circuit of beneficence is complete, representing the character of the great Giver, the law of life."

On that same page 21 is found how sin originated: "In heaven itself this law was broken. Sin originated in self-seeking. Lucifer, the covering cherub, desired to be first in heaven. He sought to gain control of heavenly beings, to draw them away from their Creator, and to win their homage to himself. Therefore he misrepresented God, attributing to Him the desire for self-exaltation."

Sin originated in self-seeking, and that is death. Love gives; love forgets self. God forgot Himself when He gave Jesus. God so loved the world that He gave His Son, His only Son. God is a giver, and by giving, God was telling us that He was giving us life. The love He gives is giving us life. Won't you now become a giver? Won't you love the way He loved?

Self-renouncing love that flows out to others is the law of life. The Dead Sea only receives, and therefore it dies. As soon as we have a cycle where loves flows into us and out of us to others, we begin to live. Give of yourself. Suddenly the channels are opened, and life begins to come back. We cease to die and begin to live. God's law is the law of life, because it is the law of love. The law of God is not a negative thing, but a positive giving of good to others. I give my supreme love to Him, and my selfless love to my neighbors. As I follow the law of love and give of myself, I live everlastingly.

God, the source of all life, has given this marvelous love until we might love Him, until we might give because of Him, and that we might live with Him in a personal relationship. "In My Father's house are many mansions; if it were not so, I would have told you. I go to prepare a place for you. And if I go and prepare a place for you, I will come again and receive you to Myself; that where I am, there you may be also." John 4:1-3. Jesus tells us not to be afraid that He has gone away, because He is coming back to take those who love Him to their beautiful mansions, so He can live with them and never part again. He wants to receive His bride, the pure church, for He said through the apostle Paul, "For I have betrothed you to one Husband." 2 Corinthians 11:2. Those who love Him will keep His commandments, and they are not grievous. We delight to do His will. It's a pleasant thing to love and to walk hand-in-hand with Jesus, with Him in my mind and heart all the day long. How pleasant is the Christian life—so wonderful, and the world will take note that we have been with Jesus.

This is my prayer for us: Loving Father in heaven, we've known a little of Thy love in the past, but we long for a full revelation of the beauty of Jesus, of His loving grace. We long to be joined unto Him in a perfect union, forsaking all others in a total commitment, unmindful of self, clinging to Him because He is the one altogether lovely. He is the lily of the valley. He is the bright and morning star. He is the desire of all ages and of all nations, the Precious One who wants to be our lover, who wants us to be joined to Him, who wants us to live with Him throughout all the ages of eternity and never part again. Lord, help to us comprehend more deeply this great love story revealed in the Bible, and to respond by loving Thee supremely and our neighbors as ourselves. We ask in Jesus' name. Amen.

CHAPTER 9: GOD'S GIFT TO THE GUILTY

An appropriate beginning to this chapter is found in the words of the Psalmist: "The upright shall dwell in Your presence." Psalm 140:13. What is accomplished by God's presence? In the previous chapter we discussed God's great love and how He loves us as His bride. The Bible has so much to say about the greatest gift that God gave to mankind. "For God so loved the world that He gave His only begotten Son, that whoever believes in Him should not perish but have everlasting life." John 3:16. That is extremely simple language, but did He really give us His Son? Did He give His Son, just to take Him back again? Do we still have Jesus, or have we lost Him? Some people think that Christ was taken away from us, and that we no longer have the presence of God with us.

Let's do a little Bible study, beginning in Luke: "And the angel said unto them, Fear not: for, behold, I bring you good tidings of great joy, which shall be to all people. For unto you is born this day in the city of David a Saviour, which is Christ the Lord." Luke 2:10-11. To whom was Jesus born? Just to the shepherds there in the field? Note that the angels said the good news of the Savior was to be "to all people."

The Old Testament teaches the same thing in a verse that we have heard and sung many times. "For unto us a child is born, unto us a Son is given: and the government shall be upon His shoulder: and His name shall be called Wonderful, Counsellor, The mighty God, The everlasting Father, The Prince of Peace." Isaiah 9:6. Unto *us* the Son was given.

I don't know how many years I was a member of the church before I read my Bible correctly about this. The Bible says that He was born to us, and He was given to us, and this is God's greatest gift to mankind. The package was a human package, with divinity all wrapped up in it. God gave His only Son.

If He is born to us, is He ours? If a child is born to you, does he or she belong to you? You say, "This is my son," or "This is my daughter," or "These are my children." Why? Because they are born to you. You have given them life and provided for them. They're yours. Now, if God has given Jesus to us, if He is born to us, then Christ is really ours.

Let's try to nail this question down properly. Is He really ours? Recall that when Stephen was being stoned after Jesus ascended to heaven, he saw the heavens opened, and there he saw Christ at the right hand of the Father. Notice the language: "But he, being full of the Holy Ghost, looked up stedfastly into heaven, and saw the glory of God, and Jesus standing on the right hand of God,

And said, Behold, I see the heavens opened, and the Son of man standing on the right hand of God." Acts 7:55-56.

Who was there at the Father's right hand? It was "the Son of man." That means that Jesus belongs to mankind. If you are the son of John, you are the son that belongs to John, right? If you are the son of the king, you are the son who belongs to the king. If Jesus is the Son of man, He is the Son who belongs to man. So after Jesus went back to heaven, Steven saw Him there—the Son of man.

"I saw in the night visions, and, behold, one like the Son of man came with the clouds of heaven, and came to the Ancient of days, and they brought Him near before Him. And there was given Him dominion, and glory, and a kingdom, that all people, nations, and languages, should serve Him: His dominion is an everlasting dominion, which shall not pass away, and His kingdom that which shall not be destroyed." Daniel 7:13-14. This bestowal indicates the end of the investigative judgment. No longer high priest, Jesus returns for us as King.

The New Testament teaches the same thing. "For there is one God, and one mediator between God and men, the man Christ Jesus." 1 Timothy 2:5. The One who mediates for us is a human being, having been tempted in all ways of life as we are now; and that man is Christ Jesus. Soon Christ is coming back in all His glory, and in the glory of the Father, with all the holy angels. Whose Son is He when He comes back to this earth?

We find the answer in some of the signs of His return. "For as the lightning cometh out of the east, and shineth even unto the west; so shall also the coming of the Son of man be." Matthew 24:27. "And then shall appear the sign of the Son of man in heaven: and then shall all the tribes of the earth mourn, and they shall see the Son of man coming in the clouds of heaven with power and great glory." Verse 30. "But as the days of Noah were, so shall also the coming of the Son of man be." Verse 37. "And knew not until the flood came, and took them all away; so shall also the coming of the Son of man be." Verse 39. "Therefore be ye also ready: for in such an hour as ye think not the Son of man cometh." Verse 44. The phrase "Son of man" is repeated often.

It's always the Son of man who is coming back, not the Son of God. Several times Matthew could have said "the Son of God," but those verses do not say that. You can find the same thing in Mark 13:26 and 34, and in Luke 21:27 and 36. In no way am I attempting to say that Jesus is not the Son of God, but God has given His Son away. The Bible says that. We can now claim Jesus as ours. God has given His Son to be ours, and always ours. And whether when He first went back to heaven, or now, or in the future, He was, is, and always will be the Son of man, the

One who belongs to you and me. We literally possess God in Jesus. Did you know that He is ours? God has given us the gift of His Son, but have we received Him?

The first chapter of the book *Desire of Ages* is probably loaded with more spiritual information than you will find almost any other place. "In taking our nature, the Saviour has bound Himself to humanity by a tie that is never to be broken. Through the eternal ages He is linked with us. 'God so loved the world, that He gave His only-begotten Son.' John 3:16. He gave Him not only to bear our sins, and to die as our sacrifice; He gave Him to the fallen race." *Desire of Ages*, p. 25. Jesus was given to the fallen race to assure us of His inimitable counsel of peace. God gave His only begotten Son to become one of the human family, forever to retain His human nature. Whose is He? He is ours. Forever and everlastingly, He is ours.

"The parable of the wedding garment opens before us a lesson of the highest consequence. By the marriage is represented the union of humanity with divinity." *Christ's Object Lessons*, p. 307. When God came down in the person of Jesus in human form, a marriage was taking place. The separation that had been there for generations, for years and years and years, was now bridged by one Person. Christ took away all the separation—all the division that sin had made. God was no longer separate and far away from man. God was in man, with man, living in a human being, and living as man. God was like that. God came down, and we had Immanuel—God with us.

"To bring humanity into Christ, to bring the fallen race into oneness with divinity, is the work of redemption." *Bible Commentary*, Volume 7, p. 927. You need to hang around that one a while; don't drop it too quickly. To bring humanity into Christ, to bring the fallen race into oneness with God—a union of marriage—is the work of redemption. You can describe it many ways, but this is the heart and soul of it. Uniting God and man is redemption. Redemption brings divine power for human beings. "Without me ye can do nothing." John 15:5. "I can do all things through Christ which strengtheneth me." Philippians 4:13. In Christ, I can do all things, but without Him I am so helpless.

The quote from the *Commentary* continues: "Christ took human nature that men might be one with Him as He is one with the Father, that God may love man as He loves His only-begotten Son, that men may be partakers of the divine nature, and be complete in Him." When God made it possible for the fullness of the Godhead to dwell in a Person possessing a human body, He was making it possible for every human being to possess the Son of God. If He could dwell in the body of Jesus, He can dwell in us. He was establishing a precedent, or a concept. He wants to be *in* us—part of us—not merely with us. We are to receive

Him. He is to abide in us, and we are to abide in Him, and a divine unity is to take place, a complete oneness like unto marriage. An ideal marriage is the only parallel we really have of this. The physical, emotional, and mental oneness that we have in marriage is yet a minimal description of Christ in you, the hope of glory. It's just a very small picture of what it can be, for we can become so intimate with Jesus that it is difficult for the human mind to grasp it.

The gift of Jesus to us is a love gift. God gave Him to us to woo us and to draw us to Him with lovingkindness. In giving Jesus, He says that He wants us to be His, to be with Him. He cannot bear to be apart from us, even though we have sinned and separated ourselves. He draws us back to Him by this love gift of His precious Son. That gift accomplishes all that man would ever possibly need. Everything is wrapped up in Jesus. In Him is the fullness of the Godhead. There is nothing we can ever imagine we would need that is not in Jesus. The only place we can find righteousness is in His righteousness. We can't find righteousness in ourselves; we can't find it in a preacher or anyone else, so we should stop looking at people. And we cannot find life in a science laboratory. We can find it only in Christ.

All goodness is in Christ; every good thing is in Him. The Father is the giver of every good gift, and the greatest of all those gifts is Jesus. Somehow we have to go back and comprehend the fullness of the package, and I say that very reverently. We need to better understand the completeness of the Gift. Jesus was the greatest thing that heaven could bestow upon mankind. The most precious One is in Christ, and God in His omniscience was planning for all our needs throughout eternity in the one gift of Jesus. We ought to stand back amazed and marvel at what God has given us. Paul calls Jesus God's "unspeakable gift." 2 Corinthians 9:15. There is no one like Him. There is nothing like it. If you love good gifts and the giver of good gifts, you ought to love the Father supremely, and Christ, who gave Himself.

"As a man Christ ascended to heaven. As a man He is the substitute and surety for humanity. As a man He liveth to make intercession for us. He is preparing a place for all who love Him. As a man He will come again with power and glory, to receive His children." *Bible Commentary*, Volume 5, p. 1126. Here we see the love story we portrayed in the last chapter—that wedding relationship.

As a man Jesus will come again with power and glory to receive His children. It should cause us joy and thanksgiving that God "hath appointed a day, in the which He will judge the world in righteousness by that Man whom He hath ordained." Acts 17:31. We may have assurance forever that the whole unfallen universe is interested in the grand work—that Jesus came to our world to accomplish the salvation of man. The logic here is difficult to follow, perhaps, but if God became man, if heaven gave Jesus, God now lives with us. We can have assurance forever that all of heaven is interested in our salvation, and that God has a plan that works. It *has* worked. It *will* work. And one of these days it will triumph gloriously. This is what God is offering us.

When the angels announced that God had become man, they gave some good news. "Glory to God in the highest, and on earth peace, good will toward men." Luke 2:14. The gift of Jesus brought good will to men. Man alienated himself from God, so God came to man with a good Gift. He can give only good gifts; He never gives bad gifts. He came with a gift to show His good will towards those who were His enemies.

If God gave His Son to die for us, do we still want to be His enemies? It is good will to men—undeserved favor by God demonstrated in His precious gift. We are in His good graces. We are no longer separated. We are no longer alienated; we are now friends. We are joined, divinity with humanity, and that tremendous gap that sin had made has been bridged totally by Jesus. There is, therefore, no separation at all in Christ. Immanuel has come.

"For if, when we were enemies, we were reconciled to God by the death of His Son, much more, being reconciled, we shall be saved by His life." Romans 5:10. Reconciliation has taken place. The most marvelous chapter on this is 2 Corinthians 5. We can read the last part of that chapter over and over again. There is so much there. When we get discouraged, let's read it, please. "And all things are of God, who hath reconciled us to Himself by Jesus Christ, and hath given to us the ministry of reconciliation; To wit, that God was in Christ, reconciling the world unto Himself, not imputing their trespasses unto them; and hath committed unto us the word of reconciliation." 2 Corinthians 5:18-19.

Do you know what the word *reconcile* means? It means "to restore to favor." Reconciliation is always the nicest between lovers, isn't it? I have often sat in my office while marriage counseling with two people who are totally alienated. I watch them fighting and quarreling—literally hating each other. We sit there and talk over their problems and try to get some understanding and some communication back and forth, and then I pray with them. It's so nice to see them stand up with tears in their eyes and kiss each other and embrace. Reconciliation is like that when love is involved. Literally, when God took human flesh, He was throwing His arms around us, kissing us, and saying that He loves us and can't let us go. God is asking, "Don't you love Me?" It was a total reconciliation, so far as God was concerned, when He gave Christ to the human race. God gave everything He had to claim us. What more could He do that He hasn't done to establish His love? What greater Gift could He give to prove that He loves you? How much more do you want? What will it take to make you believe that He loves you? What else could He do?

Do you understand God's side of this matter of reconciliation? I know you are as I am. We sit here and our brains are like stones, sometimes, in His holy, embracing presence, and we just don't respond. It just doesn't sink into our gray matter. Then we go our way and try to earn His favor, and that is total unbelief. How can we earn what we already have? It isn't by striving that we please God. It is by believing what He has already done for us. We cannot accomplish what He has already done! He already loves you. You are already friends. No alienation. Christ has come. God is with man, not separate anymore.

It is terrible unbelief, worse than the heathen, to read this and go away and believe He is far away from you. It's a terrible thing. You can't make Him love you by being better. He loved us while we were yet enemies. I'm just as guilty as you are about this; don't feel like you are the only one in the world like that. Somehow we just don't comprehend the enormity, the greatness, of God's compassion and love for us. He knew we were sinners. He knew all the things that we would do that are so evil and bad. Still He loved us. There are some humans who can love a person, maybe a spouse, who does terrible things against them. They still love them. Here we get little pictures of God. He wants to love us.

The angels heralded to those of us here on earth, "… Peace, good will toward men." Luke 2:14. That is literally what happened when God came to live with us, and reconciled us to Him. We are in His favor now. It's not that someday we will be in His favor; we stay in His favor so long as we continue to receive Him.

The shepherds who saw and heard the angels proclaiming the arrival of the Savior "made known abroad the saying which was told them concerning this child. And all they that heard it wondered at those things which were told them by the shepherds." Luke 2:17-18. This was all part of the reconciliation. "God was in Christ, reconciling the world unto Himself." 2 Corinthians 5:19.

If I accept that as a fact, then I realize that God wants to be with me, that He has accomplished everything necessary to be with me, and that I am in His good graces, no matter what I have done. I can't do anything to bring myself into His favor. I already was in His favor, even when I had no knowledge of God, or when I thought that God somehow was an enemy. "To the praise of the glory of His grace, wherein He hath made us accepted in the Beloved." Ephesians 1:6. God proved His acceptance of us through giving us His only Son. That's how desirable we are to Him. He but waits for me to receive and believe the gift that is mine in Jesus.

This is the very first step in the life of a victorious Christian. There is no Christianity until we accept the goodness of God bestowed in Jesus to man. All of Christianity is God's doing for us. We never find Him; He always finds us. It's the shepherd who finds the sheep, not the sheep that finds the shepherd. We should never say, "I found God." No, we didn't. He was hanging around all the time. We ran into Him every day, practically. It's just that we are so blind and deaf that we have a difficult time accepting the fact that He was chasing us and desiring us all the time. I could tell you many experiences about being chased by God around the world, literally.

God loves us. He has never given up on us. As sinful as we might be, as guilty as we might be, He still loves us. We can come just as we are, like the prodigal, and He will throw His arms around us, put His robe around us, and get us all cleaned up. He does the job. The prodigal son didn't do it; the father did it. Then Jesus presents us faultless before the Father's throne. *We* don't present ourselves faultless before Him. How can we say that we can do the things that only God can do?

Too often we find ourselves in some sins and bad habits that we can't overcome, and after many prayers and many sins, we say, "Well, He doesn't hear me anymore. I must have sinned away my last day of grace. I must have committed the unpardonable sin. I'm no longer acceptable to Him." That isn't the way it is at all. Those of us who feel guilt usually get things backwards. We start in the wrong place. We're trying to get rid of our sins so that God will like us and accept us, but that isn't it the way it is. That is the cart before the horse. Instead, it's "God loves me. God has accepted me. God will receive me. When will I receive Him? When will I believe in Him with all my heart because He is so good?" And as soon as we embrace Him and the fact that He loves us, for the first time we're able to do something different by His power and strength and grace. Before that time, we could do nothing. Without Him, we can do nothing. And may I translate *nothing* for you? It means *not one thing*. Somehow we have difficulty believing things like that—this idea that we can't do a thing without Him. We are always trying to do everything without Him.

When I first receive Him, it is because He has taken the first step and come to me. He first loves me. When I respond by receiving and embracing and believing Him, for the first time divinity abides in my heart, and then I'm no longer weak. I'm weak through the flesh, but strong through Christ and divine power. Humanity and divinity have become wedded, or joined. Then God can function in me.

Too often we pray as though God were way over there someplace, and we say, "Send some kind of help!" Do we send our prayers eight gazillion or more miles away to be heard, and then something is sent all the way back to us, like an enabling power? No. God has come down; He is here. God gave us Jesus. Who will become believers and embrace Him right now, and right here? Jesus promised to send us His Spirit after He left the earth, and if we have His Spirit, we have Jesus.

The devil has deceived us for so long. Please, don't misunderstand me. I'm not trying to be critical. I'm trying to help us to see what God has already accomplished. Why don't we accept and believe it? All victory over sin comes by the fact that we believe with all our hearts that Christ has embraced us just as we are. We believe that God has come into us when we receive Him and believe that we're reconciled, not alienated. He is not far away.

I must confess that, as a pastor, I still have trouble with this. And I'm embarrassed because I do, but I want to encourage you by my embarrassment, if you don't mind. You shouldn't mind. I shouldn't mind. But I do have problems practicing the presence of Christ, as some people call it. And sometimes I pray and pray, "Lord, please walk into the pulpit with me because I don't want them to listen to some fellow standing up there with an empty head like mine. I want them to hear God." And I plead, "Lord, You speak to them. You walk in there and preach." Do you think that those were good prayers? No. They were erroneous, and I prayed them hundreds of times.

You see, He has *already promised* that He is with us *always*, even to the end of the world. "I'll never forsake you. You are precious to me. I will use you. I want messengers. I called you. How can you believe I won't go with you? How can you possibly doubt?" So my problem, you see, is in not believing, isn't it? Not believing. You go off to visit someone who has a terrible problem. Are you consciously aware that God has promised to speak through you and be in attendance with you? Do you immediately claim the promise that He said He will be with us? "Lord, You said You will be with us always. I'm not qualified to minister to anyone. I'm not good enough; but You have come to me. You want to live in me. You want to use me. Help me to believe that you go with me. Help me to believe that."

The most difficult time we have is when we commit the same sin for the hundredth time, or the five-hundredth time, or the ten-thousandth time. It doesn't matter how many times we do it. He is still with us. We're still sinners whether it's the first time we sinned or the last time, right? We have always been sinners. Do you think there is a problem with God dwelling with sinners? Jesus came down to live with sinners when He took human flesh.

Jesus walked every day with Peter. How would you like Peter for your roommate? Really, I mean that. How would you like James and John, the sons of thunder, for roommates? You could hear them two floors below and ten rooms down the hall. That's what "sons of thunder" means, doesn't it? Those guys were loud, with violent tempers—just typical fishermen. They could probably turn the air blue with their "colorful" language. And they walked with Jesus for more than two years. These are the kinds of sinners Jesus lived with. They weren't exactly polished up, you know.

On the night that the officers and priests took Jesus prisoner, there was Peter—denying, cursing and swearing. Those apostles weren't exactly righteous people, were they? They weren't like that at all. Yet Christ lived with them all of those years. He grew up in that home in Nazareth, of all places. The question was asked: "Can there any good thing come out of Nazareth?" John 1:46. He lived with those unbelieving stepbrothers and stepsisters. What was it like to live in that house in Nazareth, from infancy on up?

Then during His ministry, He liked to go down to the home of Lazarus, Mary, and Martha. If I understand anything about Mary, she was the one out of which He cast seven devils; she was probably the one caught in adultery. And that is the home in which He stayed much of the time. Would you live there? Would you like your pastor to live there? Imagine spreading the word, "Did you know that Brother Lehman goes over there to that harlot's house? I wonder what He's doing over there?" Jesus went over there many nights. All those nights He spent at the house of Lazarus! Didn't that tarnish His reputation? Were people suspicious of Him?

People also said of Jesus that He was "a friend of publicans and sinners." Matthew 11:19. Some of those sinners were harlots. When you are feeling guilty, do you ever stop to think about all of this? Jesus dwelled with people—with sinners— just like us. He dwelled with the proud, the arrogant, the unbelieving. He witnessed vile sins and all sorts of corruptness, just like He sees in us. He walked with them. He loved them. He wanted to be with them. All day long, early in the morning until late at night, until He could hardly find the time to be with his Father.

Early in the morning, the disciples came out and told Jesus that people were seeking Him. Already He had been out there praying, trying to find a little time with His father. Then all day long He spent with people just like us. Do you know what it's like to work with people all day long—even sixteen hours a day? You want to run to the woods someplace and hide to get away from people. But He wanted to be with us. He so loved us that He would abide with us. Most of all, He wanted to be in us—in our thoughts day after day. God gave Him to live in us, to be with us, to be part of humanity.

Sin no longer separates because Jesus took care of those sins. "God was in Christ, reconciling the world unto Himself, not imputing their trespasses unto them; and hath committed unto us the word of reconciliation." 2 Corinthians 5:19. *The English Bible* says, "No longer holding man's misdeeds against him." *The*

Living Bible says, "No longer counting men's sins against them." He took our sins that had once separated us from God *out of the way*. "Behold the Lamb of God, which taketh away the sin of the world." John 1:29. He has taken our sins all away. Do they separate us from Him any longer? The Father laid them on Jesus, and He carried them all away. Are they gone? Then are we still separated? Or are we united with God? Just take the Bible like it is. Jesus bore our sins away. God did not hold them against us. He laid all the guilt of those sins on Christ—all the punishment—and Jesus took care of the whole thing. We are no longer separated.

The wedding has taken place when you believe this with all your heart and accept Jesus. Humanity and divinity are united in Jesus. Our sins do not separate us any longer. I am perfectly joined to Him when I reach out and say, "My Lord and my God, my Savior," and I embrace Christ. When Thomas said, "My Lord and my God," he said a huge mouthful. He could have said, "My Master, my boss." Jesus is the One who tells me everything to do. Ask Him to rule over you, to control you, to take care of your thoughts… take care of your hands… take care of your ears and your tongue… take care of your stomach and your taste… take care of your feet. "Control me completely, my Lord and my God." God has come down to live in us. Will you permit Him to be God and Master of your life?

Let's take a close look at Ephesians 2:13-19, for these verses talk about our relationship with Jesus. First, verses 13 and 14: "But now in Christ Jesus ye who sometimes were far off are made nigh by the blood of Christ. For He is our peace, Who hath made both one, and hath broken down the middle wall of partition between us." There is no separation. That wall of partition has been broken down. Then verse 15: "Having abolished in His flesh the enmity, even the law of commandments contained in ordinances; for to make in Himself of twain one new man, so making peace." He joins Himself to us. Finally, verses 16-19: "And that He might reconcile both unto God in one body by the cross, *having slain the enmity* thereby: And came and preached peace to you which were afar off, and to them that were nigh. For through Him we both have access by one Spirit unto the Father. Now therefore *ye are no more strangers and foreigners*, but fellow citizens with the saints, and of the household of God." Jesus abolished—He eliminated—the alienation and the enmity that once existed between God and man. That enmity does not exist anymore! We have been reconciled to God.

The wedding has taken place; God has joined to us. The wedding day is a happy day, isn't it? God has come down. Man is accepted in Christ. God has embraced us. Sins no longer separate us. When does this take place? It has already been accomplished. It's not in the future, nor only way in the past. To those who grasp all this, "now then we are ambassadors for Christ." 2 Corinthians 5:20. We should be preaching and witnessing about all these things. Christ sends us as emissaries out into the world.

So far as Christ is concerned, we are reconciled to God, and there is no enmity, no division, no separation. Our sins and guilt were taken from us and placed upon Christ on the cross, and we accept Him as our Savior and allow Him to take over and possess us like a loving spouse. It's an amazing thing: the One who was wronged pleads with us to accept Him into our lives, moment by moment.

What has God given to the guilty in the person of Jesus? Why should we persist in feeling guilty over anything? Why? There is only one way you can have guilt for any length of time, and that is by unbelief. There is no other way. There is no reason for us to go on with this nagging, harassing, vicious cycle of guilt, night and day, week after week. There is no reason, because God has reconciled all unto Him.

I know you struggle as I do to believe this, and there is another struggle, too. We fight against our sins to gain His favor. How foolish. It isn't that way. Until we are united in spiritual marriage with Jesus, we will never be preachers for God. We'll never be missionaries; we'll never be witnesses; and we will never be Christians. Until we know with all our hearts and souls that Christ has come into our lives, that He walks and talks with us, that He abides with us, we can never be His emissaries. What a glorious life it is to be in Christ! Even His glory beams out of our faces when we really receive Him. May He help us today to find out what God has done for us, and what God has given to this world that He loves so much. Jesus is ours. What a gift!

Here is my prayer for each of us: Loving Father in heaven, stir up our dull senses. Open our dead minds. Come into our very beings and revive us. Resurrect us from lethargy, from unthinking, from this unbelief that we have. Take away all this unbelief that seems to make us strive to please the One who is already pleased with us, who desires us so much that He gave His Son to woo and to win us and to be joined to us. Lord, come and make us Christians, believing with all our hearts that Jesus has come down to be ours. Help us to walk daily with a sense of Your holy presence. Walk with us wherever we go, and grant us that by faith, our eyes will be opened, our ears and all our other senses quickened, that we might know and be assured that God abides with us and in us, if we receive Him. In Jesus' name I pray. Amen.

CHAPTER 10: HOW THE GUILTY GET INTO HEAVEN

We have talked about the accessibility of heaven to us. Even though sin brought about a separation between God and man, we may be joined by a love and marriage relationship with Christ. Now we want to look into the consequence of being joined with Christ in this love relationship.

There is an unusual contradiction in the Bible. "So He drove out the man; and He placed at the east of the garden of Eden Cherubims, and a flaming sword which turned every way, to keep the way of the tree of life." Genesis 3:24. If I understand this correctly, God was saying, "You are not welcome. Stay out." Is that right? When Adam and Eve sinned, He drove them out of the garden and put a guard there, an angel with a flaming sword. To me, that says, "Keep out. You are not welcome here." Many people feel that is the way it still is, but somewhere between Genesis 3:24 and Revelation 22:17, the story changed. The verse in Revelation reads: "And the Spirit and the bride say, Come. And let him that heareth say, Come. And let him that is athirst come. And whosoever will, let him take the water of life freely." How did the signs get changed from "Keep out; you are not wanted," to "Whosoever will, let him come?" This is really what you find between the pages of Genesis 3 and Revelation 22. Some people don't realize that things changed between those texts—changed *drastically*. I want to give you a couple of illustrations of how unwanted people get into forbidden and restricted places, for it seems that the garden was like that.

When I was a small boy, we lived close to a railroad track. In fact, we lived close to two of them. That is the place I grew up, and it was a wonderful place to us. It wasn't bad at all. There was a railroad track on one side of our house, and a railroad track on the other side where my grandmother lived. The trains used to rumble by our backyard and, fortunately, the last train each night came through at 9:15 PM, or we would never have gotten any sleep. The first train in the morning was about 7:00 AM. Hopefully, we had had enough sleep during the night, because as the trains went by, the whole house would shake. But after a while, we hardly noticed.

Those big, black steam engines were something very special to us, and we kids would run out right beside the track, just as close as we possibly could, and gape there with our mouths wide open, you know, looking at the engineer and the fireman as each train would go by. We would watch those brakemen jump off, and the switchmen and others do their thing. The greatest thing in the world imaginable to us was to ride in one of those big steam engines. When I got a little older, I used to hitch a ride on some of those locomotives. Some bad things happened occasionally. Not too far from our house was a roundhouse. You know what a roundhouse is, don't you? That's the garage for those big steam engines. In the roundhouse they used to work on the steam engines and do repairs, oil and grease them, and so on. I used to sneak up there when I was a boy and go snooping around, even though there were big, red signs all around there that read "Keep out!" Everybody I played with wanted to go inside a roundhouse, but we didn't dare do that. We would probably get pitched out on our ears. But even though we were afraid of something happening, we always would hang around the roundhouses with great anticipation and envy. I loved the idea of getting inside to see what the workmen were doing and what those big engines looked like on the inside.

One day my grandfather, who worked on the railroad, came by and took me downtown shopping with him. He didn't have a car, so we walked. That was a common thing in those days. On the way we took a shortcut, which we usually did, through the freight yards. And there was a little red shack where he went over to talk to a man. He told me to wait while he visited this fellow. Just about a hundred feet out in front of that red building was the switch engine, that great big thing, you know, and no one was in it. There it was, just throbbing away, pulsating a little bit and hissing as the steam came out. When Granddad came out, he saw me just staring at that thing with envy. I was literally drooling. He asked, "How would you like to go for a ride?" I wasn't sure I knew what he meant. He took me by the seat of the pants because I was too short to climb the ladder (the steps were so far apart), and he boosted me up to the top of the steps and into the cab of that great big steam locomotive. Then he climbed up behind me, and he sat me in the engineer's seat. At least I thought it was the engineer's seat, but today I'm not so sure.

There was a great big lever in there, taller than I was. He pushed it forward, and said to me, "Push that big brass handle there." I tried, but it wouldn't budge, so he put his big hand over mine on the handle and pushed a little bit. The steam started coming out all around. It came up through the windows until the whole cab was full of steam. Pretty soon the engine started to rumble, and that huge steam locomotive began to move! And I was driving it! I was just bug-eyed; I could hardly believe it. It was just as good as going to heaven, and so far as I was concerned, probably better. Granddad watched me carefully; he was right there by my side. After a little while, he reached up and pulled that lever back, and the engine stopped. He eased that brass handle back, then he pulled a different lever and told me to push the same brass handle forward. That time I pushed harder, and the steam started coming out again, and the locomotive went in reverse. We stopped it right back where it was supposed to be.

Then Granddad said, "Let's go downtown." I didn't want to go downtown, so he took me by the hand and led me down the ladder. I felt about ten feet tall. I walked to town as an engineer, all of eight years of age.

We walked back home down through the same place by the roundhouse. Suddenly, he decided he had to go see a friend in there. He came and got me and said, "Come along." We walked right by those *Keep Out* signs and into the roundhouse. Granddad walked up to a bench and started talking to a fellow, and I just started running up and down among the train engines. There were many of them parked in there—the really big engines. I just had a glorious time, and nobody said a word to me.

I was where I didn't belong, and everything was just fine. No one kicked me out, and I wasn't even afraid to be there. If anyone had asked me why I was there, I would have said, "That's my granddad over there." That's all it would take—just to have my granddad there.

Later on, when I was married and had been in the Air Force, we went on our first trip to California. In my heart I was still a boy when it came to airplanes. We went out to Mountain View, California. As we drove down the freeway, we went past a NASA facility, where I saw all the latest jets parked. I still could drool, like I did about those big steam engines, when it came to airplanes. But I couldn't get into that place. We were eating our evening meal that night when, somehow, it happened to come out of me that I wanted to go out to NASA to try to get a close look at those jets. As it happened to be, my wife had an uncle who worked there. He mostly just drove a truck around the place. He hardly knew anybody at the facility; he wasn't important. A couple of days later, he asked me if I would like to go out to NASA and just ride around. Of course! So he drove us around, then parked by a dock. He said, "I know a fellow in there," and he introduced me to him. The man was an aircraft engineer. He asked me if I was interested in jets, and I told him that I had been an Air Force pilot in the war. "Come on along," he said. And I literally walked all around inside the largest wind tunnel in the world at that time.

They could not operate that wind tunnel just anytime they wanted to. It operated by electricity and drew thirty-five million watts of power to run four electric motors. I walked all over the roof, inside the chamber, in the control room, just every place. Then I walked outside to the ramp, where he started telling me about all the latest jets and their test gear, and how fast they would go, and so on. He told me everything about every one of the planes except for one that was still classified. And he even gave me some idea about that one. So I went every place, past all the signs forbidding entrance and through all the restricted places.

No one asked me a question or even looked at me. I went walking away just as happy as could be.

How did I get into all of those forbidden places? I've actually been telling you a tremendous amount of gospel, whether you understand it or not. I was permitted in those places because I was with the right individual. I walked right in. No questions asked because of the person I was with. With Grandfather, it was easy. With that engineer at NASA, it was just as easy. I was perfectly welcome because they were welcome. You might think that is an oversimplification, but it really is not. Our access into heaven is guaranteed when we walk in with Jesus. When we abide in Him, and He abides in us, we get into heaven because of Jesus, and there is no other way into there. No other way.

You are always welcome in Christ, and you are always locked out apart from Christ. I don't care how good you get to be, you can never enter heaven except through Christ. If any man be in Christ, he is welcome in heaven. If we are not in Christ, we are not welcome. Friends, it's time we began to realize that everything that heaven has is available to us in the person of Jesus. When God gave His Son, He was giving us all heaven. As we receive Him, God says, "If you keep close to Him, if you abide in Him and He in you, you can walk right into heaven, and all of heaven will say, 'Welcome!'" Isn't that right?

All this is taught in the Bible. "But now in Christ Jesus ye who sometimes were far off are made nigh by the blood of Christ. For He is our peace, who hath made both one, and hath broken down the middle wall of partition between us." Ephesians 2:13-14. Those verses tell how all this separation has been taken away, and how all the forbidden places are made accessible in Christ. How has heaven been made accessible to us? It tells us right there in verse 13: "But now in Christ Jesus ye who sometimes were far off are made nigh by the blood of Christ."

Jesus is our peace, having broken down the separation. He abolished the enmity, thus making peace. "And that He might reconcile both unto God in one body by the cross, having slain the enmity thereby." (Verse 16.) "For through Him we both have access by one Spirit unto the Father." (Verse 18.) Through Jesus, whether Jew or Gentile, we have access through Him. Our sins are no longer held against us; we are no longer locked out. He has taken away all those sins.

"In Whom we have boldness and access with confidence by the faith of Him." Ephesians 3:12. This enlarges it even more and gives us more confidence. In Christ, we have boldness and access to the Father with confidence. We don't have to come with a feeling of fear and worry and concern, if we gain access through Christ. In Christ, we come with boldness and have access with confidence. Isn't Paul a marvelous writer? He wants to assure us, but he knows we will doubt, so he drives the point home with this strong language so that every one of us will know it's available to us. We don't have to worry about it.

These things are not very well accepted by many Christians these days, and I have to spend a lot of time establishing this in your mind. Paul also tells us that we may have, "… therefore, brethren, boldness to enter into the holiest by the blood of Jesus, by a new and living way, which He hath consecrated for us, through the veil, that is to say, His flesh." Hebrews 10:19-20. In other words, come right into the throne room of God by a new, living way.

The Bible teaches that we can come with boldness, yet most of us say, "You know, if I could get only my tippy toes inside the gate…." No one will enter that way. There will be nobody who barely gets into heaven. All will have an abundant entrance into heaven, isn't that right? We can't get in without Christ, and all in Christ will be welcomed into heaven. All the angels will be singing, welcoming us there.

Now, some people ask, "But how can that be when I am such a sinner?" They think that sinners aren't welcome there. At one time, sinners were *not* welcome there, but sinners are now welcome there. Things have changed from Genesis 3:24 to Revelation 22:17. Christ has taken away all our sins. As our High Priest, He has gone into the most holy place. He took His blood; He took His righteousness. In the blood and righteous of Christ, we have access with confidence and great boldness. He has taken away all our sins because the Father laid upon Him the iniquity of us all. We don't have to worry about that. As the song goes, "I lay my sins on Jesus, the precious Lamb of God." And the Father says, "Come." We have all been accepted in the Beloved, and we're all welcome.

In the hymn book there is that marvelous song "A Mighty Fortress is Our God." The second stanza reads like this: "Did we in our own strength confide, Our striving would be losing, Were not the right man on our side, The man of God's own choosing. Dost ask who that may be? Christ Jesus, it is He. Lord Sabbaoth, His name, From age to age the same, And He must win the battle." You see, Christ the man, who took all my sins and died for them, was called forth from the tomb by the Father Who said, "Your sacrifice is sufficient." Then the Father received Jesus into the highest heaven as a human being who had been contaminated with all our sins. If the Father will take that Person, a man who received all our sins—if He will accept Jesus the man into the highest heaven—will He not receive us from whom He has taken the sins? Does that make sense to you? He takes the one contaminated with our sins. Shall He not also take those who have been cleansed from their sins?

When we receive Christ, the Father receives all from whom the sins have been taken away by the Lord Jesus. So with the right Man, we may come to the

Father. Recall the experience of Christ at the Jordan River when He was baptized. After He came up out of the water, He prayed on the banks of the Jordan; and as He prayed, we are told that the heavens opened, and the Father was heard saying, "This is My beloved Son, in Whom I am well pleased." Matthew 3:17.

There is a comment on this in the commentary, and you will be amazed at what it tells you there. "The prayer of Christ in behalf of lost humanity cleaved its way through every shadow that Satan had cast between man and God, and left a clear channel of communication to the very throne of glory. The gates were left ajar, and heavens were opened, and the Spirit of God, in the form of a dove, encircled the head of Christ, and the voice of God was heard saying, 'This is My beloved Son, in Whom I am well pleased.'" *Bible Commentary*, p. 1078.

Then we are told the results of that prayer: "The voice of God was heard in answer to the petition of Christ, and this tells the sinner that his prayer will find a lodgment at the throne of the Father. The Holy Spirit will be given to those who seek for its power and grace, and will help our infirmities when we would have audience with God. Heaven is open to our petitions, and we are invited to come 'boldly unto the throne of grace, that we may obtain mercy, and find grace to help in time of need.' We are to come in faith, believing that we shall obtain the very things we ask of Him." Ibid.

So heaven is wide open. Christ opened it up when He prayed on the banks of the Jordan. On the same page, the commentary goes on to tell about Satan's reaction to this: "He understood that this communication from the throne of God signified that heaven was now more directly accessible to man than it had been, and the most intense hatred was aroused in his breast. When Satan led man to sin, he hoped that God's abhorrence of sin would forever separate Him from man, and break the connecting link between heaven and earth. When from the opening heavens he heard the voice of God addressing His Son, it was to him as the sound of a death knell. It told him that now God was about to unite man more closely to Himself, and give moral power to overcome temptation, and to escape from the entanglements of satanic devices."

One more on page 1079: "In our behalf the Saviour laid hold of the power of Omnipotence, and as we pray to God, we may know that Christ's prayer has ascended before, and that God has heard and answered it. With all our sins and weaknesses we are not cast aside as worthless. 'He hath made us accepted in the beloved.' The glory that rested upon Christ is a pledge of the love of God for us. It tells of the power of prayer,—how the human voice may reach the ear of God, and our petitions find acceptance in the courts of heaven. The light that fell from the open portals upon the head of our Saviour, will fall upon us as we pray for help to resist temptation. The voice that spoke to Jesus says to every believing soul, 'This is my beloved child, in whom I am well pleased.' Through the gates ajar there streamed bright beams of glory from the throne of Jehovah, and this light shines even upon us. The assurance given to Christ is assurance to every repenting, believing, obedient child of God that he is accepted in the Beloved."

There is much more there. Please go read more of the quotation about how God opened heaven to us when Jesus became a human being in order to live with us here. The secret of all of this is having the right Man on our side. When God identified Himself with humanity in the person of Jesus, He literally bridged all the separation. He was saying, "Come. All are welcome. The doors are open. Your prayers are heard. You have access in Christ. Come boldly to the throne, and find the grace and the help that you need."

Now, if you are still having trouble believing some of this, let's look at some of the illustrations Christ gave. "Then said Jesus unto them again, Verily, verily, I say unto you, I am the door of the sheep. All that ever came before Me are thieves and robbers: but the sheep did not hear them. I am the door: by Me if any man enter in, he shall be saved, and shall go in and out, and find pasture." John 10:7-9.

What does that mean? "I'm the One who gives you access. Come in through Me, and you are accepted. The door is always open when you come in through Me." "Jesus saith unto him, I am the way, the truth, and the life: no man cometh unto the Father, but by Me." John 14:6. Here Jesus used a little different terminology. He could have said that another way: "Every man can come if he comes through Me." Isn't that correct? He is not trying to exclude people; He is trying to exclude the *other ways*. "*I* am the way to the Father. Every man may enter heaven by coming through Me."

There is another illustration that Christ gave: "… And I will give unto thee the keys of the kingdom of heaven." Matthew 16:19. What does that tell us? Suppose I should give you the keys to my house and I say, "Here are my keys." What does that mean to you? "Come in and out as you please. Make it your own home. Do whatever you want there." Suppose I give you the keys to my car. What does that mean? "Drive it as you please." Jesus said that He has given us the keys of the kingdom of heaven. It means that we have access there; we have an entrance there. Why would anyone stay outside? Come on in.

We can offer this entrance to other people. We are to announce to everyone, "Come. Jesus has opened heaven for you. He has given you the keys. Use the keys and come right in. What are you waiting for?" And yet we go on and on believing that someday we might be good enough to get in. When you say, "Oh, if I can just barely get inside," you are really saying, "I don't believe a word you're saying." Christ didn't make it barely possible for us to get in, or just for the very best to enter, or just for the strongest-willed people, did He? That isn't what He has done. He knew that we were all sinners. He knew that He would have to do something to give all sinners access, to make it possible for them to enter that place. So He came down and took all the sin of all sinners upon Himself, and the Father said that what Jesus did was sufficient. He died for all people. So when the Father accepted the Man Jesus, He was saying that all are accepted in Christ. This is a fact, friends.

God cannot lie. It's time we began to be Christians by believing, first of all, God's word, and accept it as absolute, concrete fact on which we can hang our whole souls. We can actually claim for ourselves that abundant entrance into heaven through Christ. The whole problem is in accepting Christ. What did God give us when He gave us Jesus? He gave us the keys. He gave us the door. He gave us the way. He gave us access. He gave us heaven. He gave us all of heaven when He gave us Jesus.

When you have time, I wish you would go back and read about Noah. Try to figure out how Noah survived a catastrophic flood. The Bible says that Noah was righteous, but after the flood, I find him doing some pretty terrible things, don't you? And I ask myself, "Why did God save *him*? He doesn't seem too righteous to me." If Noah can make it, I can make it, and not by my own works. How did Noah and his family obtain salvation from the flood? How did this come about? It's so simple that I missed it for years and years. I still miss it because I don't think about it enough. The righteousness that Noah did was building an ark. You wouldn't think that building an ark was very righteous, but God told him that the earth would be destroyed by a flood, and Noah believed that. And God told Noah that in order to be saved, he had to build the ark. So day-by-day for those many years, Noah built the ark, and by building the ark, he was really preaching. Building that ark was a tremendous sermon, and he kept preaching it all the time he built it. I don't mean that he didn't preach sermons, but his greatest sermon was the building of the ark. "The flood is coming. God has said so. It's true, and I believe it." Noah kept building the ark, and the people kept laughing and laughing because it had never rained. Finally Noah, his family, and the animals entered into the ark; an angel shut the door. For seven days there was no flood, but then the waters came.

Why were Noah and his family saved? Because they were in the ark. It's that simple. The word *ark* doesn't mean only a boat, because there is the ark of the covenant in the temple, and that is not a boat. What does the word *ark* mean, then? It means "a place of refuge; a place of safety"—a place where something or someone can be hidden, sheltered and protected. The Israelites kept the ten commandment law inside the ark, which was a secure place for such a precious item. In Noah's day, all of man and beast that went inside the floating ark were preserved alive.

God made a provision for the flood, but He made *only one* provision, not many. He told Noah to build an ark wherein he and his family would be safe. The ark was built with space for many, many souls, but of those living just before the flood, only those eight persons believed the 120-year "seek safety" message of the ark-building. God was sending a literal flood of judgment, but He was also providing a place of safety from it, a place of protection for those who would believe Him. As the biblical account reveals, all but eight souls rejected His warning and offer of refuge. They ridiculed the very idea of a flood.

The ark, as I understand by what the apostle Peter wrote, is a symbol of the salvation found in Christ. If I went into heaven by myself, I would be destroyed. If I marched up to the New Jerusalem as the wicked do at the end of the millennium, I'd be destroyed right away. I don't have access in myself, but in Jesus I can hide, and I'm "safe evermore," as the song says. I can get inside through Jesus. I can flee to Him as a refuge for my soul, and there as I hide in Jesus, I am safe.

At the end of the millennium, when fire comes down from heaven, you'll find out the reason why the righteous are not destroyed. It is because they are safe in Christ in the city. They have followed the Lamb wherever He goes. But those on the outside are not hiding in Jesus, and they are vulnerable.

This is the story that the Bible teaches about salvation. A simple review is this: God gave His Son. That Son was to wed divinity to humanity—the coming together of God and man. The gap caused by sin was bridged so that I could be in Christ, and He in me. Jesus made that possible. Before that can happen, though, God must take all my sins away; so He laid them all on Christ, the Lamb of God, and Jesus bore them away to the cross.

In this unity, I am joined to Christ. If I could find access to that railroad roundhouse through my grandfather, and if I could find access to NASA through an engineer, where can I go with my Brother, the Son of God? But Christ must make me His brother. Not until He united divinity and humanity could I have access; but now, when I am one with Jesus, a relative, a son of God, a child of God, all those restricted places are accessible—every one of them. And in Christ I can go marching right in, and the angels of heaven will say, "Lift up the everlasting gates," just as they did for Jesus Himself. "Welcome the King and His saints!" The angels will sing His praises throughout the ages of eternity.

When we get to heaven, and we meet people we knew on earth, we could ask them, "How did you get here?" I assure you that there will be no one in heaven who will say, "I worked so hard. It was a terrible ordeal, but I made myself righteous enough and here I am." There will be no one like that in heaven. Never. They will all be dead. Who says so? "Lord, Lord, have we not prophesied in Thy name? and in Thy name have cast out devils? and in Thy name done many wonderful works?" Matthew 7:22. But Jesus has to tell them, "I never knew you: depart from Me, ye that work iniquity." (Verse 23.) Does that sound like iniquity? They had cast out devils and healed the sick. That sounds like works of righteousness to most of us; but they weren't, really, because they were trying to earn their way to heaven. Their righteousness was all filled with selfishness and the power of Satan, for the devil can bless righteous works so long as they are filled with ego. He loves to do that, and he even will give you a few souls on your ego trip, until you can say you've won many to God. But no, you didn't. You never won one person, nor have I. Only Christ wins souls. The Lord can use a good recording device to win souls better than he can use a self-righteous Pharisee, can't He? Really! But He'd rather have a voice from the living—our voices—testifying of His wonderful saving grace.

Really, friends, we don't stop to understand that we can do nothing without Him. We are just helpless. But with Christ, we can do all things. God has adopted the whole human family and married Himself to all humanity and made us sons and daughters of God in Jesus. We are His relatives, and He will welcome us into His home. He can hardly wait to come back and take us to those mansions He is preparing for us. Jesus wants to live with us. He has made heaven accessible to all who will join with Him. But first, we must become *believers*.

For years we have been afflicted with a spiritual disease, thinking that we are true believers because we believe the Sabbath and the truth about the state of the dead. Those indeed are precious truths, and so are standards and the prophecies. But who believes that heaven is open to us? Who believes that Jesus has come down to give us an abundant entrance into the kingdom? Who believes that Jesus took away our sins—that He is joined with us in a perfect unity so that He fully controls our lives? Who believes that? We can see all the Sabbath arguments as perfectly as possible. We can do all kinds of missionary work, and still be unbelievers in the accessibility created by Christ.

Jesus hasn't come because we think we are not ready—even though He made heaven ready and open when the Father accepted Him. It's all been open for close to two thousand years. Christ was a man who took all my sins to the cross. He had an abundant entrance into heaven and was welcomed by the angels. My sins are gone in Christ. May I not have that entrance? The apostle Paul says, "Let us therefore come boldly unto the throne of grace, that we may obtain mercy, and find grace to help in time of need." Hebrews 4:6.

Do you understand what God has given to us? Jesus came down as a baby in that manger in Bethlehem, but what an enormous package He was. What a precious gift! Just how full was heaven's gift? How complete is the reconciliation? How wonderful is the adoption that every human being has in Jesus, if they will believe it and receive it. And how tremendous will be our entrance into heaven. God is still waiting for the day when the fullness of the consequences of His gift in Jesus are finally materialized—when millions of saints stand on the sea of glass and praise God for giving us Jesus, and for making heaven wide open through Christ. Then with those new voices we will have, we will join the angelic voices and praise Him from whom all blessing flow. The heavens will ring for years with the praises of the redeemed because Jesus has literally opened heaven, and we've all walked in. And the most blessed thing of all is that our precious Jesus, who was at one time a tiny bundle of humanity and divinity, is ours forever.

Don't ever think again, "If I can just somehow sneak in...." May our hearts just thrill as we encompass all the fullness of the gift of Jesus, and let us believe with all our hearts that heaven is ours in the Lord Jesus. Let us thank Him every day, never because of our own goodness, but always because of that tremendous Gift. Think, "Heaven is mine. Thank you, Lord."

My prayer for us all is this: Loving Father, we're just so human, and we're so weak. We spend so much time looking at ourselves, and we're so concerned that we're not good enough. So we keep striving to be good enough, always forgetting that Jesus accomplished everything that we want. Please forgive us. Help us to understand better than we do how much God so loved the world. He couldn't stand to be separated from us. We are the apple of His eye—His own creation. That ultimate plan to make mankind in His own image was a precious plan. He'll not be satisfied until He sees us rejoicing in the fullness of God. To give His precious Son to buy us back from sin and slavery was an enormous sacrifice, an inestimable gift. Jesus is the Pearl of great price. Oh, help us to realize that if God would give so much, surely He wants us, and we are desirable to Him. We are precious in His sight. Help to us look and see what God has done for us and believe it with all our hearts. We praise Jesus and thank Him forevermore for His kindness and grace and mercy. Lord, open our eyes and our ears and our minds; take away all the cobwebs and all the self. Help us to behold the goodness and the fullness of God, and the marvelous gift of Jesus. Grant that someday, very soon, we will have that welcome into heaven. We ask in the wonderful name of Jesus. Amen.

Chapter 11: When You Offend Your Lover, What Do You Say?

Perhaps the biggest problem facing most of us is this: How can I ever dislike what I enjoy? That is what this chapter is all about—how to dislike what we enjoy. Whether we like it or not, sinners enjoy sin, and most will tell you that they do. Some say they love their sins.

I'm talking about sinners in general. They say, "Let's go over to the bar and enjoy a drink." They say, "Let's enjoy a movie tonight." Just watch people as they take a puff on their cigarettes; see their fascination as they watch the smoke slowly ascend. There seems to be something charming about it; it seems like they're enjoying it. People who drink will just sit and sip and sip, as though there is something very special about it. If you have never tried it, by the way, it really is firewater. I'm not suggesting that you try it, but if you do, you will find that out in a hurry. I know some of these things because I have not always been a Christian.

Some people even enjoy losing their tempers. When they do so, they become "king of the roost," so to speak, and everybody scatters. When they are dominating, they just come alive. They are thrilled and energized. They revel in their domination. After a while, they might have some unwanted repercussions, but at the time it's certainly enjoyable.

The Scriptures tell us that we need to hate sin. "Hate the evil, and love the good." Amos 5:15. "Abhor that which is evil; cleave to that which is good." Romans 12:9. Sometimes we think that if we could just communicate to people how bad sin really is, they would hate it. So we have spent hours and hours and years and years telling people in various ways how abominable sin is. And people say, "Oh, yeah? I don't believe it." Isn't that the way it is? We tell people how bad sin is, and they ask if there is something wrong with us. They tell us to "try it; you'll like it." We answer, "Just wait until you get down to the end of the road. Then it's not so enjoyable." And they respond, "It's a long way off." Somehow, we think that by education, by proof, by more knowledge, we will make people see that sin is abhorrent, and they will cease to like it, and stop sinning.

A doctor can prove to an alcoholic that he is killing himself with alcohol, but he still drinks. The same thing happens with tobacco and all sorts of other bad things. Proof just does not accomplish the job because we, as sinners, like sin. We go on saying we enjoy it, even if it's going to kill us. You know, we'll never stop sinning that way. When you try to take sin from those who enjoy it, it's like taking candy from a baby. It's like trying to rescue a drowning man. He'll drag you under with him. Sins are so much a part of the people we are trying to save from their sins, it's like attempting surgery without anesthetics, like trying to cut something out of them. It's very painful. They don't want to let go of what they enjoy so much. It's like cutting off an arm or a leg or a tongue. "I like my sins. I need to do those sins. Don't take them from me." People literally just scream out in agony—literally. So sin is a part of ourselves, and we can't help people just by telling them that sin is bad. Sin won't go away that way.

This is a very big problem. How are we sorry for that which we enjoy? We really must face this problem squarely, or we will miss a huge part of Christianity and will not bless or help people at all. We must go back and find out what sin is, which hopefully you have seen, to some extent, so far in this book. I don't want to rub your nose in the dirt too much. Sin is transgression of the law, and the law is love. Obedience is supreme love for God, and loving our neighbors as ourselves. In Christianity, this is illustrated by the laws of a marriage contract in which we are united to Christ, where we are one with Him in a precious love relationship.

We all enjoy love very much, but we actually are confronted with two loves, or two enjoyments: the enjoyment we have with Christ and our fellow men, and the enjoyment we have with sin. Obviously, these two loves conflict. Which one gives you the greatest pleasure? Which one blesses you the most? Which one offers you the most? Which one loves you the most? Will you sit down and look at the two loves that we have? In marriage, when Christ came to join divinity and humanity in that marriage contract of the law, we give ourselves to our Mate, and that is what we say in our vows. Especially does the wife give herself to her husband, and remember that the Husband of the church is Christ.

As church members, we give ourselves to Christ. We give Him our all. Jesus said to "love the Lord thy God with all thy heart, and with all thy soul, and with all thy mind." Matthew 22:37. We love Him by giving Him ourselves. He has won us by His tremendous love. We gladly give ourselves to Him.

In addition to our heart and soul and mind, which He talks about there, we give Him something else: "I beseech you therefore, brethren, by the mercies of God, that ye present your bodies a living sacrifice, holy, acceptable unto God, which is your reasonable service." Romans 12:1. Give Christ your bodies. We use this verse for health reform, but use it now for our marriage to Christ. "What? know ye not that your body is the temple of the Holy Ghost which is in you, which ye have of God, and ye are not your own? For ye are bought with a price: therefore glorify God in your body, and in your spirit, which are God's." 1 Corinthians 6:19-20.

Literally, then, as we come to Him, He is asking for all of us. He is not demanding; He is not exacting. He tells us that He gives Himself, and that includes all the fullness of the Godhead. He gave His body to save us. He gave us everything that He had. Can't we give ourselves to Him—heart, mind, soul, and body? When we have entered into this relationship, as we profess to have done in baptism and conversion, then sin becomes unfaithfulness to our Mate, our Spouse, our divine love partner. All sin is an offense against Him. All sin. All of our affections of the heart, the mind, the soul, and the body have been given to Him. All our energies, all our interests. How can we turn our affections and energies away from Him and give them to someone else or something else?

If we offer to somebody else that which we dedicated to Him, that is exactly like adultery. Our Husband claims these things, and He is jealous, and He wants us. He wants all of us. Marriage is exclusive. Why should we give ourselves unto those to whom we are not married? Why should we be joined to them when the Lord loves us so much? It doesn't matter what type of sin it is. All sin is giving affections or energy or something to someone else. When we do so, we are saying, "Well, I'm not sure I love you anymore. I'm not sure you love me, and I think I might like this something else better." And after a while, you become a polygamist, or a spiritual swinger. There are many like that nowadays, just going everywhere with their affections. They have not really landed in one place and stayed with the Lord.

This is a different concept of sin than we are used to—this alienation of affections, or giving of our love to someone else. "Nevertheless I have somewhat against thee, because thou hast left thy first love." Revelation 2:4. And, may I say, left thy first lover, also. The problem we have is that we have left Him. We didn't lose Him. There wasn't some mistake where He went to sleep and couldn't find us again. We left Him. We have taken our affections and placed them on someone else or something else. We left Him, our first lover and our first love.

All sin is like that. We wonder what is wrong with sin. We ask, "Tell me what is wrong with doing this?" And then we have a big argument about what is so bad and what is so good about it. That's not where it is; it never was that. There is not too much wrong with sin until we are so close to Jesus that He is most precious to us. Sin won't seem so bad until we love Him supremely with all our affections of body, mind, soul, and heart. Then suddenly there is something wrong in leaving that love, in bringing about that separation and that alienation.

Joseph, one of the sons of Jacob, had the right concept of this when he was tempted by Potiphar's wife. "There is none greater in this house than I; neither hath he kept back anything from me but thee, because thou art his wife: how then can I do this great wickedness, and sin against God?" Genesis 39:9. Potiphar, Joseph's master, had given him all this authority, second only to Potiphar in his house.

The first time I perceived what it was saying, I noticed that he didn't say, "I'm offended by you, and I'd be doing some great evil and adultery." He recognized that he would be harming a man who had been kind to him. But when it came down to giving into that sin or not, he asked how he could do such a great wickedness and sin against God. In what way would he have sinned against God? If you read very carefully, keeping in mind this concept of marriage, you'll discover an interesting thought. "And the LORD was with Joseph, and he was a prosperous man; and he was in the house of his master the Egyptian. And his master saw that the LORD was with him, and that the LORD made all that he did to prosper in his hand." Verses 2-3.

Joseph's earthly father was not there. His brothers had failed him. He was way down there in Egypt by himself, but he really wasn't by himself. The Lord was with Joseph. God walked with Joseph; they were tied together in that far-off land. They worked together, and Joseph dwelled with God while living in Egypt, the symbol of the world and of sin. He walked with God. He knew God, and God knew him. The Lord was precious to him, and he knew that he was precious to the Lord. Then there came someone to take his affections from the Lord, and he said he could not do such a terrible thing against His God. He could not give His affections to that woman.

Adulterers always defend their actions by saying they love each other, but the love found in adultery is an extremely selfish kind of love. Let them ask themselves, "How much do you love the husband of the woman (or the wife of the husband) with whom you committed adultery? How much do you love the children of that marriage? How much do you love them?" Love is giving. Love is self-forgetful. Love is self-denying and self-renouncing. Adultery is not love. It is lust, and we do not think about others. But Joseph thought about his God. He could not give to that woman his heart and body when he had given them to the Lord. It just wasn't possible. That is a right concept of sin. Joseph would hurt neither his Lord nor his master. Maybe the woman thought she was hurt, but she wasn't hurt. He was doing her a favor, a real blessing.

Now, let's suppose that you are tempted, and you commit a sin against your Lord and Master Jesus. Go back and put in the basic truth of Joseph's story. Don't just stop with the bare bones of the literal interpretation. First, we are tempted to sin against Christ, to whom we are perfectly joined in a marvelous love affair. While you indulge in the sin, you might not feel guilty. You may have a few pangs of conscience, but a little while later you indulge it again. Do you feel guilty about this? If the situation were a wife who commits adultery, and the husband finds out, then the wife eventually has to face her husband. And fellows, think about all this in terms of your being part of the church, which is the bride of Christ. The wife faces her husband, who knows all about the sin, and he is weeping. He doesn't say anything. He doesn't condemn. He doesn't criticize. He doesn't look down the end of his nose at her. He doesn't point the finger. He is weeping. His love has been taken away from him. He had told his wife that he loved her with an everlasting love, that he had drawn her with lovingkindness. In his heart, he asks, "How can I let you go? But you want to go, and I can never force you to stay." There is no love in force. Love does not demand or exact. "If my love doesn't hold you, I have lost you. So I can't criticize, or I'll drive you away. All I can do is love you. Why don't you love me?"

As the wife stands there before the husband who does not condemn—as she stands there before one who is so filled with love for her that he is hurt by the alienation of her affections—as she stands there and realizes that she has been giving her affections to someone else who doesn't really love her like this husband—how does she feel? She feels genuine guilt, a heaviness of heart. She gulps. She has regret; she has remorse and sadness. That is guilt, and it's the only proper kind of guilt.

When we sin against Christ, then the marvelous Comforter, the gift of God's love, comes down and makes plain to us that we love another—that we have not appreciated, or have done despite to, the incredible love He has shown for us. We don't feel good about it one bit. We don't know what to say, and we can't speak, and we wish we could die; but Christ doesn't condemn us. He wants us to come back, and we want to go back, but we can't figure out how. This is heaviness-of-heart guilt that is so close to repentance that it can hardly be separated from repentance for sin. They're just so close together, for almost as soon as we discover what we have done to Him and our hearts feel this way, we are filled with sadness and sorrow. That kind of heart-sorrow guilt and repentance are very similar. One comes first and the other usually comes right after it, if we still have any feelings at all.

The Bible tells us that this repentance is a gift of God. "Him hath God exalted with His right hand to be a Prince and a Saviour, for to give repentance to Israel, and forgiveness of sins." Acts 5:31. Also, there is this: "The goodness of God leadeth thee to repentance." Romans 2:4. As He stands there hurt and weeping, His goodness is shining out, and that is what breaks our hearts. That is what makes us feel guilty and sad at the same time, almost. We ask ourselves, "How can I hurt the One who loves me so much?"

A description of this goodness of God is found in *Steps to Christ*, pages 26 and 27: "Christ must be revealed to the sinner as the Saviour dying for the sins of the world; and as we behold the Lamb of God upon the cross of Calvary, the mystery of redemption begins to unfold to our minds and the goodness of

God leads us to repentance. In dying for sinners, Christ manifested a love that is incomprehensible; and as the sinner beholds this love, it softens the heart, impresses the mind, and inspires contrition in the soul." The goodness of God leads us to repentance.

Do you know what *contrition* is? It's a knotting-up of your heart. You feel like you've got a lump there, like a huge cancer of some kind, and it physically gnaws like when your stomach is in spasms. It gnaws away, and it hurts and won't go away so quickly. Contrition is part of repentance. This contrition comes when we go to the cross, because through the cross is revealed this love that is incomprehensible—this love that says, "I cannot let you go, even though you have sinned. You have gone away into spiritual adultery, but I cannot let you go. I want you back. I will pay for all those sins, and take them all away so that you can come back. I still want you. Please come back."

This thought is continued: "And as Christ draws them to look upon His cross, to behold Him whom their sins have pierced, the commandment comes home to the conscience. The wickedness of their life, the deep-seated sin of the soul, is revealed to them. They begin to comprehend something of the righteousness of Christ, and exclaim, 'What is sin, that it should require such a sacrifice for the redemption of its victim? Was all this love, all this suffering, all this humiliation, demanded, that we might not perish, but have everlasting life?'" Ibid, p. 27. Here is that genuine guilt. We exclaim, "What is sin, that it should require such a sacrifice for the redemption of its victim? Was all this love, all this suffering, all this humiliation demanded that we might not perish, but have everlasting life?" We really have to look at the cross, because without the shedding of blood there is no remission, or putting away, of sin. It is not just the blood being shed; it's the love manifested at Calvary, the heart that was willing to give all for us. God was giving Himself.

At Calvary, we see ourselves punishing God with our sins. When we kneel down to confess our sins, we must kneel down at the foot of the cross. Jesus earned the right to forgive sins at the cross. He did not automatically have that right; He *gained* it. He *earned* it. And in our minds' eyes, we must come to the place where He gained it, and kneel down there, and see Him dying for our sins.

In the Old Testament there is such a vivid picture of all this. Back then, when a man sinned, he had to bring a sacrifice. If you haven't been on a farm or a ranch, probably a sacrifice doesn't impress you much. According to the Bible, the man had to bring the most perfect animal he had. It couldn't be the one he thought would die tomorrow because it was so sick. It had to be the best he had. 2 Corinthians 8:12.

On the farm where I grew up, we had one of those orphan lambs that we raised in the kitchen with a bottle and that had become a pet. When it was a year old—the age of a sacrificial animal—whenever I walked out into the yard, he would come up and hit me on the thigh because he wanted a bottle. "Give me something to drink." We called him Bucky. He was always bucking us on the thigh, wanting a drink of milk. That is how he got the bottle when he was young. Instead of bucking his mother, he would buck some of us for something to drink. He loved that. He was a friend, and he would tag along behind us all over the farmyard.

Suppose one day you sinned—one of those sins you love so much that are so enjoyable. Imagine yourself having to find a sacrifice, and the sacrifice is Bucky. You would bring to the courtyard that precious animal, that friend, that innocent victim that has done nothing wrong. The priest would tie him down and then hand you the knife you were to use to kill him. All this is because you enjoyed sin. You see, friends, we have left something out of our Christianity. We have almost thrown away the cross. We hate it because we feel miserable there.

In Old Testament days, there was no forgiveness until you brought a sacrifice. *No forgiveness.* Can you imagine yourself slitting the throat of a pet animal like Bucky? Can you think the thoughts that would race through your mind about that sin you enjoyed? You say to yourself, "I didn't realize that what I was doing involved anything like this. This animal doesn't deserve this." You feel so horrible that you are tempted to let your animal friend go, but you want forgiveness, so in agony of soul, you kill your innocent friend and watch him kick and twitch until he is dead.

Have you ever killed an animal? I grew up in a non-Christian home. We used to go hunting a great deal. When I was a little guy, I was more like a fetching dog, not a hunter. I would chase and round up all the pheasants others had killed, or the rabbits, whatever it was, and I didn't enjoy that one bit. I just got tired of chasing everything all the time like an errand boy. I longed for the day when I would have a gun, and be a man. I would be the hunter. Then the conquests and the victories would be mine. I could hardly wait. I begged and begged my father for a gun, and he told me that I could have a gun when I could buy one for myself.

So I worked and worked and worked. You won't believe what a gun cost in those days. I could get a new gun for less than seven dollars. That was half a week's wage, and I worked long hours to earn that much money. I finally had my first shotgun. I can recall either the first or second time we went out to hunt with the neighbor man Ed, who always joked and teased me a lot. Shotgun shells cost a nickel apiece. It took me a long time to get a nickel, so I never wasted a shotgun shell. We were walking across a big field when a jackrabbit got up and started running off. I aimed my gun to shoot at it, but we didn't shoot jack rabbits because most of them had disease, so we couldn't eat them.

When I lowered my gun, Ed said, "What's the matter, Billy? Afraid you couldn't hit it?" He needled me and intimidated me and ridiculed me until I determined I was going to show him. By then the rabbit was way off in the distance, but I fired at it and hit it. Boy, was I happy. I took off on a dead run after that rabbit to prove to Ed that I was a man. When I got to it, I saw that I had hit the hind carcass of the animal. There he was, still up on his front legs but with his hind legs bent off to the side. Tears were running down the fur of its cheeks! Suddenly, I wasn't a man. In fact, I wished I were dead.

Well, here came Dad and Ed, and there I was, and I wanted to be a man, but I didn't want to kill. I had heard that rabbits would cry, but I never heard one cry until then. They tell me that deer will cry, too, by the way. I looked at that animal, and I watched Dad and Ed. Remember, shells were expensive, and we didn't waste them. Back then, if you were a man, you would take the heel of your boot and grind the animal's head into the ground. The pressure was on, and I got closer and closer until, almost in blindness, I lifted my boot and brought it down hard on his head, crushing it. Then I couldn't sleep all night.

If you have never killed, you don't understand a lot about the death of Jesus. It was our sins that killed Him. We may say, "Jesus died two thousand years ago." That is true, but "by every sin Jesus is wounded afresh." *Desire of Ages*, p. 300. You know, what we think is confession is really just a cop-out, an evasion of reality. When we kneel before bedtime to confess our sins, we become the biggest cowards in the world. We think that the Lord will forgive us because we say, "I'm sorry that I sinned today. Good night, and please give me restful sleep." We don't think another thing about it until the next day. Then our sins come back to haunt us. We wonder why we keep thinking about them. It's because the sins are not gone. They have not been taken to the cross and given to Jesus, to bear our guilt and penalty. When we do go to the cross, we hardly ever linger there. We rarely, if ever, spend a thoughtful hour there with our sins, asking, "Why did He die for me? Is my sin really so horrible that it required the death of God's only Son?" If we would meditate on that last question, the Holy Spirit will reveal the answer.

When we finally comprehend that He so loved us that He gave up His life with His Father forever by dying for us—and that we manifested utter selfishness by going out and loving other things more than Him, to the point that we forgot all about Him and loved sin and the world and ourselves more than Him—and that we gave away all that we had dedicated to Him—we realize what is so wrong with sin: it breaks His loving heart afresh. All that agony He expressed on the cross shows that we are torturing Him again with our sins. He knows that unless we repent, those sins will cause us to be eternally lost. That fearful fate compels Him to give all for us, because He loves us and wants us with Him eternally. The love of God is also what leads us to repentance. Our ingratitude and lack of love for God is revealed to our stricken hearts, and He offers us precious forgiveness and peace. When we leave the foot of the cross, we will be walking on cloud nine, let me tell you. We will be just way up in the sky. Do you know why? Because our heavy load of guilt has been lifted off us and placed on Jesus.

Some athletes train with weights on their shoes. The weights are removed before a race, and suddenly they can run faster than ever. Jesus says, "Come unto me, all ye that labour and are heavy laden, and I will give you rest.... For my yoke is easy, and my burden is light." Matthew 11:28, 30. His yoke is easy, and His burden is light. Suddenly, you are just flying through the air, and everything is just wonderful. Wonderful! You know that He loves you, and you can never forget it. The next day when one of those temptations come back, do you say you need another hour at the cross? Another hour watching that rabbit that you killed? Not in a thousand years. Never. I hate that contrition. I don't want it. I don't want to have to go back there. Yet at the cross, you exclaim, "Lord, save me, lest I die!" And you will love Him supremely and hate the sins. Remember that at the beginning of this chapter, I asked, "How can I ever dislike what I enjoy?" Are you beginning to understand the answer to that question?

I have been talking a lot about His love, and what a precious gift Jesus is to all of us. Do you love Him? He wants to know, straight out. Jesus fully confessed His love for us in public, hanging naked on a cross after being scourged twice with the Roman whip. Are we afraid to tell anybody that we love Him? I've been chicken too often, haven't you? He just wants to know. And when we run around committing spiritual adultery, giving our affections to others and to the world, He wants to know if we have heart sorrow for our waywardness. That is all. We don't like phonies, and neither does God. We don't like liars; don't tell God lies. If you love Him, tell Him. If you are sorry, tell Him. He has told you how much He loves you in spite of your sins. What do you want to tell Him? When you offend your divine Lover, what do you say? If you want to tell Him you love Him and you are sorry, then make this prayer your own:

Loving Father, all of us down here are like each other. Not a one of us is better than another, and yet we are all different. We have to come to You in our own way, in our own time, and You have been so patient with us. You will keep on waiting and worrying and working until we respond, and I'm personally grateful that you waited for me. We get so embarrassed about confessing our love for the

Lord. Do forgive us for being so afraid. We are just so weak, and we comprehend so little of Thy marvelous love, but we still confess that we love Thee, and we truly are sorry. We would like to promise we could do better, but all our promises are like ropes of sand. We promise and promise, and fail and fail, and all we can say is, "Forgive us." We want to be so filled with this marvelous love that our hearts are changed, that we will hate those things that hurt our Lover. We love Thee and Thy divine grace and powerful presence. We would be like Jesus. Take over our whole being—not only our minds and our hearts and our souls, but our bodies. Make us like Jesus, because He lives in our affections, because He lives in our minds, because He has our interest and our esteem, our devotions, our gratitude and affections. Lord, literally consume us with all of your love. Grant that our confession today, strengthened by Thy sweet Spirit, will be a testimony that goes on and on and on, until we can see our precious Lord face-to-face and there, throughout the ages, tell Him how much we love Him. We ask in Jesus' name. Amen.

CHAPTER 12: COMMUNION: WORTHY OR UNWORTHY?

The communion service is most precious. As you find more and more of the love of Christ in your heart, the communion service will be something that you will always want to partake of.

We partake of the communion with our fellow believers. The family of God will be the family that goes on and on throughout all eternity. Our church families are just little parcels of the heavenly family that we will all join when we gather on the sea of glass.

We need to begin to understand what it's like to be brothers and sisters, a term we have forgotten for a long time ago. But as Christ comes into our hearts and divinity and humanity are combined, we see the same evidence in others. They become so precious to us because it's the same Jesus, and we're all united in that one body. I hope to assure you that those who feel unworthy to participate in communion are the very ones who ought to do so.

"For as often as ye eat this bread, and drink this cup, ye do shew the Lord's death till He come. Wherefore whosoever shall eat this bread, and drink this cup of the Lord, unworthily, shall be guilty of the body and blood of the Lord. But let a man examine himself, and so let him eat of that bread, and drink of that cup. For he that eateth and drinketh unworthily, eateth and drinketh damnation to himself, not discerning the Lord's body." 1 Corinthians 11:26-29.

These few verses have kept thousands away from communion services for many, many years. In my estimation, it's all because we do not understand them, and that's a tragedy. We think that this is a service reserved for only the very finest Christians, the ones who give no evidence of sin of any kind in their lives. Some think that if we have any sin, we cannot be there. We would be there "unworthily," and that is damnation, according to verse 29. We don't want that, so we have convinced ourselves that, by attending the communion service, we would bring additional condemnation upon ourselves.

This is such a misunderstanding. I wish we didn't have to talk about it, but we do. Who was it that Jesus invited that night of that first Lord's Supper? The Bible tells us very plainly that the disciples were still disputing about who would have the highest place in the kingdom. That was not exactly humility. That's one reason we should partake of the ordinance of humility.

They were all invited to that final meal with Jesus. There was Peter, who would soon deny his Lord with cursing. There was Thomas, almost totally unbelieving. There was even Judas, as you know.

If *worthy* means *sinless*, how would we rate Peter, Thomas and the rest of them? We must look at these folk honestly. Could they possibly partake readily, unless they were sinless? But we know they were not sinless. They were very sinful, and yet Jesus instituted the Lord's Supper with that group of people. You see, salvation in all of heaven's blessings is a gift of grace, which is favor to the unworthy, to the undeserving. And the communion service is part of that favor. It's an ordinance of grace, not of merit. It's for sinners to partake in, not for those who are sinless, necessarily.

What does it mean to "eat and drink unworthily"? Why did Paul write this? What is it all about? Since it doesn't mean *sinless*, what does it mean? Why does he say that if people "eateth and drinketh unworthily," they will bring curses upon themselves?

Notice the theme of service in verse 26: "For as often as ye eat this bread, and drink this cup, ye do shew the Lord's death till He come." In this service there is a demonstration, a recalling of those events concerning the Lord's death. They were to partake in remembrance of Jesus. They were to break the bread and drink of the wine. The symbolism is great in this service.

It is not only remembering that He died; it is remembering for whom He died. This was made plain by Paul: "But God commendeth His love toward us, in that, while we were yet sinners, Christ died for us." Romans 5:8. So again, we must remember not just that He died. He died for us—each one of us—while we were yet sinners. There must be a personalized, individualized recalling of this fact.

Secondly, we must remember for what He died. The Bible makes that plain, also. "For I delivered unto you first of all that which I also received, how that Christ died for our sins according to the scriptures." 1 Corinthians 15:3. Therefore, when we partake of this service, do we remember these things? Do we see not only that He died, but He died for us and for our sins? Do we perceive and remember these reasons that He died? Do we recall that He agonized for us, that He bled, that He suffered? That He was beaten for us? Do these thoughts enter our minds? Or is it just a ceremony that we attend because it's required of us?

As we break the bread along with our brethren, do we ask ourselves, "Why am I breaking His body and drinking His blood?" Or do we just think about other things? As we do these things and recall that it was for our sins and for each one of us as a sinner, then we are remembering our place, our part in the Lord's death—that we, by our sins, by our lives, have required this. We caused His death. His death was for us.

If we understand and think on this as we partake—if we perceive the role of each of us sinners individually and the result of our sin—we partake worthily. If we do not perceive this, we partake unworthily. That is not only my interpretation; the Bible teaches that so clearly: "For he that eateth and drinketh unworthily, eateth and drinketh damnation to himself, not discerning the Lord's body." 1 Corinthians 11:29. That person doesn't perceive the Lord's body, the suffering, the agony, the reason He died—for whom and for what. He doesn't see this. He doesn't apply the precious blood and all the agony. In saying Jesus died for the sins of the world, we tend to generalize what He did and get the focus off us individually. That is not what it's about. There must be a personal application to each of us as we partake. As we break the bread and drink the wine, these emblems must bring to focus in each of our minds, "It was for me."

It's so easy for us to feel that we are qualified. If we have a strong will, if we are concerned only about external behavior, if we're not concerned about our hearts, if we forget that often we're severe with other people, if we justify this by our brightness or by our virtue, our office or seniority or something else, then we eat unworthily, not recognizing that He died for us personally, individually, no matter how good we might seem to ourselves. His death was required because of each one of us, as if we were the only one.

We assume too much, sometimes. Those who go to church but sit through a communion service without partaking, or those who stay away, may be saying, "I cannot partake because I'm too sinful." Those are the very ones who would partake worthily. If that is their reason for not partaking, their spiritual eyesight is clear. They recognize quickly that it was for them that Jesus died, and they could not have any hope except for His death.

Some of us have so much confidence in ourselves that we go in an almost casual manner, and just sit there. We partake of the bread and juice, not realizing that we have caused this remembrance, this recalling that He died for us. If we would partake worthily, we must ask the question the disciples asked of themselves when Jesus said, "… One of you shall betray me. And they were exceeding sorrowful, and began every one of them to say unto him, Lord, is it I?" Matthew 26:21-22. Is it not conceivable that we each could be so corrupt, so vile, as to betray the One we profess to love with all our hearts? How can it be? But around the circle they went: "Lord, is it I?"

The Bible tells us Judas would have been suspect by the absence of his asking the same question, and so even He asked, "Lord, is it I?" As we all sit through the communion service, it is not enough to know that we are there, that it is the right thing to do. Some way, each of us must discern the Lord's presence in what He has done for each one of us personally, and we must discern what we are in relationship to Him. We must ask ourselves, "Lord, is it I?" And the truth should come home to my heart and to your heart.

We all admit that we have betrayed Jesus at some point in our lives. By our sins, we caused all His agony, heartache, and suffering. It was while we were yet enemies that He did that for us, because He loved us so much. As each of us partakes in this service, we must not lock Him out. We must look at Him on the cross, and see *Him*—not just the symbols, but in our mind's eye, see Jesus there for each one of us. You must see Him there, just for yourself, and I must see Him there, just for me.

There is a special quality found in the Lord's Supper. As you perceive this as an individualized service, one of the few services that we have that is for each individual, the Lord will come so close to you. Literally, as you partake of Him, internalizing these emblems, if your mind dwells correctly on these thoughts, the Lord comes into your heart. This sense of cleansing by the blood of Jesus and the death of Christ becomes a reality. He brings purity. He brings cleansing. He brings forgiveness. He brings hope. He brings peace. And as you leave the Lord's house, you walk with joyful, calm assurance. "The Lord has forgiven me. I am a child of the King. He is mine, and I am His. We have been together during that service, and He will never forsake me."

Every time you partake in the ordinance of the Lord's Super, pray that His sacred presence manifests to each one of us. Just sit there and meditate, comprehending all the meaning of the question: "Lord, is it I?" We, in relationship to the cross, know for sure that Christ has died for our sins, and they are all taken away.

My prayer for those who partake in the communion service is this: Loving Father, the sweetest fellowship in all the earth is to walk and talk with Jesus, to abide with Him, to commune with Him, to come into union with Him. He has come down that He might be one with us. May our hearts be open to fully receive Him. As our minds recall the precious gift on Calvary—all the suffering that we might be free, that we might be forgiven, that we might be received, that we might be sons and daughters of God—help us to comprehend these things. Grace each service in which we participate by Thy presence, and grant us faith to perceive that the Lord is here, where He has promised to be. May we not only join in sweet fellowship with the Lord, but may we be drawn closer to one another until that precious day we can be with Jesus and never part again—brothers and sisters of that glorious family of our Heavenly Father. We ask this in Jesus' name. Amen.

CHAPTER 13: GOOD NEWS FOR THE GUILTY

Some of the best news in the Bible is this: "For God so loved the world, that He gave His only begotten Son, that whosoever believeth in Him should not perish, but have everlasting life." John 3:16. There is that sweet hymn by Charles Wesley with these lyrics: "Love divine, all loves excelling, Joy of heaven to earth come down; Fix in us thy humble dwelling; All thy faithful mercies crown! Jesus, Thou art all compassion, Pure unbounded love Thou art; Visit us with Thy salvation; Enter every trembling heart." This hymn has really been the theme of our entire study on *God's Love Affair with the Guilty*.

When God gave His Son, Jesus became ours, and we became His. Heaven was adopting the earthly family. Jesus belongs to us; He is ours. God so loved us that He gave Him. If we could but realize what we have in Jesus—just a faint glimpse of what this is all about—then we would talk more about God so loving the world and giving us Jesus. Remember that Christ is ours eternally. We shall never lose Him. We may leave Him, but we cannot lose Him. He is always ours, if we choose to have Him.

If a child of a king becomes your brother, you'd become a child of a king, also. If the son of a king is your brother, then are you also the son of a king. When the Son of God becomes our brother by becoming human, we become children of God, do we not? This is illustrated in a verse written by the apostle John: "But as many as received Him, to them gave He power to become the sons of God, even to them that believe on His name." John 1:12. I hope that text makes much more sense than it has in the past. The word in Greek there is not truly *power*; it's not strength. It's not like an electric motor or something. He gave them *authority* or *right*, which is the real meaning of the Greek work translated *power*. To those who receive Him, He gives the right or the authority to come into being that instant as sons of God.

What are we waiting for? Are you with me? Centuries ago, God so loved He gave. He gave from the foundation of the world, the Bible says. He physically came. God came down embracing all humanity, taking humanity. He became ours, and we can receive Him. The instant we receive Him, we have the right or the authority to come into being, right then and there, as children of God. Not someday, when we get good enough. We'll never be that good. God is the giver of every good and precious gift, and the greatest of all His gifts was His one and only Son. Heaven is adopting us in the person of Jesus.

When we receive Him, not only do we become Christians, but we receive something else that is fantastic: "But when the fullness of the time was come,

God sent forth His Son, made of a woman, made under the law, To redeem them that were under the law, that we might receive the adoption of sons. And because ye are sons, God hath sent forth the Spirit of His Son into your hearts, crying, Abba, Father. Wherefore thou art no more a servant, but a son; and if a son, then an heir of God through Christ." Galatians 4:4-7. It is God's desire to adopt us as sons and daughters!

Here it is again, because it is so wonderful to hear: "And because ye are sons, God hath sent forth the Spirit of His Son into your hearts crying, Abba, Father. Wherefore thou art no more a servant, but a son." Now listen to this: "And if a son, then an heir of God through Christ." We need to read the sequence. The Father gives His son, so that we might be adopted; and when this adoption occurs, we receive His Spirit. That means God abides in us individually, in the person of God, the Holy Spirit. Wherefore we are no more servants but sons, and then as sons, heirs of God through Jesus Christ our Lord.

We can spend a long time in that text, because these things go by our ears just like jet planes, and all they leave is noise. We must stop and think about these words. If we receive the Son of God, the Father makes us sons along with Him, and His sons are heirs. That means we are very, very rich, because our Father has the cattle on a thousand hills. In His kingdom and city, the streets are even paved with gold. It's not stored in a vault somewhere; it's put out there for everybody to walk on. And His treasures are much greater than gold and silver. He has the treasures of patience, neatness, peace and joy, happiness, and glad tidings—all the things that cannot be bought. These are all the things we receive in Christ as heirs of God.

"God has adopted human nature in the person of His Son and has carried the same into the highest heaven." *Desire of Ages*, p. 25. Jesus is still human, you see? He took our human nature with Him to heaven. "It is the 'Son of man' who shares the throne of the universe. It is the 'Son of man' whose name shall be called 'Wonderful, Counselor, The mighty God, The everlasting Father, The Prince of Peace.'" The great "I Am" is the liaison between God and humanity, laying His hand upon both God and man, upon both heaven and earth. "He who is holy, harmless, undefiled, and separate from sinners" is not ashamed to call us brethren. Hebrews 7:26. He is not ashamed. Are we ashamed to call him Brother? "In Christ, the family of earth and the family of heaven are bound together. Christ glorified is our Brother. Heaven is enshrined in humanity, and humanity is enfolded in the bosom of infinite love." *Desire of Ages*, p. 25-26.

I wish my brain were big enough to comprehend all these things. "The family of earth and the family of heaven are bound together," tied inseparably in Jesus. Christ is one Person, and in Him are both divinity and humanity. He stays with us because He is ours; He is our Brother. When we receive Christ, heaven comes into us. God Himself comes into us.

We have made Christianity so many different things, but in its utter simplicity, it's receiving what God gave and what God gives. It's just reaching out and embracing Jesus and comprehending the fullness that God has given to us in this magnificent gift. Jesus is marvelous.

Suppose that the President of the United States was your brother. Would you have some power? Some influence with others? Suppose the richest man in the world was your brother. Wouldn't you consider that to your advantage? What is it like, then, when God is our Brother? What is that like? He is, you know. We must just let this go over and over in our minds for hours, because our brains are so feeble, ruined by television and newspapers and magazines. We can't quite comprehend the mysteries of God that He has revealed to us. These are great, enormous thoughts that God has given to us.

The Bible says in Galatians 4:7: "Wherefore thou art no more a servant, but a son; and if a son, then an heir of God through Christ." We have become sons and daughters by receiving Him as God's gift to us; and if sons and daughters, then we are automatically heirs of God. This immediately changes all of Christianity. We have to throw away many of our old concepts. We haven't put Christianity in the context of God adopting humanity and making us heirs.

In the Bible we are told what happens to an heir: "Then shall the King say unto them on His right hand, Come, ye blessed of My Father, inherit the kingdom prepared for you from the foundation of the world." Matthew 25:34. We inherit the world. We don't deserve it, we don't work for it, but we inherit the kingdom!

Here's another verse that talks about inheritances and heirs: "And every one that hath forsaken houses, or brethren, or sisters, or father, or mother, or wife, or children, or lands, for My name's sake, shall receive an hundredfold, and shall inherit everlasting life." Matthew 19:29. We inherit the kingdom. We inherit everlasting life.

Here's another text on inheriting all things: "He that overcometh shall inherit all things; and I will be his God, and he shall be My son." Revelation 21:7. Again, we inherit the kingdom, everlasting life, and all things that God has to give us. Nothing is withheld. All that God has belongs to His children. Is that not true? We must become members of His family, though. To accomplish that, God adopts us as His sons and daughters. Then we belong to His family; we are His children. We inherit all these things.

How do we obtain an inheritance, then? By trying to be an heir? What do we do to become heirs? We just have to belong to the family; isn't that right?

God makes us members of the family. In order to make this plan work, God sent His Son down, and has adopted all who have received His Son. He says that we all are His children now. Jesus has become our Brother by becoming human. God and man are joined together. If we accept Him into our lives—truly, fully receive Him by faith, we have the right to be sons and daughters of God. Now we are His children. Now we belong to the family. Now we are heirs. The kingdom is ours. Everlasting life and all things are ours.

It is not by trying to be good that we become heirs. We inherit everlasting life and the kingdom by being heirs, not by trying to be good. And because I am an heir and because I know I inherit all these things, I'm so grateful, and I respond by loving Him for His great love. Now I'm a different person, too. The change in my life is a response to God making me an heir. It's not by *trying* to be an heir, then. It's *because I am* an heir. God has made me that.

Inheritance is usually the result of a will. When we read the Bible correctly, we will find the will. I hope we can put all this legal language together, for the Bible is filled with much legal terminology, through and through. We almost have to be attorneys, sometimes, to understand all the legal terms used in the Scriptures. We should understand this one nicely, though: "And for this cause He is the mediator of the new testament, that by means of death, for the redemption of the transgressions that were under the first testament, they which are called might receive the promise of eternal inheritance." Hebrews 9:15. That is His will, right there in Hebrews 9:15. It's a simple one, but never was there a more important one in all of human history. It says that His death would bring about the bestowal of the inheritance, which is the "redemption of the transgressions," which results in the beneficiaries receiving eternal life.

Now, the one who writes a will or who dies, leaving a will, is called a *testator.* The will is his or her "last will and *testament.*" Jesus is the testator, but what does verse 15 mean when it says that Jesus is the "*mediator* of the new testament"? The word *mediator,* as used in the Greek in Hebrews 9:15, means the one in the middle or midst, working between the parties to unite them. He or she "mediates" peace between them. Jesus, in man's behalf, satisfied the claims of God upon mankind, and in so doing, guaranteed mankind a new and better covenant. So Jesus fills two roles to ensure our redemption.

We know the death of the testator is necessary before the terms of the will can be carried out. *The Living Bible* words verses 16 and 17 in Hebrews 9 thus: "For where a testament is, there must also of necessity be the death of the testator. For a testament is of force after men are dead: otherwise it is of no strength at all while the testator liveth." This Bible paraphrase indirectly calls the good news of the gospel a *will*, because it refers to a testator. That interpretation is perfectly legitimate from the Greek language. So the will goes into effect only after the death of the person whose it is. No one inherits anything until it is proven that the person who signed the will is dead. While the testator is still alive, no one can prematurely receive any of those things he has promised to them in the will.

Therefore, "by virtue of His death," "by means of His death," the death of God's Lamb, the benefits of the new testament can now be ours. The law is now written in our hearts of flesh; it no longer remains outside us. We are told what inheritance Christ has willed to distribute to His beneficiaries: an "eternal inheritance," eternal life. We are told who the beneficiaries of the will are: "those who obey God's call to enjoy the promises," "they which are called." Who in their right mind would not obey God's call to enjoy the promises? Who would turn such an invitation down? Although the Testator names every human being a beneficiary, according to His great love for mankind, does everyone actually become a beneficiary? Is that what the verse says? No. Everyone will have the *opportunity* to become a beneficiary. By becoming heirs, we are named in that will. All of heaven's adopted sons and daughters will be beneficiaries; but lest I be understood to be saying that everyone is an heir, and everyone is given this inheritance, I remind you that "many are called, but few are chosen." Matthew 22:14. Why are few chosen? It isn't that the will has any legal limitations; its terms are broad, generous, and apply to all. Any person may receive the gifts of inheritance. If we do not become heirs, it's that we disqualify ourselves because of unbelief. The gospel tells us that "… whosoever believeth in him should not perish, but have everlasting life." Belief is the only stipulation of the will. The beneficiaries must believe, or they lose their part in the inheritance intended for them.

Not only is Jesus the testator and the mediator, but because He passed from death into life again, He can also be the executor of His own will. A female executor is called an executrix, but in this case, the executor is Jesus. "Behold, the Lord cometh with ten thousands of his saints, to execute judgment upon all…." Jude 1:15. An executor does the bulk of the work related to a will. He ensures the terms, conditions, and dispositions of the will are carried out as the testator intended and directed. Knowing how much He loves us, this is very good news. He guards our interests in this matter from start to finish. From testator to executor, He is on our side; He wants us to receive the promised inheritance. By whatever means necessary—people, Bible, periodical, book, but usually by His emissary, the Holy Spirit—He contacts every beneficiary before the will's final distribution. Absolutely everyone is designated an heir in the will. There is no shortage in what He wants to give to every single person; He can give and give and never run out. The Executor tells us that the testator's possessions are about to be distributed.

What is His to give is about to be given. Having life in Himself, He will give us eternal life. He encourages us to submit to the easy terms of the will; He's done everything to make that acceptance easy. Why miss such a wonderful opportunity?

Jesus fills another role for us, too. "If any man sin, we have an advocate with the Father, Jesus Christ the righteous." 1 John 2:1. He is our advocate—and a voluntary one. We don't hire him, in an impersonal way, to do a job for us. He volunteers Himself for this role. Why? Because we need him; we need an advocate. What does an advocate do? A dictionary says an advocate "comes forward in behalf of and as the representative of another." Jesus is our "substitutionary, intercessory advocate." He comes forward as our substitute, to protect us from negative things; and he comes forward as our intercessor, pleading our cause before God, representing us, claiming us as His brethren. We're family to Him, and He shares everything He has with us—even His robe of righteousness. He does everything for us, because we don't know how to do anything. If we didn't have an Advocate, we would never be adopted into the family of God; we wouldn't benefit from the will; we wouldn't receive the eternal inheritance. But we *do* have an Advocate, and we know that He is untiring in His efforts for us. Our Advocate is our High Priest; we can't get a more qualified advocate than that. If we fall into sin, and turn to God immediately for forgiveness when we realize our sin, that sin is pardoned instantly, through the intercession of our Mediator, or Advocate. As testator, He wants to give us what is promised in His will, and as advocate, this is one way He accomplishes that objective.

Although we know God is omniscient, knowing all things, we can imagine the courtroom scene depicted in the book of Daniel. We see Jesus in heaven right now, in the investigative judgment, examining the record books hopefully, listening attentively to the witnesses as they testify before the Judge. The witnesses are the "ten thousand times ten thousand" angels that stand before the Judge, who is the Ancient of days, our heavenly Father. Jesus, our Advocate, sees that because of His generous provisions of grace, an innumerable host of heirs have, by faith, met the terms and conditions of the will. Legally and lovingly in heaven's eyes, they are no longer servants, or friends, or potential heirs. They are *brethren*, co-heirs with Him. They will be given eternal life and all the riches inherent in being children of the King. What a marvelous thought! He and we rejoice! All those souls, saved by believing and trusting in His righteousness, not their own.

So the investigative judgment is not all sour grapes and criticism, as some people think. Jesus our Lord—Christ our righteousness—is well able to present us "faultless before the presence of His [Father's] glory, with exceeding joy." Jude verse 24. He also will execute, or carry out, the final steps of the will: the actual delivery of the inheritance to the true heirs. That is the executive judgment, the last phase, and it happens at His second coming. This is unsurpassably wonderful news for those that "love His appearing;" they are prepared for His return. Then "this mortal shall have put on immortality" (1 Corinthians 15:54) and the Executor will have completed His duties in that office.

There's more to the story, though. Before Jesus left this world, He decided to do something about executing the will down here, as well. Take note of this, as found in *Acts of the Apostles*, p. 27: "Before ascending to heaven, Christ gave His disciples their commission." I hope we never forget these words. This is the heart of our message, and some of us don't even know it is there. What is that commission? "He told them that they were to be the executors of the will in which He bequeathed to the world the treasures of eternal life."

Have we been fulfilling our commission as executors of God's will? Have we been telling people about this will? Or are we preaching everything else but the will? If we leave this out, we are failing in our commission. We are to be executors of the will. This is our primary duty. He commissioned us to be executors of the will in which He bequeathed to the world the treasures of eternal life. This is the gospel for this time. This is our job, assigned to us by Christ before He went back to heaven.

Our work as executors includes searching out and notifying every potential heir by every possible means. We have the delightful task of saying to every person, "You are an heir." That is what we call missionary work. We have made it everything else but this. Christ never assigned the kind of missionary work that many people are doing. Our missionary work too often is what some people call a galling duty. It's viewed as unwelcome as sticking our chins into a buzz saw, but it was never meant to be like that. He gave us the commission to become executors of the will wherein we tell people, "You are in Jesus' will; you are an heir! Jesus has bequeathed eternal life to you. If you receive Him, you will receive an eternity of peace, vigor, and joy."

There's a caveat here. We tell people they are heirs already, because Jesus died for them already. All provisions have already been made for them to be heirs; there remains only the disposal of the gifts in the will. However, do you remember that they have to become part of the family first, to be heirs? They have to believe in Christ, their Savior and Lord and Brother. That's Who He is. They must receive Him, even as they must be received as adopted brethren, if they are to be co-heirs. That's the legal reality of it. Hebrews 2:11 tells us exactly who are heirs: "For both he that sanctifieth and they who are sanctified are all of one: for which cause he is not ashamed to call them brethren." If Jesus calls them brethren (and sisters, of course), that means that like Jesus, they are children of the heavenly Father, adopted into the family of the King of kings.

Although everyone's name is listed in the Testator's will, testifying to the Testator's love for all mankind, not everyone will comply with the will's one limitation or condition. Those who are heirs are "they who are sanctified," which in the Greek means "being sanctified." They are converted souls. Those are the ones Jesus calls brethren. Those who hate Him are not His brethren. He loves them, but if they are rejecting Him, they aren't "being sanctified." There are elements of repentance, obedience, and character change that the brethren manifest that those who love the world do not. Still, He pities them and loves them; he knows that they are playthings of the devil. He wants all to join the heavenly family, so He has commissioned us to tell others about His will, as revealed in the gospel, and the inheritance He desires to give them. He wants to give them "the treasures of eternal life." Imagine that! We think eternal life is a treasure in itself, but He wants to give unknown multiples of "treasures of eternal life." How very generous is our Savior, to share so many treasures with His brethren.

"And He said unto them, Go ye into all the world, and preach the gospel to every creature." Mark 16:15. We have used this text for many years, but we have had a different idea about it before. Now we have a better conception of the gospel. Our heavenly Father wants to, and will, adopt us. The Holy Testator's will has only one stipulation, one requirement, for those who would be heirs. As many as fully receive Him, by faith, they become sons and daughters, and therefore heirs. Tell every person—the whole human family—that they are heirs if they are family members. Even more encouraging, if they are not born into the family—and none of us are—they can choose to belong to the family! Those who accept Christ are heirs. God wants everyone to belong to His family. John 1:12 says, "But as many as received him, to them gave He power to become the sons of God, [even] to them that believe on his name."

This matter of inheritance is right in the first angel's message. "And I saw another angel fly in the midst of heaven, having the everlasting gospel to preach unto them that dwell on the earth, and to every nation, and kindred, and tongue, and people." Revelation 14:6. As we discussed earlier, after a testator's death, the executor of that person's will is legally accountable for contacting every living heir who is named as a beneficiary of the will, wherever each one is to be found. Otherwise, he or she can be sued. They must be searched out; they must be informed. They must be given an opportunity to accept or reject the terms of the will. Executors are to exhaust every means, print or media, to do this.

Sometimes we leave out the following important aspect of the gospel: "And this gospel of the kingdom shall be preached in all the world for a witness unto all nations; and then shall the end come." Matthew 24:14. We are to preach the gospel of what? The kingdom. We inherit the kingdom, so never leave that out when preaching the gospel. The end will not come until we have found every person that could be a possible heir. Not until the work of us executors is completed, by notifying all the heirs, will the end come. Everyone must have an opportunity to accept the tremendous good news of the kingdom. We say that the gospel is the good news, but we often don't stress that it is the kingdom of God that people inherit. Please don't leave that out. When they've all been notified and have made their decisions to accept or reject their inheritance, then He returns.

We launched into this commission over a century ago, and yet today we hardly ever find anyone saying, "You can be an heir to the kingdom." Perhaps this has something to do with why Jesus hasn't returned. He will not come when we finish going into all the world with medical missionary work or teaching the state of the dead. He won't come then. We can have institutions and churches and hospitals and schools in all the countries of the world, but that won't cause Him to return. He is not going to come back until every human being has been told that he or she is an heir. They must be told that their name is in the will, and then we leave it up to them to accept or reject the terms of the will, which is to accept Christ with all their heart.

That is what it's all about. We can never hasten Christ's coming by going out to various places with a general message. We must have the good news of the *kingdom* to present to people. Until our preaching and our teaching and our Bible studies contain the good news of the kingdom, we're not fulfilling the commission. Our own children often don't even know it. Many in the church pew do not know it. And yet we think that we are finishing the Lord's work.

Therefore, to accomplish this legally, we must use every news media, all the public notices, every species of communication—every kind and variety. This is our authorization, or commission, for public evangelism. Evangelism is a bad word to some Christians. It's bad because we haven't been doing the work Christ assigned to us. Public evangelism is to notify heirs. There is no other reason for it. It isn't to become showmen. We don't need great eloquence to inform heirs. We use the methods of communication available to the human family to inform them that they are heirs. That is what evangelism is for. This doesn't just mean big meetings. It also means personal evangelism, and any type of public work. The whole commission for public soul winning is to notify people that they are heirs.

This is so different from what we have made it. To notify heirs is a delightful task. It really is. It's not a miserable work; it's the most pleasant work ever committed to mankind. Can you imagine telling people that their names are written in Christ's will and that they can belong to the family of God? Then to tell them that they are going to inherit everlasting life, the kingdom, and all things? If we fulfilled our commission as Christ gave it to us, people would think that we are the greatest news bearers. There is nothing finer than that.

I almost hate to mention this, but years ago there was a TV program called *The Millionaire*. A billionaire would write a cashier's check for one million dollars to some person he had selected. A certain man had the job of finding that heir and telling them about the money. People had different reactions to being told that they were now in the possession of one million dollars. And there were terms to receive the money, just as there are terms to someone becoming an heir to the kingdom of God.

Our work is like the man who had to search out that new millionaire and notify him or her; he had the pleasure of seeing the reactions on their faces. Christ has made it our commission to go search out the heirs. This is genuine missionary work. This is carrying out the gospel commission. Everything else is human invention. It really is. And it's time we went about our Father's business, not our inventions of His business. We can do this without a university education, don't you think? I hope that even boys and girls can do this. Perhaps they can do it better than some of us.

I hope the Lord doesn't have to take somebody from the plow to replace me because I have too much education. I honestly hope that. But I have read about that in the *Testimonies*, haven't you? I just don't comprehend in all my book learning that the Spirit of God is telling me go out and inform people that they are heirs, and ask them if they know how to claim their inheritance. I am to ask them if they have tasted the goodness of the Lord. That goodness is Christ, and if they accept that fact, then I am to invite them to become sons and daughters of God, so they can receive what the Divine Testator has willed to give them.

Many would rejoice and give thanks as to how good God is to us. This is such a different work. In our public evangelism and personal effort to win souls, in our visits to people, we are to inform them of the death of their Brother. I hope you pay close attention now. Inform them first that their Brother has died, and then, as executors of the will of Christ, declare to people the good news. Isn't that our duty and their entitlement? Isn't that their right to know? After all, He is their near relative, a kinsman. If your Brother has died, and you are His brother or sister, you would say to each person, "I, as an ambassador and representative of our

Brother, the Lord, Jesus Christ, do hereby notify and inform you that our Brother has died and left a will in which your name is written as an heir. I am proclaiming the following to you: According to His will, you are to receive eternal life, a place in His everlasting kingdom, and as a prince or princess, a share in all the possessions which are His. Would you please make certain to be present at His return, when He gives out His inheritance to all the heirs and to takes you home to His kingdom?"

We are to say all that in a pronouncement, and if they believe it and receive Him, then they are heirs. If they believe the truth of the word of God, they can walk happily, knowing that they are children of God. They need not worry about how good they are. The terms of the will do not include that. The terms are that they accept Jesus; He is responsible for making us good. It is His goodness—His righteousness—that we receive that makes us good. Of ourselves, we have nothing good. In Him, all things are good. When we receive Him into our hearts and become His children, His goodness abides in us. That is the heart and soul of righteousness by faith.

Then, because of our belief, our faith, we begin to thank Him and to love Him. We live a life of gratitude and praise and love, which is the fulfilling of the law. There is no other route to fulfillment. None. We can try to be good enough to be heirs, but we won't make it. We must become believers in the truth of God—that through Christ we have been made heirs of His kingdom.

We could spend a lot more time on this matter of the good news of the kingdom and our commission to be executors of Christ's will. I know you will put this book down and forget everything you just read, because you are just as I am. How quickly we forget. Someday we are going to have to stop long enough in one place, and think long enough, and believe long enough, until we know we are children of God. We might not find that basic truth in school or church, but we must find it, and we must believe it. Parents, when you know you are children of God, your children will love you. The generation gap will be gone. People will see a new kind of Christianity that they have never seen before; and for the first time, you will become a preacher of the gospel.

Honestly, you cannot preach the gospel until you are a child of God. I can't, either. It's just all pushing air; that is all it is. It's just empty words. But when you are a believer, and you know that you are a son or daughter of God, then you start to speak to people about it. The conviction comes out. It just radiates and reaches out and tells everyone, "Hey, you are an heir, too." And many who discover that they are heirs of the kingdom of God will shout, "*Hallelujah!*"

Someday our churches will ring with rejoicing. Do you know that? "Before the final visitation of God's judgments upon the earth there will be among the people of the Lord such a revival of primitive godliness as has not been witnessed since apostolic times. The Spirit and power of God will be poured out upon His children." *The Great Controversy*, p. 464. Someday we will really sing, and the organ will not be able to play louder than we can sing, no matter how big it is. Someday our hearts will be filled with jubilation, and we will greatly rejoice in the truth that God has given to us.

To adopt us as children, Christ had to accomplish a very strange thing. He had to become our nearest relative—not just a relative, but the nearest one. This is a principle that the Lord established in the Old Testament, in the book of Ruth. Ruth had appealed to Boaz for marriage, "… Spread therefore thy skirt over thine handmaid; for thou art a near kinsman." His response to her explained the law that the nearest kinsman had first right or duty. "And now it is true that I am thy near kinsman: howbeit there is a kinsman nearer than I. Tarry this night, and it shall be in the morning, that if he will perform unto thee the part of a kinsman, well; let him do the kinsman's part: but if he will not do the part of a kinsman to thee, then will I do the part of a kinsman to thee." Ruth 3:9, 12-13. This talks about the right of a near kinsman or relative. There was a priority to be followed. God placed in His word this wonderful law about the prerogatives, rights and duties of a close relative. If you, because of poverty, had been sold into slavery, a close relative could buy you out of slavery. If you had to sell your property because of poverty, he could buy back your property. For the childless widow of a near relative who had lost her husband, such as Ruth, the closest relative had first right to marry her. For the male offspring of that union, he would hold in trust the property so that he or they would have a name in the Promised Land. That was very important. If there were no male children, their place in the Promised Land was lost. Their name wasn't there; somebody else's name was there. These and many more things could be accomplished by the closest relative. Applying this spiritually, through sin, we lost our place in God's Promised Land. We became slaves of Satan. Jesus wanted no one between Himself and His beloved. He would become our nearest kinsman—One such as ourselves, in human flesh, to redeem us from bondage to sin and Satan, and give us a new, glorious future. Therefore, He, as the Son of God, made a way that we, too, may be sons and daughters of God. He became our Kinsman-Redeemer.

How close did He come when He became a near Kinsman or Brother? There was an incident where Jesus was told that His mother and brothers were outside and wanted to see Him. "Then one said unto Him, Behold, Thy mother and Thy brethren stand without, desiring to speak with Thee. But He answered and said unto him that told Him, Who is My mother? and who are My brethren? And He stretched forth His hand toward His disciples, and said, Behold My mother and My brethren! For whosoever shall do the will of My Father which is in heaven, the same is My brother, and sister, and mother." Matthew 12:47-50.

Here is a wonderful comment on this: "All who would receive Christ by faith were united to Him by a tie closer than that of human kinship. They would become one with Him, as He was one with the Father. As a believer and doer of His words, His mother was more nearly and savingly related to Him than through her natural relationship. His brothers would receive no benefit from their connection with Him unless they accepted Him as their personal Saviour.... It was to redeem us that He became our kinsman. Closer than father, mother, brother, friend, or lover is the Lord our Saviour." *Desire of Ages*, p. 327. Did you get that? Closer than father, mother, brother, friend or lover is Jesus our Savior. When He became our relative, He came very close.

Another quote sheds more light: "All who would receive Christ by faith were united to Him by a tie closer than that of human kinship. They would become one with Him, as He was one with the Father. As a believer and doer of His words, His mother was more nearly and savingly related to Him than through her natural relationship." Ibid, p. 325. So Christ becomes closer to those who receive Him than any relative they have. They would become one with Him as He was one with His father.

Can you imagine that about Mary, who carried Him in her own body? Our spiritual relationship with Jesus is even closer than the mother-child relationship between Jesus and Mary. Remember that when God so loved the world, He gave us Jesus. He came down, but He wasn't just coming down to the world. He wasn't just physically coming to all people. He was coming right inside of us. Even closer than the physical-emotional relationship He had with His mother is the relationship we can have with Christ. There are things we never told our mothers that we would tell Jesus. Isn't that right?

In order to make us heirs—children of the Father—He comes closer and closer to us. He becomes closer than our parents, closer than our natural brothers or sisters, even closer than our own husbands or wives. He becomes closer than a child to its mother, born from her body. He comes in closer than anyone else, that He might save us by making us sons and daughters of the King. He is the loving, nearest relative who adopts us; and thereby we become heirs of everlasting life, heirs of the kingdom, and heirs of all things. Think of it: sons and daughters of God in the family of heaven! All this is ours! And the Lord tells us that when this good news is preached in the entire world for a witness unto every nation, then shall the end come.

Do you love Jesus? How soon do you want Him to come back? Friends, the day has come that with our faces lighted up, our Bibles under our arms, we should go around proclaiming to every human being, "You are an heir. The treasures of heaven are all yours." That should make each one so very happy. "Come and join us in telling every soul." Heirs of the kingdom! Stand up, and shout and sing! Jesus is coming, and soon the inheritance will all be ours!

Dear friends, it's time to fulfill the gospel commission by taking the good news of the kingdom everywhere. May God help us to be on fire with the good news and have every soul rejoicing because God is so good to us.

CHAPTER 14: A SAFE PLACE FOR THE GUILTY

All through this book I have tried to give you hope, and in this final chapter I pray that you will find the most hope of all. "This know also, that in the last days perilous times shall come." 2 Timothy 3:1. In these last days, we all have problems. Some people think that their problems are because they are either divorced or single. That isn't necessarily the case. I know married people who feel like they can hardly wait until they are divorced. To them, marriage is pure hell. What I'm trying to tell you is, whether you are single or married, life is extremely difficult. Sometimes there are no solutions to the problems we have. In these very difficult times, many of our problems are simply due to the fact that we are living in the last days. Did you know that?

Almost everyone is suffering from insecurity. I think I see some who are not, but after I visit with them for a while, I discover that they have fears, too. The reasons for the anxiety and fears are many. We cannot be sure of our jobs. At one time in the past, if we had worked at the same place for thirty years, we could be sure we could retire from that job with a secure income. Not anymore. People who have worked many years on a job can suddenly have their jobs taken away from them, and they have no recourse. In fact, we cannot be certain of anything anymore. My daughter tells me that she hates to see all that money taken out of her check for Social Security. She doubts that she will ever get any of it back. I know that many of you feel the same way. All types of fears. No one these days is really secure unless they are a super-Pharisee, or perhaps they have believed the power of positive thinking for so long that they can't see reality. Reality tells us that life is very uncertain. People are worried about nuclear wars and collapsed economies. Many are worried about the environment. Toxic waste is being found in people's backyards and is causing all kinds of problems. A person can't tell if that beautiful river going by his house is filled with poison. There is just so much that we don't know anymore—so much uncertainty.

All around us are threatening dangers. It's been that way for a long time, and it's getting worse. Our money might not be worth a thing tomorrow. We may think that we can have security and money and houses and lands and investments, but that is not true anymore. We can lose it all overnight. We can take all the precautions we can think of, and tomorrow it could be gone. I could go on and on about all types of things. There is insecurity in the church today, too. We used to think our church was safe, but now we have problems in the church: funds and false doctrines and credibility and all sorts of things, until people are losing their confidence in the church. They are losing their confidence in ministers and professors in our universities. We are even, to some extent, losing our confidence in each other.

Wherever you go, there are serious problems like these. We are told that everything that can be shaken will be shaken. It's just a very insecure time. Yes, "in the last days perilous times shall come." We have always believed this. We have always taught that it's going to be this way. But when times do get perilous, we say, "I can't believe it; and I don't like this." That's the way things are, though. We cannot escape this peril by changing our locations or vocations or whatever, because wherever we go and whatever we do, there is going to be insecurity there today.

You know something? As a pastor, I think this is all wonderful. You probably want to say, "You must be crazy." No, I think it's wonderful. One reason is that for so many years, we have trusted in things. We have trusted far too much in materialism. I can remember the depression days very well. I wish all of you could realize what it was like back then. Back then, you could not predict where your next meal was coming from, yet, in some ways, it was a pretty good time. Really. It wasn't all that bad when almost no one had a job, when thousands stood in lines at soup kitchens and brought home a one-gallon syrup pail full of food for the day—powdered milk and a few other items—and that was for a whole family. I stood in lines many times; my father was too proud to do that. I was always envious of those who stood in the soup kitchen line to eat. We lived a simple existence. We may not have had nice homes and fancy clothing and cars and vacations, and all the things we think today are so nice, yet it was a still a good time. We didn't think it was so bad.

But you know, when times got better, I think we started to trust in *things*, and not in God. Preaching becomes extremely difficult when people have so much. They won't come to Lord in all their need because they don't feel much need. Oh, we say we have a lot of needs, but if we get enough money and a nice enough home and a nice enough marriage, we live like we don't need the Lord anymore.

It's easy for the preacher when people get so needy and so upset and so insecure that they cry out to the Lord and ask, "What are we going to do?" I thank the Lord for those days. If that is too nasty for you, forgive me, will you? But it's wonderful when people become very needy and cry out to God in their desperation. I think it makes Him happy. He waits for many years for some people to call upon Him in their great need. Thank the Lord that today many are crying at last. It's a good thing. Don't be upset at your insecurity. So many others are that way nowadays. Thank God that He is still there waiting for us to cry out to Him so He can answer our prayers. He is just delighted—always waiting, like a loving father.

What do we do about insecurity like this and all the fears we have? What do we do about all the threatening dangers? What can we do about some of our teachings and doctrines that seem to hold a guillotine over our heads? Where is the safe place for us in these times with all our insecurity? I'd like to suggest that the safe place is found in the experience of a builder in the Bible. We already talked about him in a previous chapter, but let's revisit the story and see what else we can glean from it.

What did Noah build? Did he build a boat? Recall that he built an *ark*. Do you remember why it was called an ark instead of a boat? It's quite simple, really, but at the same time, there is a little confusion about this. "By faith Noah, being warned of God of things not seen as yet, moved with fear, prepared an ark to the saving of his house; by the which he condemned the world, and became heir of the righteousness which is by faith." Wow, righteousness by faith was available way back in Noah's day!

I just want you to think a little, because I believe that many people read about Noah and what he built, and it doesn't even dawn on them what they are reading about. It didn't dawn on me for many, many years. God's plan was for Noah to build an ark, and He gave the plans to Noah and told him to build it. God never said to Noah, "Build a boat." The plans He gave him were for a boat, yet the Bible always calls it an ark. You will find it called an ark in Genesis 6: 14, in Genesis 7:1, and in Hebrews 11:7. It is always called an ark, and never a boat. When you understand the meaning of that, you will love the Lord more than you ever have in the past.

What is an ark? It's a place of safety, or a place of refuge. The two tablets on which God wrote the ten commandments were put into an ark for safekeeping. They were put into that marvelous, gold-covered box called the ark of the covenant to keep them safe there and preserve them. Noah and his family were preserved in safety in a different ark during the flood. So an ark is not just a boat or a box of special design; it's a place of safekeeping. God said, "Noah, I want you build a place of refuge for my people—a place where it's safe when the storm comes." God told Noah that a flood was coming, and He wanted to preserve His people in the ark. He wanted them to stay alive, and not die like those who were not in the ark. So the Lord devised a plan for them to keep them safe.

You could say that God's idea for the ark was the plan of salvation back in Noah's time. The ark was a place where they could be safe from all the peril, all the danger, all the flood waters. God invented a refuge. Please never forget it. It wasn't Noah's idea, was it? It was God's idea. He wanted a place where His people could be safe in the storm. God told Noah to preach repentance to the people for one hundred and twenty years. "Don't miss a soul. Tell them there is a place that is going to be safe when the flood comes." That was our loving, heavenly Father's idea. He didn't want anyone to die; He wanted them all to live. Noah was to build a huge ark so that there would be room for not only the animals, but for as many as might repent. If need be, God would have had Noah build twenty or thirty arks; He wanted to save lives. So as Noah hammered and preached that there was a terrible time of destruction coming, he invited everyone to enter the ark, where they would be safe from the storm. It was as if God was saying, "You don't have to die. You don't have to learn how to swim or build your own floating vessel. I will provide a place where you can be safe. I have the plans for it, and I have the man that is going to build it."

God has always desired and planned for us to have a safe hiding place called an ark. Think of it sort of like a game refuge when the hunting season is on. The birds and animals flee to that place; they know they can't be shot there. Believe me, hunting season for human souls has been going on for a long time. The devil and his angels have been out there shooting at us day and night, yet many do not know where to hide. Many of our problems come simply because the devil is out there shooting at us. The Bible reveals this. "And the dragon was wroth with the woman, and went to make war with the remnant of her seed, which keep the commandments of God, and have the testimony of Jesus Christ." Revelation 12:17.

Who are the remnant people? Do you know who they are? If you have never been shot at by the devil, then you probably don't know. You may have a theory about it, but if you feel like you are being shot at all the time by the devil and his host of fallen angels, you are probably part of that remnant. That is really what all the trouble is about. It's hunting season on God's remnant people. If you don't flee into the refuge, you might get shot. That is all there is to it. If all the time you are kicking yourself and wondering, "How come these bad things always happen to me?" then get into a safe place, and you won't be hit by the devil's bullets anymore. That is what God is telling us. Find out where it's safe. A lot of our problems arise simply because we are standing outside God's ark of safety and are therefore vulnerable. It's like being exposed on top of a rock where anybody can see and hit us. We have to get to someplace where we can hide. "Come down, family, and get inside the ark." That is what the Lord is saying. He is appealing to us to come into the place of refuge where it's safe. We don't have to stand outside and drown. "Come on inside." Send preachers to proclaim it loudly and clearly. "Get inside the ark while you can."

When the terrible flood of waters came, Noah and his family were preserved in the ark. The ark was a miracle in itself. "The ark was severely rocked and tossed about. The beasts within expressed by their varied noises the wildest terror, yet amid all the warring of the elements, the surging of the waters, and the hurling about of trees and rocks, the ark rode safely. Angels that excel in strength guided the ark and preserved it from harm. Every moment during that frightful storm of forty days and forty nights, the preservation of the ark was a miracle of almighty power." *Spiritual Gifts*, Volume 3, p. 70. The Lord would not let the ark perish. God said to build it, and said that in it Noah and his family would be safe, and they were safe.

Now, the most important question about this ark is this: Why were Noah and his family spared, and not the others? Please don't misunderstand this, and please forgive me if I think that almost all of us have misunderstood this. Why were they spared when others were destroyed? We touched on this in a previous chapter, but it is so important that we need to look at it again. We want no misunderstandings. Noah was a sinner, was he not? In his day, had not *all* sinned and come short of the glory of God, just as it had been since the days of Adam? Then why save some sinners and destroy other sinners? Are some sinners better than other sinners? Sometimes in our secular views, we think so, but the Lord doesn't think so. Why were some sinners saved and some lost? Just think about it for a little while. The Bible says that "there is none righteous, no, not one." Romans 3:10. There were none righteous in Noah's day. Was not Noah found intoxicated after the flood? (See Genesis 9:20,21.) Was not his son Ham, who was also in the ark, found guilty of quite a strange but terrible moral sin? That is what the Bible teaches. Yet both Ham and Noah were in the ark. The Bible even calls Noah a righteous man. "And the LORD said unto Noah, Come thou and all thy house into the ark; for thee have I seen righteous before me in this generation." Genesis 7:1. With seeming contradictions like that, are we sure that we have righteousness all figured out?

I'd like to have a long discussion with you on this matter; but instead of teaching you, I would like to ask you some very probing questions because I'm not sure we understand this business of righteousness. I know many assume that they do. I know we have a lot of quotations and everything else we could use to portray our opinions. But I have many questions I'd like to ask you from the Bible about righteousness. I'll start with these: Why did God call Noah righteous when he had these problems or sins or imperfections or whatever you want to call them? Some would even call them crimes. Why was he saved and others were destroyed? Why was Ham there? You must give correct answers, by the way, or you are going to have a lot of trouble with your own Christianity.

I'll try to give you some correct answers. The main reason (and be careful about this)—the main reason God called Noah righteous is that Noah was a believing sinner. He was a sinner, but he was a *believing* sinner. The ones outside were unbelieving sinners, and you must examine that a little bit. Noah demonstrated his belief by responding to God's instructions to build that ark. He spent one hundred and twenty years building that ark. That is really some belief. In other words, God directed him to do something, and he did it. You may not call building an ark righteousness, but Noah followed God's instructions to the letter. He followed *God's* directions. He did that. Since Noah *believed* what God said, he did what God *told him to do*. He *first* believed God, did he not? He *believed* what God said, and *then* He *acted* on what God had said. There were other believers, also, and they helped Noah build, though they went to their rest before the horrors of the flood came.

All of that demonstrated his belief in God's warning to the people. God loves human beings enough to warn them. Some don't believe that, but He warns us because He wants us preserved, and not destroyed. He is "not willing that any man should perish, but that all should come to repentance." Therefore, the warnings are not threats. They are not predicting our doom. God is saying that He does not want us vulnerable. He doesn't want us to be lost. He wants us inside, where it's safe. That's a pretty merciful and long-suffering God, don't you think?

Noah believed in a loving, compassionate God who didn't want anybody destroyed. He was fully convinced that God was a good God. Not too many believe that, even today. But since God is a compassionate Person who loves His children dearly, He did not want them to be destroyed if He could prevent it. He said that He had a place of safety for Noah; Noah believed in a God like that, so he built the ark. He *believed* that God was that way. Part of his belief was based on how God was showing His great mercy toward all when He said, in essence, "Make a refuge for my people." All of them, anyone who would come in, would find a refuge—a nice, safe hiding place. All were invited.

So God was providing all of this—a place of protection and safety. For one hundred and twenty years He showed all His mercy and kindness to let all kinds of persons know that there would be a safe place when the flood came. God wasn't just warning and threatening people. He told them through Noah that a flood was coming, but assured those who believed Him that they didn't have to be afraid. He said, "I want to save you. Will you go where it's safe? Or will you not believe me and stay outside where it is not safe?" It was the difference between belief and unbelief, right? It was that simple. And finally He told faithful Noah, "Come thou and all thy house into the ark; for thee have I seen righteous before Me in this generation." Genesis 7:1. Noah was to bring all his family—his wife, his sons, and their wives—into safety.

We have a terrible time with our belief, or our unbelief; the Jews were lost because of unbelief. Sometimes I am frightened that we are so much like them. God was saying, "I don't want you to die. I want you to live, and I will provide a place where you can live so that you never need to die. Come on into the safe place."

I'd like to give you the reason Noah and his family were saved and the others were lost. There is only one reason: Noah believed God, just as Abraham did. "Abraham believed God, and it was counted unto him for righteousness." Romans 4:3. That is justification by faith. God did not say that Abraham was righteous, and it did not say that he accepted Christ's righteousness. It says that Abraham *believed God*. And his belief in what God said was accounted as righteousness, which is justification. His *belief* was accounted as righteousness. That's justification by faith. Paul wrote a lot more in Romans about that than we realize. So Abraham first believed God. And so did Noah. Their belief in what God said was accounted to both of them for righteousness.

Noah's belief had several aspects. First, he believed that a flood was coming—something totally unheard of—just because God said it would come. Secondly, Noah had tremendous confidence in God's love for His children, His people, even if they *were* sinners. He believed that God still loved them, wanted to forgive them, and wanted to provide for them. That love was shown in the 120-year grace period, full of Noah's pleas to repent and join him in the ark. Thirdly, Noah believed in, and did not question, God's method of provision for the saving of His children. And lastly, because Noah believed all of this, he acted upon his belief and built the ark. Then he brought his family into the ark with him, as God directed him to do. Because of that faith in God and His provision for their safety, Noah and his family were preserved. So his faith was demonstrated repeatedly over a long period of time.

Although Noah had character imperfections and sinned after the flood subsided, he was preserved in the ark, and his family with him, simply because he followed the directions and believed in God's goodness to sinners. Many people still do not believe in God's provision for sinners. Many who go to church don't believe that. They don't believe that God is that good. They think that when they get good enough, then God will accept them. *We* even pray that way, which means that we do not believe that God has made provision for us. We hope someday that we are able to get inside heaven, when we will somehow be qualified to get in there.

Noah did not obey in order to become righteous or to be saved. Again: he did not obey to become righteous. He obeyed because He believed God. And his belief in God was counted to him as righteousness. So he wasn't *trying* to be righteous. That wasn't the purpose at all. He simply believed that God would preserve him and his family and all others who would believe in God's mercy. Because he believed that, it was accounted to him for righteousness. Be careful what you think about righteousness, or you'll have some problems.

Do you know that we are still saved in the very same way as Noah? We are saved in the exact same way. Here is a difficult verse in the Bible: "Which sometime were disobedient, when once the longsuffering of God waited in the days of Noah, while the ark was a preparing, wherein few, that is, eight souls were saved by water. The like figure whereunto even baptism doth also now save us." 1 Peter 3:20-21. Peter is making a parallel between the ark and the flood, and baptism.

This verse in the King James version is difficult, so here it is in the Lamsa translation (also called the Modern English version): "In the days of Noah, when the Spirit of God had patience, He commanded an ark to be made in the hope of their repentance, but only eight souls entered into it, and were saved by its floating upon the water. You also are saved in that very manner by baptism." Baptism is like entering into the ark, a place of safety.

The Phillips translation of verse 21 reads like this: "And I cannot help pointing out what a perfect illustration this is of the way you have been admitted to the safety of the Christian 'ark' by baptism." The ark that Noah prepared is a perfect illustration of the way you are admitted to the Christian ark (or place of safety) by baptism. It is all about a Christian refuge—a place of refuge for today in these difficult times, and also for in the future when fire comes to destroy the earth.

Peter is teaching that in the New Testament, there is an ark of safety that God has provided. Do you know what that ark is? We enter that ark by baptism, according to Peter. We will find it in Galatians 3:27, where it reads, "For as many of you as have been *baptized into Christ* have put on Christ." "Baptized into Christ" is the key phrase. It's also found in Romans 6:3: "Know ye not, that so many of us as were *baptized into Jesus Christ* were baptized into His death?" The concept here is essentially the same as what Peter wrote about. It's something we get inside of, and there we are protected from all the elements that would destroy us.

It isn't just *believing* in Christ, but being *baptized into Him*. He is the hiding place where I am safe and preserved. Jesus is God's ark of safety provided for us.

Don't forget that baptism is a dying to self and a rising to live for Christ. "For ye are dead, and your life is hid with Christ in God." Colossians 3:3. He is hiding us in a place of refuge, where the enemy can't take pot-shots at us. It's a place where we are preserved—where we are kept by God's power. So Christ is likened in the Bible to the ark of safety. Baptism is an entering by faith into Jesus, where we are preserved because we are hiding in Him. "Hiding in Jesus, I am safe evermore."

I like the words of the hymn titled *The Haven of Rest*: "The tempest may sweep o'er wild, stormy deep; but in Jesus I'm safe evermore." There are many other hymns about this. I wonder how many times we sing them and they hardly make any impression on our minds at all. Another example is *Jesus, Lover of My Soul*: "Hide me, Oh my Savior hide, till the storm of life is past. Other refuge have I none, hangs my helpless soul on Thee." Many marvelous gospel hymns teach that our refuge, our ark of safety, is Christ.

It seems to me in these days that we do not know how to hide anymore. We do all kinds of praying and worrying, but I don't think we know how to hide. I think I am just as guilty of this as you may be. We sit out there so vulnerable, and we don't know where to go to hide. We wonder why things keep happening to us. I think that people in bygone years, when they had less materialism, knew where to run to find a safe place to hide.

I recall that my father and I were fishing one Sunday in a river near home. He never had a car so we had to walk. I even thought that was fun. We were spending one Sunday afternoon fishing there on the edge of a huge pasture on the edge of town. There was a terrible storm coming in from the northwest, as it does in the Dakotas. We didn't mind a little rain and wind, but that storm looked different. As we gazed off across that field, the wind became more and more violent, and then we saw a tornado coming. Dad realized that there was no place to hide right where we were, but about a block way was a big railroad trestle that had huge granite piers holding up the railway bridge. We raced down there with our fishing gear and dove in behind one of those piers that were solid rock. "On Christ the solid rock I stand." We watched that tornado go whizzing by, tearing up the sod and the trees, and finally going down the hill. We came out from our hiding place, looked around fearfully, and hoped there was no more of the tornado on the back end of it. It's nice to have a hiding place.

God has provided a spiritual and emotional hiding place where you can flee. We have to know how to hide in Jesus, and to know what that means. There are ways of doing it, and the hymnbooks are just filled with concepts of hiding in the Refuge.

In the Bible there are several illustrations of this hiding—*even when you are very, very guilty*. "Then ye shall appoint you cities to be cities of refuge for you; that the slayer may flee thither, which killeth any person at unawares. And they shall be unto you cities for refuge from the avenger; that the manslayer die not, until he stand before the congregation in judgment. And of these cities which ye shall give six cities shall ye have for refuge. Ye shall give three cities on this side Jordan, and three cities shall ye give in the land of Canaan, which shall be cities of refuge. These six cities shall be a refuge, both for the children of Israel, and for the stranger, and for the sojourner among them: that every one that killeth any person unawares may flee thither.... If the slayer shall at any time come without the border of the city of his refuge, whither he was fled; And the revenger of blood find him without the borders of the city of his refuge, and the revenger of blood kill the slayer; he shall not be guilty of blood." Numbers 35:11-15, 26-27.

These verses talk about the six cities of refuge. They were God's provisions for someone who *accidentally* killed somebody. The bad thing about those cities is that the one who killed never got a fair trial right away. Back then, there was what was called the "right of private vengeance." If you killed me, for example, my brother had the right to kill you and never be taken to trial. This right of private vengeance still exists today in some places in Africa. However, so long as you hid in a city of refuge, the one seeking vengeance could not get to you to get even. Believe me, the devil is waiting just outside those city gates, so to speak—waiting for us to step outside, away from our Refuge. The moment we do, if the devil can't get us physically, he will get us emotionally or mentally. He is a dirty fighter. We must realize that many of these attacks on us that we call trials are not because there is something wrong with our emotions or our brains or our marital situation or being single. They are attacks by an enemy. Not all of them, but many of them are. And the devil always kicks us when we are down. Have you ever noticed how problems come in big bunches? They come like a tidal wave to just wash away every hope we ever had. The devil fights like that. So God provided cities of refuge where sinners could be safe.

Here is a quote about that: "The cities of refuge appointed for God's ancient people were a symbol of the refuge provided in Christ. The same merciful Saviour who appointed those temporal cities of refuge has by the shedding of His own blood provided for the transgressors of God's law a sure retreat, into which they may flee for safety from the second death. No power can take out of His hands the souls that go to Him for pardon. 'There is therefore now no condemnation to them which are in Christ Jesus,' ... that 'we might have a strong consolation, who have fled for refuge to lay hold upon the hope set before us.'" *Patriarchs and Prophets*, p. 516. Even transgressors of God's law "have a strong consolation" in Christ, to Whom they "have fled for refuge." Sinners are doomed, but God has a place to hide them from the second death. They are preserved because they are in the hiding place, and not because they are so good. Christ is the city of refuge— the hiding place—for those guilty of transgressing God's law.

How do we escape from the second death? By being in the hiding place, which is Jesus, the Ark. Not because we're so good—no more than Noah was—but because we are in the hiding place. Who may flee there? The transgressors of God's law, or sinners, may flee there. "Who is he that condemneth? It is Christ that died, yea rather, that is risen again, who is even at the right hand of God, who also maketh intercession for us." Romans 8:34. We have an enemy trying to destroy us, and we have a Friend trying to preserve us. This is the great controversy. Our job is to make sure that others come into the hiding place. Our job is not to criticize and condemn others who might not have the light of truth that we do, or else they might lose hope. Our job is to intercede in their behalf and lead them into the hiding place. Noah preached that the refuge of the ark was for guilty sinners. Yes, even Noah and his family members were sinners, but they were *believing* sinners.

"From the end of the earth will I cry unto Thee, when my heart is overwhelmed: lead me to the Rock that is higher than I. For Thou hast been a shelter for me, and a strong tower from the enemy. I will abide in Thy tabernacle for ever: I will trust in the covert of Thy wings." Psalms 61:24. All this is about protection—about a safe place.

The wise man wrote: "The name of the LORD is a strong tower: the righteous runneth into it, and is safe." Proverbs 18:10. Do you remember the towers that were in the old fortresses? The towers were the strongest places. Again, this is describing a hiding place, a refuge.

"Satan trembles and flees before the weakest soul who finds refuge in that mighty name." *Desire of Ages*, p. 131. The devil takes off and runs when we find refuge in the name of Jesus. We do not defend ourselves with our righteousness, because we don't have any. We defend ourselves in the name of Jesus, and the devil takes off and runs. And, by the way, we have to chase him away all the time. When we are down and on a guilt trip, plead the precious name of Jesus so the devils will scram! "Get out of here!" We have the right to do that. We may plead Jesus' name, and God will intercede and chase the devil right out of our lives. We don't have to sit and suffer guilt all the time.

"Turn you to the strong hold, ye prisoners of hope." Zechariah 9:12. The language here is telling us to get inside the Stronghold. When we read in the New Testament about the straight and narrow path, do we know what that is talking about? Some people think it is talking about a very confining lifestyle. No. It is talking about the pathways that go up to the mountaintop, where all of the fortresses are. The enemy has a terrible time laying siege to a fortress that is on a mountaintop. The straight and narrow ways are the paths that go up the mountainside, heading up to the fortress at the top. You never want to be outside the fortress after dark, because there are thieves who will attack you. The word picture in the Bible about entering in through the "strait gate" concerns those who are pressing to get into the fortress before dark. Jesus is trying to get us to a safe place when He says that "narrow is the way, which leadeth unto life." Matthew 7:14. That text is all about getting into the safe place. It's not talking about how good you are, but it does say that we must stay on that path.

"For I will pass through the land of Egypt this night, and will smite all the firstborn in the land of Egypt, both man and beast; and against all the gods of Egypt I will execute judgment: I am the LORD. And the blood shall be to you for a token upon the houses where ye are: and when I see the blood, I will pass over you, and the plague shall not be upon you to destroy you, when I smite the land of Egypt." Exodus 12:12-13. If the Israelites were inside their homes with the precious blood on the doorposts, eating of the paschal lamb and bitter herbs, they were safe from the angel of destruction. God saved the first-born son of those who complied with the conditions. Later on, God required that every first-born son be purchased back from God. That is because God, in His great mercy, spared the first-born sons who were by faith under His blood. Therefore, the first-born sons belonged to God. Parents had to buy their sons back from God for a temple shekel each.

This is discussed in *Patriarchs and Prophets*, page 274: "Furthermore, the first-born of both man and beast were to be the Lord's, to be bought back only by a ransom, in acknowledgment that when the first-born in Egypt perished, that of Israel, though graciously preserved, had been justly exposed to the same doom but for the atoning sacrifice." Now, what was the reason that the first-born of the Israelites did not die? They were exposed to the destroying angel, were they not? They were sinners, too. They "had been justly exposed to the same doom but for the atoning sacrifice." Not unjustly, but justly in danger. They were not preserved because they were so good or so much more perfect than the Egyptians. They were preserved because they were under the blood of the lamb, symbolic of Jesus. That was the only reason. They were saved by the blood, and so are we. Don't forget that the Israelites were exposed to the same doom as were the Egyptians. It was the "atoning sacrifice" that made all the difference. No wonder the devil hates the cross and seeks to diminish its importance in our salvation.

The Israelites were exposed to the angel of death, but they did not die because they were in the hiding place, under the precious blood. They had followed God's instructions for safety because they believed that God would preserve them. They believed He would do what He told them He would do. Therefore, because of their belief, they did not die. That is righteousness. In Hebrews chapter 11, Paul brings out the actions that other people of other times did that God told them to do, and they were accounted righteous, also. Go read that whole chapter when you have time.

I want you to see in hellfire, in the destruction of the wicked in the second death, something similar that will happen to God's people as happened in the ark during the flood, in the cities of refuge, and during the Passover in Egypt. I pray that this will give you hope. Did you know that Psalms 91 tells us that the righteous will see the death of the wicked? "He that dwelleth in the secret place of the most High shall abide under the shadow of the Almighty. I will say of the LORD, He is my refuge and my fortress [this is talking about a place of safety]: my God; in Him will I trust…. Thou shalt not be afraid for the terror by night; nor for the arrow that flieth by day; Nor for the pestilence that walketh in darkness; nor for the destruction that wasteth at noonday. A thousand shall fall at thy side, and ten thousand at thy right hand; but it shall not come nigh thee. Only with thine eyes shalt thou behold and see the reward of the wicked. Because thou hast made the LORD, which is my refuge, even the most High, thy habitation; There shall no evil befall thee, neither shall any plague come nigh thy dwelling." Psalms 91:1-2, 5-10.

Before the fire comes down from heaven to destroy the wicked, God's people are safe in the New Jerusalem. "And they [the wicked] went up on the breadth of the earth, and compassed the camp of the saints about, and the beloved city: and fire came down from God out of heaven, and devoured them." Revelation 20:9. The wicked go up to attack the holy city, and fire comes down to devour them, but the saints are right there in the city—the New Jerusalem. "While the earth is wrapped in the fire of God's vengeance, the righteous abide safely in the Holy City." *Story of Redemption*, p. 429.

"When the flood of waters was at its height upon the earth, it had the appearance of a boundless lake of water. When God finally purifies the earth, it will appear like a boundless lake of fire. As God preserved the ark amid the commotions of the Flood, because it contained eight righteous persons, He will preserve the New Jerusalem, containing the faithful of all ages, from righteous Abel down to the last saint which lived. Although the whole earth, with the exception of that portion where the city rests, will be wrapped in a sea of liquid fire, yet the city is preserved as was the ark, by a miracle of Almighty power. It stands unharmed amid the devouring elements." *Bible Commentary*, E. G. White Comments, Volume 7, p. 986.

This says that the righteous in the holy city are exposed to the same doom as the wicked. They are justly exposed, as were the first-born of the Israelites in Egypt. Why is that? It is because the Israelites were sinners, and so are those who will be in the Holy City. If we have sinned just once, we should be on the outside of the holy city when the earth is wrapped in a sea of liquid fire. The only reason we are not—the only difference—is that we have fled to the Refuge which is Christ. "Hiding in Jesus, I am safe evermore." When we are baptized into Christ and truly hide in Him, believing that He is the sinner's dear refuge, we have peace.

As I hear people expressing all their fears and doubts about the judgment, the plagues and the second death, I sometimes wonder if we have ever discovered that Christ is the Ark of safety. Do we know anything about Him at all? There are too many fears, too many doubts among God's people. I would not give you false hope; a true Savior-sinner relationship implies a close walk with Him. "Can two walk together, except they be agreed?" Amos 3:3. It's a vastly different thing to walk with Jesus when we know His provision for our present safety, and His provision for the rest of our lives. Then we have a *reason* to walk with Him. We have a reason to be thankful. He has already saved us. He has already made a plan for our escape. He is not waiting for us to be good enough to escape. So sin and guilt are vastly different when we look at it in the context of hiding in Jesus. When we are hiding in Him, it's difficult to sin. When we are assured of salvation in Christ and protection by Him, it's difficult to sin. How can we sin against the One who is so good to us and who has made eternal provision for us?

It's not about trying to be good enough. It's about not hurting the One who has been so good to us. It's a different reason for living. We have a reason to live because we know that we are going to be hidden and protected. Why be afraid? We are assured that "perfect love casteth out fear." 1 John 4:18. That includes all fear, even the second death. We can have consolation, for the Lord will take care of us.

There is a marvelous hymn titled *How Firm a Foundation, Ye Saints of the Lord* with these lyrics in the first and last stanzas: "How firm a foundation, ye saints of the Lord, Is laid for your faith in His excellent Word! What more can He say than to you He hath said Who unto the Savior for refuge have fled? ... The soul that on Jesus hath leaned for repose I will not, I will not, desert to his foes; That soul, though all hell should endeavor to shake, I'll never, no never, no never, forsake!" Jesus is a solid refuge, and we can always flee to Him. We need have no fear; there is total protection there. No enemy can get at us. God would empty all heaven before He would allow the devil to get at us in our refuge.

Sometimes we just sit and fight all by ourselves. We get into our problems and we say, "Woe is me!" That is so self-centered. We just dig ourselves deeper and deeper into our problems, and have more and more fears and guilt, and more depression and discouragement. Yet all the time, the safe place from the enemy's darts is right there beside us and we won't get inside. We keep looking at our dismal circumstances. We always water the weeds, and not the flowers and vegetables. Then the weeds get so big, they can provide shade for us, and it's gloomy all the time. Stop thinking about the weeds and all the difficult circumstances, and start watering the flowers and the vegetables and the fruit, that they might grow and give us hope.

I had an experience in the war that helps me to understand very graphically what this hiding place is. I flew what they called "The Hump." We flew over the Himalayas into China, hauling aviation gasoline. We flew over six hundred miles into enemy territory when I first started flying there. When we flew aviation gasoline, we used to say, "Rub some of the fuel between your fingers and watch it blow up." That was hardly an exaggeration. The fuel was about 130 octane. We had an awful lot of airplanes blow up as we learned by experience how to safely haul that highly flammable fuel. The designation of my aircraft was C-109. We called them "C-one-o-booms," and "C-crash," because that's what happened all the time. We had to have humor like that, or we would have died from fear.

One evening about 7 PM, they called my crew and me down to the flight line to fly a trip over "The Hump." Our aircraft was loaded with barrels of fuel. The operations officer called me back to his office and told me there were some problems. We received our gasoline from a big pipeline that ran down two rivers. When they shut the pipelines down, they filled them full of water, because otherwise we had to prime them. Whenever they stopped flowing fuel into the barrels, they pumped water into the pipelines and aimed the pipes into the swamp to dump the water. The problem was that, by mistake, they had been filling the fuel barrels and gasoline trucks with water. So the gasoline trucks would drive up to be filled with aircraft fuel, but instead they were filled with water.

They filled up twelve airplanes with water. Each plane could hold about five thousand gallons of liquid, so that was a lot of water. They didn't know that this problem existed until they went out to drain the sumps. The water was heavier than the gasoline, so the engineers drained the water out of the bottoms of the fuel tanks on the planes until they could see the fuel. And the water just kept pouring out. They had a terrible time draining the water from all of the plane fuel tanks. All day long they had been draining water out of the fuel tanks. I was told that I would be the first one to go out. If nothing happened to me, they would send more planes out. I said, "Thanks a lot." The engineer told me that he had personally checked my plane a dozen times and it seemed that all the water was gone from the fuel tanks. He said, "There is no water in that airplane's fuel tanks."

So I was told to head out towards China. If I did not radio back within two hours, they would assume that all was okay, and they would send another plane out. My crew and I had lived through many perilous times, so this was just one more of them. We took off and headed for China. We climbed up to 16,000 feet. I had a student pilot that I was checking out. He was supposed to be flying the airplane and I was supposed to be his co-pilot. I was grading him on the flight. It then came time to put the two inboard engines on auxiliary fuel tanks. That involved turning two levers just ninety degrees, a simple procedure. I reached over and pulled those two levers down and BANG! BANG! BANG! BANG! There was such a terrible noise that it scared all of us half to death. It was like bombs going off. I quickly put the levers back where they were, and then we started checking all the gauges. We realized that we had lost one engine completely and another one was slowly going bad. We had a full load of fuel and only two good engines.

We radioed back to the base and told them we were returning home. It took a long time to get back; meanwhile, the worst storm the base had had in over twenty years was hitting hard there. In that part of India, it rains. It rained 465 inches on average each year at our home base. On our way back, we hit that violent storm and couldn't get near the base, so we circled back and forth over the jungles of eastern India. While we were up there on two bad engines and nursing a third one, we began to wonder how long we could stay flying. We circled the base for five hours until the middle of the night.

Finally they radioed us to come in at about 1,000 feet from the southwest, and hopefully we would be able to find the airfield. The bad thing about going down to 1,000 feet was that there were mountains nearby that rose to 1,500 feet. If we went in too far in the pitch black of night, we would end up slamming into a mountain. I flew in at 1,000 feet. All five of us were in the cockpit, just straining to see some sign of light. We continued to fly at that same altitude, hoping to see a light from the airfield. It was my job to say when we had to gain altitude to keep from slamming into a mountain, but I couldn't see a thing.

I finally said, "Let's get out of here!" I rammed the throttles to maximum power and headed back up to a higher altitude, but just as we started to climb, I saw the most beautiful thing you could ever see in your whole life. I saw that little beacon light going round and round. I can fully relate to how wonderful it was for Jesus to say that He is the light of the world. After all those hours up there facing death, there was nothing like seeing that beacon of light! In just a few seconds, we were landing on the airstrip. Later, I saw fellows in my crew lean down and kiss the ground. We had reached the haven of rest, and there is just nothing like it. What a wonderful thing when God gets us safely through our trials and we realize that He had preserved us all that time.

He has a safe place for us all, where there are no more fears, where we have peace and can sleep like a baby. Jesus is my soul's refuge, and yours. We can be safe today, and safe from future hellfire. The devil can't get at us. I beseech you to hide in Jesus, where you are safe evermore—just like those believing sinners Noah and his family.

Thank you so much, and may God bless you.

Made in the USA
San Bernardino, CA
19 April 2016